Men in Dark Times

OTHER BOOKS BY HANNAH ARENDT

Origins of Totalitarianism

Between Past and Future

On Revolution

The Human Condition

Eichmann in Jerusalem

MEN IN DARK TIMES

Hannah Arendt

HARCOURT, BRACE & WORLD, INC., NEW YORK

"On Humanity in Dark Times: Thoughts about Lessing," an address on accepting the Lessing Prize of the Free City of Hamburg in 1959, originally written in German, published by R. Piper, Munich, 1960, translated by Clara and Richard Winston.

"Rosa Luxemburg: 1871–1919," a review of J. P. Nettl, *Rosa Luxemburg*, in *The New York Review of Books*, 1966.

"A Christian on St. Peter's Chair from 1958 to 1963," a review of Pope John XXIII, *Journal of a Soul*, in *The New York Review of Books*, 1965.

"Karl Jaspers: A Laudatio," address given in 1958 when the German Peace Prize was awarded to Karl Jaspers, originally written in German and published by R. Piper, Munich, 1958, translated by Clara and Richard Winston.

"Karl Jaspers: Citizen of the World?" appeared in *The Philosophy of Karl Jaspers*, edited by P. A. Schilpp, 1957, now published by Open Court Publishing Company, La Salle, Ill. for The Library of Living Philosophers, Inc. Used by permission.

"Isak Dinesen: 1885–1963," a review in *The New Yorker*, 1968, of Parmenia Migel, *Titania. A Biography of Isak Dinesen*.

"Hermann Broch: 1886–1951," introduction to two volumes of essays in *Gesammelte Werke*, Rheinverlag, Zürich, 1955 (now Suhrkamp, Frankfurt/M.), originally written in German, translated by Clara and Richard Winston.

"Walter Benjamin: 1892–1940," originally in *The New Yorker*, 1968; introduction to a collection of his essays, *Illuminations*, Harcourt, Brace & World, 1968, originally written in German, translated by Harry Zohn.

"Bertolt Brecht: 1898–1956" appeared in *The New Yorker*, 1966.

"Waldemar Gurian: 1903–1954" appeared in The Gurian Memorial Issue of *The Review of Politics*, 1955.

"Randall Jarrell: 1914–1965" appeared in *Randall Jarrell, 1914–1965*, Farrar, Straus & Giroux, 1967.

Contents

PREFACE   vii

ON HUMANITY IN DARK TIMES:
THOUGHTS ABOUT LESSING
Translated by Clara and Richard Winston

3

ROSA LUXEMBURG: 1871–1919

33

ANGELO GIUSEPPE RONCALLI: A CHRISTIAN
ON ST. PETER'S CHAIR FROM 1958 TO 1963

57

KARL JASPERS: A LAUDATIO
Translated by Clara and Richard Winston

71

KARL JASPERS: CITIZEN OF THE WORLD?

81

ISAK DINESEN: 1885–1963

95

HERMANN BROCH: 1886–1951
Translated by Richard Winston

111

WALTER BENJAMIN: 1892–1940
Translated by Harry Zohn

153

BERTOLT BRECHT: 1898–1956

207

WALDEMAR GURIAN: 1903–1954

251

RANDALL JARRELL: 1914–1965

263

INDEX   269

PREFACE

Wᴀɪᴛᴛᴇɴ over a period of twelve years on the spur of occasion or opportunity, this collection of essays and articles is primarily concerned with persons—how they lived their lives, how they moved in the world, and how they were affected by historical time. The people assembled here could hardly be more unlike each other, and it is not difficult to imagine how they might have protested, had they been given a voice in the matter, against being gathered into a common room, as it were. For they have in common neither gifts nor convictions, neither profession nor milieu; with one exception, they hardly knew of each other. But they were contemporaries, though belonging to different generations—except, of course, for Lessing, who, however, in the introductory essay is treated as though he were a contemporary. Thus they share with each other the age in which their life span fell, the world during the first half of the twentieth century with its political catastrophes, its moral disasters, and its astonishing development of the arts and sciences. And while this age killed some of them and determined the life and work of others, there are a few who were hardly affected and none who could be said to be conditioned by it. Those who are on the lookout for representatives of an era, for mouthpieces of the *Zeitgeist*, for exponents of History (spelled with a capital H) will look here in vain.

Still, the historical time, the "dark times" mentioned in the title, is, I think, visible everywhere in this book. I borrow the term from Brecht's famous poem "To Posterity," which mentions the disorder and the hunger, the massacres and the slaughterers, the outrage over injustice and the despair "when there was only wrong and no outrage," the legitimate hatred that makes you ugly nevertheless, the well-founded wrath that makes the voice grow hoarse. All this was real enough as it took place in public; there was nothing secret or mysterious about it. And still, it was by no means visible to all, nor was it at all easy to perceive it; for, until the very moment when catastrophe overtook everything and everybody, it was covered up not by realities but by the highly efficient talk and double-talk of nearly all official representatives who, without interruption and in many ingenious variations, explained away unpleasant facts and justified concerns. When we think of dark times and of people living and moving in them, we have to take this camouflage, emanating from and spread by "the establishment"—or "the system," as it was then called—also into account. If it is the function of the public realm to throw light on the affairs of men by providing a space of appearances in which they can show in deed and word, for better and worse, who they are and what they can do, then darkness has come when this light is extinguished by "credibility gaps" and "invisible government," by speech that does not disclose what is but sweeps it under the carpet, by exhortations, moral and otherwise, that, under the pretext of upholding old truths, degrade all truth to meaningless triviality.

Nothing of this is new. These are the conditions which, thirty years ago, were described by Sartre in *La Nausée* (which I think is still his best book) in terms of bad faith and *l'esprit de sérieux*, a world in which everybody who is publicly recognized belongs among the *salauds*, and everything that is exists in an opaque, meaningless thereness which spreads obfuscation and causes disgust. And these are the same conditions which, forty years ago (though for altogether different purposes), Heidegger described with uncanny precision in those paragraphs of *Being and Time* that deal with "the they," their "mere talk," and, generally, with everything that, unhidden and unprotected by the privacy of the self, appears in public. In his description of human existence, everything that is real or authentic is assaulted by the overwhelming power of "mere talk" that irresistibly arises out of the public realm, determining every aspect of everyday existence, anticipating and annihilating the sense or the nonsense of everything the future may bring. There is no escape, according to Heidegger, from the "incomprehensible triviality" of this common everyday world except by withdrawal from it into that solitude which philosophers since Parmenides and Plato have opposed to the political realm. We are here not concerned with the philosophical relevance of Heidegger's analyses (which, in my opinion, is undeniable) nor with the tradition of philosophic thought that stands behind them, but exclusively with certain underlying experiences of the time and their conceptual description. In our context, the point is that the sarcastic, perverse-sounding statement, *Das Licht der Öffentlichkeit verdunkelt alles* ("The light of the public obscures everything"), went to the very heart of the matter and actually was no more than the most succinct summing-up of existing conditions.

"Dark times," in the broader sense I propose here, are as such not identical with the monstrosities of this century which indeed are of a horrible novelty. Dark times, in contrast, are not only not new, they are no rarity in history, although they were perhaps unknown in American history, which otherwise has its fair share, past and present, of crime and disaster. That even in the darkest of times we have the right to expect some illumination, and that such illumination may well come less from theories and concepts than from the uncertain, flickering, and often weak light that some men and women, in their lives and their works, will kindle under almost all circumstances and shed over the time span that was given them on earth—this conviction is the inarticulate background against which these profiles were drawn. Eyes so used to darkness as ours will hardly be able to tell whether their light was the light of a candle or that of a blazing sun. But such objective evaluation seems to me a matter of secondary importance which can be safely left to posterity.

January 1968

Men in Dark Times

ON HUMANITY IN DARK TIMES:
Thoughts about Lessing[1]

I

The distinction conferred by a free city, and a prize that bears the name of Lessing, are a great honor. I admit that I do not know how I have come to receive it, and also that it has not been altogether easy for me to come to terms with it. In saying this I can ignore entirely the delicate question of merit. In this very respect an honor gives us a forcible lesson in modesty; for it implies that it is not for us to judge our own merits as we judge the merits and accomplishments of others. In awards, the world speaks out, and if we accept the award and express our gratitude for it, we can do so only by ignoring ourselves and acting entirely within the framework of our attitude toward the world, toward a world and public to which we owe the space into which we speak and in which we are heard.

But the honor not only reminds us emphatically of the gratitude we owe the world; it also, to a very high degree, obligates us to it. Since we can always reject the honor, by accepting it we are not only strengthened in our position within the world but are accepting a kind of commitment to it. That a person appears in public at all, and that the public receives and confirms him, is by

[1] Address on accepting the Lessing Prize of the Free City of Hamburg.

no means a matter to be taken for granted. Only the genius is driven by his very gifts into public life, and is exempted from any decision of this sort. In his case alone, honors only continue the concord with the world, sound an existing harmony in full publicity, which has arisen independently of all considerations and decisions, independently also of all obligations, as if it were a natural phenomenon erupting into human society. To this phenomenon we can in truth apply what Lessing once said about the man of genius in two of his finest lines of verse:

Was ihn bewegt, bewegt. Was ihm gefällt, gefällt.
Sein glücklicher Geschmack ist der Geschmack der Welt.

(What moves him, moves. What pleases him, pleases.
His felicitous taste is the world's taste.)

Nothing in our time is more dubious, it seems to me, than our attitude toward the world, nothing less to be taken for granted than that concord with what appears in public which an honor imposes on us, and the existence of which it affirms. In our century even genius has been able to develop only in conflict with the world and the public realm, although it naturally finds, as it always has done, its own peculiar concord with its audience. But the world and the people who inhabit it are not the same. The world lies between people, and this in-between—much more than (as is often thought) men or even man—is today the object of the greatest concern and the most obvious upheaval in almost all the countries of the globe. Even where the world is still halfway in order, or is kept halfway in order, the public realm has lost the power of illumination which was originally part of its very nature. More and more people in the countries of the Western world, which since the decline of the ancient world has regarded freedom from politics as one of the basic freedoms, make use of this freedom and have retreated from the world and their obligations within it. This withdrawal from the world need not harm an individual; he may even cultivate great talents to the point of genius and so by a detour be useful to the world again. But with each such retreat an almost demonstrable loss to the world takes place; what is lost is the specific and usually irreplaceable in-between

4

which should have formed between this individual and his fellow men.

When we thus consider the real meaning of public honors and prizes under present conditions, it may occur to us that the Hamburg Senate found a solution to the problem rather like that of Columbus' egg when it decided to link the city's prize with the name of Lessing. For Lessing never felt at home in the world as it then existed and probably never wanted to, and still after his own fashion he always remained committed to it. Special and unique circumstances governed this relationship. The German public was not prepared for him and as far as I know never honored him in his lifetime. He himself lacked, according to his own judgment, that happy, natural concord with the world, a combination of merit and good fortune, which both he and Goethe considered the sign of genius. Lessing believed he was indebted to criticism for something that "comes very close to genius," but which never quite achieved that natural harmonization with the world in which Fortuna smiles when Virtù appears. All that may have been important enough, but it was not decisive. It almost seems as if at some time he had decided to pay homage to genius, to the man of "felicitous taste," but himself to follow those whom he once half ironically called "the wise men" who "make the pillars of the best-known truths shake wherever they let their eyes fall." His attitude toward the world was neither positive nor negative, but radically critical and, in respect to the public realm of his time, completely revolutionary. But it was also an attitude that remained indebted to the world, never left the solid ground of the world, and never went to the extreme of sentimental utopianism. In Lessing the revolutionary temper was associated with a curious kind of partiality which clung to concrete details with an exaggerated, almost pedantic carefulness, and gave rise to many misunderstandings. One component of Lessing's greatness was the fact that he never allowed supposed objectivity to cause him to lose sight of the real relationship to the world and the real status in the world of the things or men he attacked or praised. That did not help his credit in Germany, where the true nature of criticism is less well understood than elsewhere. It was

5

hard for the Germans to grasp that justice has little to do with objectivity in the ordinary sense.

Lessing never made his peace with the world in which he lived. He enjoyed "challenging prejudices" and "telling the truth to the court minions." Dearly though he paid for these pleasures, they were literally pleasures. Once when he was attempting to explain to himself the source of "tragic pleasure," he said that "all passions, even the most unpleasant, are as passions pleasant" because "they make us . . . more conscious of our existence, they make us feel more real." This sentence strikingly recalls the Greek doctrine of passions, which counted anger, for example, among the pleasant emotions but reckoned hope along with fear among the evils. This evaluation rests on differences in reality, exactly as in Lessing; not, however, in the sense that reality is measured by the force with which the passion affects the soul but rather by the amount of reality the passion transmits to it. In hope, the soul overleaps reality, as in fear it shrinks back from it. But anger, and above all Lessing's kind of anger, reveals and exposes the world just as Lessing's kind of laughter in *Minna von Barnhelm* seeks to bring about reconciliation with the world. Such laughter helps one to find a place in the world, but ironically, which is to say, without selling one's soul to it. Pleasure, which is fundamentally the intensified awareness of reality, springs from a passionate openness to the world and love of it. Not even the knowledge that man may be destroyed by the world detracts from the "tragic pleasure."

If Lessing's aesthetics, in contrast to Aristotle's, sees even fear as a variety of pity, the pity we feel for ourselves, the reason is perhaps that Lessing is trying to strip fear of its escapist aspect in order to save it as a passion, that is to say, as an affect in which we are affected by ourselves just as in the world we are ordinarily affected by other people. Intimately connected with this is the fact that for Lessing the essence of poetry was action and not, as for Herder, a force—"the magic force that affects my soul"— nor, as for Goethe, nature which has been given form. Lessing was not at all concerned with "the perfection of the work of art in itself," which Goethe considered "the eternal, indispensable

6

requirement." Rather—and here he is in agreement with Aristotle —he was concerned with the effect upon the spectator, who as it were represents the world, or rather, that worldly space which has come into being between the artist or writer and his fellow men as a world common to them.

Lessing experienced the world in anger and in laughter, and anger and laughter are by their nature biased. Therefore, he was unable or unwilling to judge a work of art "in itself," independently of its effect in the world, and therefore he could attack or defend in his polemics according to how the matter in question was being judged by the public and quite independently of the degree to which it was true or false. It was not only a form of gallantry when he said that he would "leave in peace those whom all are striking at"; it was also a concern, which had become instinctive with him, for the relative rightness of opinions which for good reasons get the worst of it. Thus even in the dispute over Christianity he did not take up a fixed position. Rather, as he once said with magnificent self-knowledge, he instinctively became dubious of Christianity "the more cogently some tried to prove it to me," and instinctively tried "to preserve it in [his] heart" the more "wantonly and triumphantly others sought to trample it underfoot." But this means that where everyone else was contending over the "truth" of Christianity, he was chiefly defending its position in the world, now anxious that it might again enforce its claim to dominance, now fearing that it might vanish utterly. Lessing was being remarkably farsighted when he saw that the enlightened theology of his time "under the pretext of making us rational Christians is making us extremely irrational philosophers." That insight sprang not only from partisanship in favor of reason. Lessing's primary concern in this whole debate was freedom, which was far more endangered by those who wanted "to compel faith by proofs" than by those who regarded faith as a gift of divine grace. But there was in addition his concern about the world, in which he felt both religion and philosophy should have their place, but separate places, so that behind the "partition . . . each can go its own way without hindering the other."

Criticism, in Lessing's sense, is always taking sides for the world's sake, understanding and judging everything in terms of its position in the world at any given time. Such a mentality can never give rise to a definite world view which, once adopted, is immune to further experiences in the world because it has hitched itself firmly to one possible perspective. We very much need Lessing to teach us this state of mind, and what makes learning it so hard for us is not our distrust of the Enlightenment or of the eighteenth century's belief in humanity. It is not the eighteenth but the nineteenth century that stands between Lessing and us. The nineteenth century's obsession with history and commitment to ideology still looms so large in the political thinking of our times that we are inclined to regard entirely free thinking, which employs neither history nor coercive logic as crutches, as having no authority over us. To be sure, we are still aware that thinking calls not only for intelligence and profundity but above all for courage. But we are astonished that Lessing's partisanship for the world could go so far that he could even sacrifice to it the axiom of noncontradiction, the claim to self-consistency, which we assume is mandatory to all who write and speak. For he declared in all seriousness: "I am not duty-bound to resolve the difficulties I create. May my ideas always be somewhat disjunct, or even appear to contradict one another, if only they are ideas in which readers will find material that stirs them to think for themselves." He not only wanted no one to coerce him, but he also wanted to coerce no one, either by force or by proofs. He regarded the tyranny of those who attempt to dominate thinking by reasoning and sophistries, by compelling argumentation, as more dangerous to freedom than orthodoxy. Above all he never coerced himself, and instead of fixing his identity in history with a perfectly consistent system, he scattered into the world, as he himself knew, "nothing but *fermenta cognitionis*."

Thus Lessing's famous *Selbstdenken*—independent thinking for oneself—is by no means an activity pertaining to a closed, integrated, organically grown and cultivated individual who then as it were looks around to see where in the world the most favorable place for his development might be, in order to bring himself into harmony with the world by the detour of thought.

8

For Lessing, thought does not arise out of the individual and is not the manifestation of a self. Rather, the individual—whom Lessing would say was created for action, not ratiocination—elects such thought because he discovers in thinking another mode of moving in the world in freedom. Of all the specific liberties which may come into our minds when we hear the word "freedom," freedom of movement is historically the oldest and also the most elementary. Being able to depart for where we will is the prototypal gesture of being free, as limitation of freedom of movement has from time immemorial been the precondition for enslavement. Freedom of movement is also the indispensable condition for action, and it is in action that men primarily experience freedom in the world. When men are deprived of the public space—which is constituted by acting together and then fills of its own accord with the events and stories that develop into history—they retreat into their freedom of thought. That is a very ancient experience, of course. And some such retreat seems to have been forced upon Lessing. When we hear of such a retreat from enslavement in the world to freedom of thought, we naturally remember the Stoic model, because it was historically the most effective. But to be precise, Stoicism represents not so much a retreat from action to thinking as an escape from the world into the self which, it is hoped, will be able to sustain itself in sovereign independence of the outside world. There was nothing of the sort in Lessing's case. Lessing retreated into thought, but not at all into his own self; and if for him a secret link between action and thought did exist (I believe it did, although I cannot prove it by quotations), the link consisted in the fact that both action and thought occur in the form of movement and that, therefore, freedom underlies both: freedom of movement.

Lessing probably never believed that acting can be replaced by thinking, or that freedom of thought can be a substitute for the freedom inherent in action. He knew very well that he was living in what was then the "most slavish country in Europe," even though he was allowed to "offer the public as many idiocies against religion" as he pleased. For it was impossible to raise "a voice for the rights of subjects . . . against extortion and despotism," in other words, to act. The secret relationship of his "self-thinking" to action lay in his never binding his thinking to results. In fact, he explicitly renounced the desire for results, insofar as these might mean the final solution of problems which his thought posed for itself; his thinking was not a search for truth, since every truth that is the result of a thought process necessarily puts an end to the movement of thinking. The *fermenta cognitionis* which Lessing scattered into the world were not intended to communicate conclusions, but to stimulate others to independent thought, and this for no other purpose than to bring about a discourse between thinkers. Lessing's thought is not the (Platonic) silent dialogue between me and myself, but an anticipated dialogue with others, and this is the reason that it is essentially polemical. But even if he had succeeded in bringing about his discourse with other independent thinkers and so escaping a solitude which, for him in particular, paralyzed all faculties, he could scarcely have been persuaded that this put everything to rights. For what was wrong, and what no dialogue and no independent thinking ever could right, was the world—namely, the thing that arises between people and in which everything that individuals carry with them innately can become visible and audible. In the two hundred years that separate us from Lessing's lifetime, much has changed in this respect, but little has changed for the better. The "pillars of the best-known truths" (to stay with his metaphor), which at that time were shaken, today lie shattered; we need neither criticism nor wise men to shake them any more. We need only look around to see that we are standing in the midst of a veritable rubble heap of such pillars.

Now in a certain sense this could be an advantage, promoting a new kind of thinking that needs no pillars and props, no standards and traditions to move freely without crutches over unfamiliar terrain. But with the world as it is, it is difficult to enjoy this advantage. For long ago it became apparent that the pillars of the truths have also been the pillars of the political order, and that the world (in contrast to the people who inhabit it and move freely about in it) needs such pillars in order to guarantee continuity and permanence, without which it cannot offer mortal men the relatively secure, relatively imperishable home that they need. To be sure, the very humanity of man loses its vitality to the extent that he abstains from thinking and puts his confidence into old verities or even new truths, throwing them down as if they were coins with which to balance all experiences. And yet, if this is true for man, it is not true for the world. The world becomes inhuman, inhospitable to human needs—which are the needs of mortals—when it is violently wrenched into a movement in which there is no longer any sort of permanence. That is why ever since the great failure of the French Revolution people have repeatedly re-erected the old pillars which were then overthrown, only again and again to see them first quivering, then collapsing anew. The most frightful errors have replaced the "best-known truths," and the error of these doctrines constitutes no proof, no new pillar for the old truths. In the political realm restoration is never a substitute for a new foundation but will be at best an emergency measure that becomes inevitable when the act of foundation, which is called revolution, has failed. But it is likewise inevitable that in such a constellation, especially when it extends over such long spans of time, people's mistrust of the world and all aspects of the public realm should grow steadily. For the fragility of these repeatedly restored props of the public order is bound to become more apparent after every collapse, so that ultimately the public order is based on people's holding as self-evident precisely those "best-known truths" which secretly scarcely anyone still believes in.

II

History knows many periods of dark times in which the public realm has been obscured and the world become so dubious that people have ceased to ask any more of politics than that it show due consideration for their vital interests and personal liberty. Those who have lived in such times and been formed by them have probably always been inclined to despise the world and the public realm, to ignore them as far as possible, or even to overleap them and, as it were, reach behind them—as if the world were only a façade behind which people could conceal themselves—in order to arrive at mutual understandings with their fellow men without regard for the world that lies between them. In such times, if things turn out well, a special kind of humanity develops. In order properly to appreciate its possibilities we need only think of *Nathan the Wise*, whose true theme—"It suffices to be a man"—permeates the play. The appeal: "Be my friend," which runs like a leitmotif through the whole play, corresponds to that theme. We might equally well think of *The Magic Flute*, which likewise has as its theme such a humanity, which is more profound than we generally think when we consider only the eighteenth century's usual theories of a basic human nature underlying the multiplicity of nations, peoples, races, and religions into which the human race is divided. If such a human nature were to exist, it would be a natural phenomenon, and to call behavior in accordance with it "human" would assume that human and natural behavior are one and the same. In the eighteenth century the greatest and historically the most effective advocate of this kind of humanity was Rousseau, for whom the human nature common to all men was manifested not in reason but in compassion, in an innate repugnance, as he put it, to see a fellow human being suffering. With remarkable accord, Lessing also declared that the best person is the most compassionate. But Lessing was troubled by the egalitarian character of compassion —the fact that, as he stressed, we feel "something akin to compassion" for the evildoer also. This did not trouble Rousseau. In the spirit of the French Revolution, which leaned upon his ideas, he saw *fraternité* as the fulfillment of humanity. Lessing, on the other hand, considered friendship—which is as selective as compassion is egalitarian—to be the central phenomenon in which alone true humanity can prove itself.

Before we turn to Lessing's concept of friendship and its political relevance, we must dwell for a moment on fraternity as the eighteenth century understood it. Lessing, too, was well acquainted with it; he spoke of "philanthropic feelings," of a brotherly attachment to other human beings which springs from hatred of the world in which men are treated "inhumanly." For our purposes, however, it is important that humanity manifests itself in such brotherhood most frequently in "dark times." This kind of humanity actually becomes inevitable when the times become so extremely dark for certain groups of people that it is no longer up to them, their insight or choice, to withdraw from the world. Humanity in the form of fraternity invariably appears historically among persecuted peoples and enslaved groups; and in eighteenth-century Europe it must have been quite natural to detect it among the Jews, who then were newcomers in literary circles. This kind of humanity is the great privilege of pariah peoples; it is the advantage that the pariahs of this world always and in all circumstances can have over others. The privilege is dearly bought; it is often accompanied by so radical a loss of the world, so fearful an atrophy of all the organs with which we respond to it—starting with the common sense with which we orient ourselves in a world common to ourselves and others and going on to the sense of beauty, or taste, with which we love the world—that in extreme cases, in which pariahdom has persisted for centuries, we can speak of real worldlessness. And worldlessness, alas, is always a form of barbarism.

In this as it were organically evolved humanity it is as if under the pressure of persecution the persecuted have moved so closely together that the interspace which we have called world (and which of course existed between them before the persecution, keeping them at a distance from one another) has simply disappeared. This produces a warmth of human relationships which may strike those who have had some experience with such groups as an almost physical phenomenon. Of course I do not mean to imply that this warmth of persecuted peoples is not a great thing. In its full development it can breed a kindliness and sheer goodness of which human beings are otherwise scarcely capable. Frequently it is also the source of a vitality, a joy in the simple fact of being alive, rather suggesting that life comes fully into its own only among those who are, in worldly terms, the insulted and injured. But in saying this we must not forget that the

13

charm and intensity of the atmosphere that develops is also due
to the fact that the pariahs of this world enjoy the great privilege
of being unburdened by care for the world.

Fraternity, which the French Revolution added to the liberty
and equality which have always been categories of man's political
sphere—that fraternity has its natural place among the repressed
and persecuted, the exploited and humiliated, whom the eighteenth century called the unfortunates, *les malheureux*, and the
nineteenth century the wretched, *les misérables*. Compassion,
which for both Lessing and Rousseau (though in very different
contexts) played so extraordinary a part in the discovery and
confirmation of a human nature common to all men, for the first
time became the central motive of the revolutionary in Robespierre. Ever since, compassion has remained inseparably and un-
mistakably part of the history of European revolutions. Now
compassion is unquestionably a natural, creature affect which in-
voluntarily touches every normal person at the sight of suffering,
however alien the sufferer may be, and would therefore seem an
ideal basis for a feeling that reaching out to all mankind would
establish a society in which men might really become brothers.
Through compassion the revolutionary-minded humanitarian of
the eighteenth century sought to achieve solidarity with the unfortunate and the miserable—an effort tantamount to penetrating
the very domain of brotherhood. But it soon became evident
that this kind of humanitarianism, whose purest form is a privilege of the pariah, is not transmissible and cannot be easily
acquired by those who do not belong among the pariahs. Neither
compassion nor actual sharing of suffering is enough. We cannot
discuss here the mischief that compassion has introduced into
modern revolutions by attempts to improve the lot of the unfortunate rather than to establish justice for all. But in order to
gain a little perspective on ourselves and the modern way of
feeling we might recall briefly how the ancient world, so much
more experienced in all political matters than ourselves, viewed
compassion and the humanitarianism of brotherhood.

Modern times and antiquity agree on one point: both regard
compassion as something totally natural, as inescapable to man

as, say, fear. It is therefore all the more striking that antiquity took a position wholly at odds with the great esteem for compassion of modern times. Because they so clearly recognized the affective nature of compassion, which can overcome us like fear without our being able to fend it off, the ancients regarded the most compassionate person as no more entitled to be called the best than the most fearful. Both emotions, because they are purely passive, make action impossible. This is the reason Aristotle treated compassion and fear together. Yet it would be altogether misguided to reduce compassion to fear—as though the sufferings of others aroused in us fear for ourselves—or fear to compassion—as though in fear we felt only compassion for ourselves. We are even more surprised when we hear (from Cicero in the *Tusculanae Disputationes* III 21) that the Stoics saw compassion and envy in the same terms: "For the man who is pained by another's misfortune is also pained by another's prosperity." Cicero himself comes considerably closer to the heart of the matter when he asks (*ibid*. IV 56): "Why pity rather than give assistance if one can? Or, are we unable to be open-handed without pity?" In other words, should human beings be so shabby that they are incapable of acting humanly unless spurred and as it were compelled by their own pain when they see others suffer?

In judging these affects we can scarcely help raising the question of selflessness, or rather the question of openness to others, which in fact is the precondition for "humanity" in every sense of that word. It seems evident that sharing joy is absolutely superior in this respect to sharing suffering. Gladness, not sadness, is talkative, and truly human dialogue differs from mere talk or even discussion in that it is entirely permeated by pleasure in the other person and what he says. It is tuned to the key of gladness, we might say. What stands in the way of this gladness is envy, which in the sphere of humanity is the worst vice; but the antithesis to compassion is not envy but cruelty, which is an affect no less than compassion, for it is a perversion, a feeling of pleasure where pain would naturally be felt. The decisive factor is that pleasure and pain, like everything instinctual, tend to muteness, and while they may well produce sound, they do not produce speech and certainly not dialogue.

All this is only another way of saying that the humanitarianism of brotherhood scarcely befits those who do not belong among the insulted and the injured and can share in it only through their compassion. The warmth of pariah peoples cannot rightfully extend to those whose different position in the world imposes on them a responsibility for the world and does not allow them to share the cheerful unconcern of the pariah. But it is true that in "dark times" the warmth which is the pariahs' substitute for light exerts a great fascination upon all those who are so ashamed of the world as it is that they would like to take refuge in invisibility. And in invisibility, in that obscurity in which a man who is himself hidden need no longer see the visible world either, only the warmth and fraternity of closely packed human beings can compensate for the weird irreality that human relationships assume wherever they develop in absolute worldlessness, unrelated to a world common to all people. In such a state of worldlessness and irreality it is easy to conclude that the element common to all men is not the world, but "human nature" of such and such a type. What the type is depends on the interpreter; it scarcely matters whether reason, as a property of all men, is emphasized, or a feeling common to all, such as the capacity for compassion. The rationalism and sentimentalism of the eighteenth century are only two aspects of the same thing; both could lead equally to that enthusiastic excess in which individuals feel ties of brotherhood to all men. In any case this rationality and sentimentality were only psychological substitutes, localized in the realm of invisibility, for the loss of the common, visible world.

Now this "human nature" and the feelings of fraternity that accompany it manifest themselves only in darkness, and hence cannot be identified in the world. What is more, in conditions of visibility they dissolve into nothingness like phantoms. The humanity of the insulted and injured has never yet survived the hour of liberation by so much as a minute. This does not mean that it is insignificant, for in fact it makes insult and injury endurable; but it does mean that in political terms it is absolutely irrelevant.

III

These and similar questions of the proper attitude in "dark times" are of course especially familiar to the generation and the group to which I belong. If concord with the world, which is part and parcel of receiving honors, has never been an easy matter in our times and in the circumstances of our world, it is even less so for us. Certainly honors were no part of our birthright, and it would not be surprising if we were no longer capable of the openness and trustfulness that are needed simply to accept gratefully what the world offers in good faith. Even those among us who by speaking and writing have ventured into public life have not done so out of any original pleasure in the public scene, and have hardly expected or aspired to receive the stamp of public approval. Even in public they tended to address only their friends or to speak to those unknown, scattered readers and listeners with whom everyone who speaks and writes at all cannot help feeling joined in some rather obscure brotherhood. I am afraid that in their efforts they felt very little responsibility toward the world; these efforts were, rather, guided by their hope of preserving some minimum of humanity in a world grown inhuman while at the same time as far as possible resisting the weird irreality of this worldlessness—each after his own fashion and some few by seeking to the limits of their ability to understand even inhumanity and the intellectual and political monstrosities of a time out of joint.

I so explicitly stress my membership in the group of Jews expelled from Germany at a relatively early age because I wish to anticipate certain misunderstandings which can arise only too easily when one speaks of humanity. In this connection I cannot gloss over the fact that for many years I considered the only adequate reply to the question, Who are you? to be: A Jew. That answer alone took into account the reality of persecution. As for the statement with which Nathan the Wise (in effect, though not in actual wording) countered the command: "Step closer, Jew" —the statement: I am a man—I would have considered as nothing but a grotesque and dangerous evasion of reality.

Let me also quickly clear away another likely misunderstanding. When I use the word "Jew" I do not mean to suggest any special kind of human being, as though the Jewish fate were either representative of or a model for the fate of mankind. (Any such thesis could at best have been advanced with cogency only during the last stage of Nazi domination, when in fact the Jews and anti-Semitism were being exploited solely to unleash and keep in motion the racist program of extermination. For this was an essential part of totalitarian rule. The Nazi movement, to be sure, had from the first tended toward totalitarianism, but the Third Reich was not by any means totalitarian during its early years. By "early years" I mean the first period, which lasted from 1933 to 1938.) In saying, "A Jew," I did not even refer to a reality burdened or marked out for distinction by history. Rather, I was only acknowledging a political fact through which my being a member of this group outweighed all other questions of personal identity or rather had decided them in favor of anonymity, of namelessness. Nowadays such an attitude would seem like a pose. Nowadays, therefore, it is easy to remark that those who reacted in this way had never got very far in the school of "humanity," had fallen into the trap set by Hitler, and thus had succumbed to the spirit of Hitlerism in their own way. Unfortunately, the basically simple principle in question here is one that is particularly hard to understand in times of defamation and persecution: the principle that one can resist only in terms of the identity that is under attack. Those who reject such identifications on the part of a hostile world may feel wonderfully superior to the world, but their superiority is then truly no longer of this world; it is the superiority of a more or less well-equipped cloud-cuckoo-land.

When I thus bluntly reveal the personal background of my reflections, it may easily sound to those who know the fate of the Jews only from hearsay as if I am talking out of school, a school they have not attended and whose lessons do not concern them. But as it happens, during that selfsame period in Germany there existed the phenomenon known as the "inner emigration," and those who know anything about that experience may well recognize certain questions and conflicts akin to the problems I have mentioned in more than a mere formal and structural sense. As its very name suggests, the "inner emigration" was a curiously ambiguous phenomenon. It signified on the one hand that there were persons inside Germany who behaved as if they no longer belonged to the country, who felt like emigrants; and on the other hand it indicated that they had not in reality emigrated, but had withdrawn to an interior realm, into the invisibility of thinking and feeling. It would be a mistake to imagine that this form of exile, a withdrawal from the world into an interior realm, existed only in Germany, just as it would be a mistake to imagine that such emigration came to an end with the end of the Third Reich. But in that darkest of times, inside and outside Germany the temptation was particularly strong, in the face of a seemingly unendurable reality, to shift from the world and its public space to an interior life, or else simply to ignore that world in favor of an imaginary world "as it ought to be" or as it once upon a time had been.

There has been much discussion of the widespread tendency in Germany to act as though the years from 1933 to 1945 never existed; as though this part of German and European and thus world history could be expunged from the textbooks; as though everything depended on forgetting the "negative" aspect of the past and reducing horror to sentimentality. (The world-wide success of *The Diary of Anne Frank* was clear proof that such tendencies were not confined to Germany.) It was a grotesque state of affairs when German young people were not allowed to learn the facts that every schoolchild a few miles away could not help knowing. Behind all this there was, of course, genuine perplexity. And this very incapacity to face the reality of the past might possibly have been a direct heritage of the inner emigration, as it was undoubtedly to a considerable extent, and even more directly, a consequence of the Hitler regime—that is to say, a consequence of the organized guilt in which the Nazis had involved all inhabitants of the German lands, the inner exiles no less than the stalwart Party members and the vacillating fellow travelers. It was the fact of this guilt which the Allies simply incorporated into the fateful hypothesis of collective guilt. Herein lies the reason for the Germans' profound awkwardness, which strikes every outsider, in any discussion of questions of the past. How difficult it must be to find a reasonable attitude is perhaps more clearly expressed by the cliché that the past is still "unmastered" and in the conviction held particularly by men of good will that the first thing to be done is to set about "mastering" it. Perhaps that cannot be done with any past, but certainly not with the past of Hitler Germany. The best that can be achieved is to know precisely what it was, and to endure this knowledge, and then to wait and see what comes of knowing and enduring.

Perhaps I can best explain this by a less painful example. After the First World War we experienced the "mastering of the past" in a spate of descriptions of the war that varied enormously in kind and quality; naturally, this happened not only in Germany, but in all the affected countries. Nevertheless, nearly thirty years were to pass before a work of art appeared which so transparently displayed the inner truth of the event that it became possible to say: Yes, this is how it was. And in this novel, William Faulkner's *A Fable*, very little is described, still less explained, and nothing at all "mastered"; its end is tears, which the reader also weeps, and what remains beyond that is the "tragic effect" or the "tragic pleasure," the shattering emotion which makes one able to accept the fact that something like this war could have happened at all. I deliberately mention tragedy because it more than the other literary forms represents a process of recognition. The tragic hero becomes knowledgeable by re-experiencing what has been done in the way of suffering, and in this *pathos*, in resuffering the past, the network of individual acts is transformed into an event, a significant whole. The dramatic climax of tragedy occurs when the actor turns into a sufferer; therein lies its peripeteia, the disclosure of the dénouement. But even non-tragic plots become genuine events only when they are experienced a second time in the form of suffering by memory operating retrospectively and perceptively. Such memory can speak only when indignation and just anger, which impel us to action, have been silenced—and that needs time. We can no more master the past than we can undo it. But we can reconcile ourselves to it. The form for this is the lament, which arises out of all recollection. It is, as Goethe has said (in the Dedication to *Faust*):

> *Der Schmerz wird neu, es wiederholt die Klage*
> *Des Lebens labyrinthisch irren Lauf.*

> (Pain arises anew, lament repeats
> Life's labyrinthine, erring course.)

The tragic impact of this repetition in lamentation affects one of the key elements of all action; it establishes its meaning and that permanent significance which then enters into history. In contradistinction to other elements peculiar to action—above all to the preconceived goals, the impelling motives, and the guiding principles, all of which become visible in the course of action— the meaning of a committed act is revealed only when the action itself has come to an end and become a story susceptible to narration. Insofar as any "mastering" of the past is possible, it consists in relating what has happened; but such narration, too, which shapes history, solves no problems and assuages no suffering; it does not master anything once and for all. Rather, as long as the meaning of the events remains alive—and this meaning can persist for very long periods of time—"mastering of the past" can take the form of ever-recurrent narration. The poet in a very general sense and the historian in a very special sense have the task of setting this process of narration in motion and of involving us in it. And we who for the most part are neither poets nor historians are familiar with the nature of this process from our own experience with life, for we too have the need to recall the significant events in our own lives by relating them to ourselves and others. Thus we are constantly preparing the way for "poetry," in the broadest sense, as a human potentiality; we are, so to speak, constantly expecting it to erupt in some human being.

When this happens, the telling-over of what took place comes to a halt for the time being and a formed narrative, one more item, is added to the world's stock. In reification by the poet or the historian, the narration of history has achieved permanence and persistence. Thus the narrative has been given its place in the world, where it will survive us. There it can live on—one story among many. There is no meaning to these stories that is entirely separable from them—and this, too, we know from our own, non-poetic experience. No philosophy, no analysis, no aphorism, be it ever so profound, can compare in intensity and richness of meaning with a properly narrated story.

I seem to have digressed from my subject. The question is how much reality must be retained even in a world become inhuman if humanity is not to be reduced to an empty phrase or a phantom. Or to put it another way, to what extent do we remain obligated to the world even when we have been expelled from it or have withdrawn from it? For I certainly do not wish to assert that the "inner emigration," the flight from the world to concealment, from public life to anonymity (when that is what it really was and not just a pretext for doing what everyone did with enough inner reservations to salve one's conscience), was not a justified attitude, and in many cases the only possible one. Flight from the world in dark times of impotence can always be justified as long as reality is not ignored, but is constantly acknowledged as the thing that must be escaped. When people choose this alternative, private life too can retain a by no means insignificant reality, even though it remains impotent. Only it is essential for them to realize that the realness of this reality consists not in its deeply personal note, any more than it springs from privacy as such, but inheres in the world from which they have escaped. They must remember that they are constantly on the run, and that the world's reality is actually expressed by their escape. Thus, too, the true force of escapism springs from persecution, and the personal strength of the fugitives increases as the persecution and danger increase.

At the same time we cannot fail to see the limited political relevance of such an existence, even if it is sustained in purity.

Its limits are inherent in the fact that strength and power are not the same; that power arises only where people act together, but not where people grow stronger as individuals. No strength is ever great enough to replace power; wherever strength is confronted by power, strength will always succumb. But even the sheer strength to escape and to resist while fleeing cannot materialize where reality is bypassed or forgotten—as when an individual thinks himself too good and noble to pit himself against such a world, or when he fails to face up to the absolute "negativeness" of prevailing world conditions at a given time. How tempting it was, for example, simply to ignore the intolerably stupid blabber of the Nazis. But seductive though it may be to yield to such temptations and to hole up in the refuge of one's own psyche, the result will always be a loss of humanness along with the forsaking of reality.

Thus, in the case of a friendship between a German and a Jew under the conditions of the Third Reich it would scarcely have been a sign of humanness for the friends to have said: Are we not both human beings? It would have been mere evasion of reality and of the world common to both at that time; they would not have been resisting the world as it was. A law that prohibited the intercourse of Jews and Germans could be evaded but could not be defied by people who denied the reality of the distinction. In keeping with a humanness that had not lost the solid ground of reality, a humanness in the midst of the reality of persecution, they would have had to say to each other: A German and a Jew, and friends. But wherever such a friendship succeeded at that time (of course the situation is completely changed, nowadays) and was maintained in purity, that is to say without false guilt complexes on the one side and false complexes of superiority or inferiority on the other, a bit of humanness in a world become inhuman had been achieved.

IV

The example of friendship, which I have adduced because it seems to me for a variety of reasons to be specially pertinent to the question of humanness, brings us back to Lessing again. As is well known, the ancients thought friends indispensable to human life, indeed that a life without friends was not really worth living. In holding this view they gave little consideration to the idea that we need the help of friends in misfortune; on the contrary, they rather thought that there can be no happiness or good fortune for anyone unless a friend shares in the joy of it. Of course there is something to the maxim that only in misfortune do we find out who our true friends are; but those whom we regard as our true friends without such proof are usually those to whom we unhesitatingly reveal happiness and whom we count on to share our rejoicing.

We are wont to see friendship solely as a phenomenon of intimacy, in which the friends open their hearts to each other unmolested by the world and its demands. Rousseau, not Lessing, is the best advocate of this view, which conforms so well to the basic attitude of the modern individual, who in his alienation from the world can truly reveal himself only in privacy and in the intimacy of face-to-face encounters. Thus it is hard for us to understand the political relevance of friendship. When, for example, we read in Aristotle that *philia*, friendship among citizens, is one of the fundamental requirements for the well-being of the City, we tend to think that he was speaking of no more than the absence of factions and civil war within it. But for the Greeks the essence of friendship consisted in discourse. They held that only the constant interchange of talk united citizens in a *polis*. In discourse the political importance of friendship, and the humanness peculiar to it, were made manifest. This converse (in contrast to the intimate talk in which individuals speak about themselves), permeated though it may be by pleasure in the friend's presence, is concerned with the common world, which remains "inhuman" in a very literal sense unless it is constantly talked about by human beings. For the world is not humane just because it is made by human beings, and it does not become humane just because the human voice sounds in it, but only when it has become the object of discourse. However much we are affected by the things of the world, however deeply they may stir and stimulate us, they become human for us only when we can discuss them with our fellows. Whatever cannot become the object of discourse—the truly sublime, the truly horrible or the uncanny—may find a human voice through which to sound into the world, but it is not exactly human. We humanize what is going on in the world and in ourselves only by speaking of it, and in the course of speaking of it we learn to be human.

The Greeks called this humanness which is achieved in the discourse of friendship *philanthropia*, "love of man," since it manifests itself in a readiness to share the world with other men. Its opposite, misanthropy, means simply that the misanthrope finds no one with whom he cares to share the world, that he regards nobody as worthy of rejoicing with him in the world and nature and the cosmos. Greek philanthropy underwent many a change in becoming Roman *humanitas*. The most important of these changes corresponded to the political fact that in Rome people of widely different ethnic origins and descent could acquire Roman citizenship and thus enter into the discourse among cultivated Romans, could discuss the world and life with them. And this political background distinguishes Roman *humanitas* from what moderns call humanity, by which they commonly mean a mere effect of education.

That humaneness should be sober and cool rather than sentimental; that humanity is exemplified not in fraternity but in friendship; that friendship is not intimately personal but makes political demands and preserves reference to the world—all this seems to us so exclusively characteristic of classical antiquity that it rather perplexes us when we find quite kindred features in *Nathan the Wise*—which, modern as it is, might with some justice be called the classical drama of friendship. What strikes us as so strange in the play is the "We must, must be friends," with which Nathan turns to the Templar, and in fact to everyone he meets; for this friendship is obviously so much more important to Lessing than the passion of love that he can brusquely cut the love story off short (the lovers, the Templar and Nathan's adopted daughter Recha, turn out to be brother and sister) and transform it into a relationship in which friendship is required and love ruled out. The dramatic tension of the play lies solely in the conflict that arises between friendship and humanity with truth. That fact perhaps strikes modern men as even stranger, but once again it is curiously close to the principles and conflicts which concerned classical antiquity. In the end, after all, Nathan's wisdom consists solely in his readiness to sacrifice truth to friendship.

Lessing had highly unorthodox opinions about truth. He refused to accept any truths whatever, even those presumably handed down by Providence, and he never felt compelled by truth, be it imposed by others' or by his own reasoning processes. If he had been confronted with the Platonic alternative of *doxa* or *aletheia*, of opinion or truth, there is no question how he would have decided. He was glad that—to use his parable—the genuine ring, if it had ever existed, had been lost; he was glad for the sake of the infinite number of opinions that arise when men discuss the affairs of this world. If the genuine ring did exist, that would mean an end to discourse and thus to friendship and thus to humanness. On these same grounds he was content to belong to the race of "limited gods," as he occasionally called men; and he thought that human society was in no way harmed by those "who take more trouble to make clouds than to scatter them," while it incurred "much harm from those who wish to subject all men's ways of thinking to the yoke of their own." This has very little to do with tolerance in the ordinary sense (in fact Lessing himself was by no means an especially tolerant person), but it has a great deal to do with the gift of friendship, with openness to the world, and finally with genuine love of mankind.

The theme of "limited gods," of the limitations of the human understanding, limitations which speculative reason can point out and thereby transcend, subsequently became the great object of Kant's critiques. But whatever Kant's attitudes may have in common with Lessing's—and in fact they do have much in common—the two thinkers differed on one decisive point. Kant realized that there can be no absolute truth for man, at least not in the theoretical sense. He would certainly have been prepared to sacrifice truth to the possibility of human freedom; for if we possessed truth we could not be free. But he would scarcely have agreed with Lessing that the truth, if it did exist, could be unhesitatingly sacrificed to humanity, to the possibility of friendship and of discourse among men. Kant argued that an absolute exists, the duty of the categorical imperative which stands above men, is decisive in all human affairs, and cannot be infringed even for the sake of humanity in every sense of that word. Critics of the Kantian ethic have frequently denounced this thesis as altogether inhuman and unmerciful. Whatever the merits of their arguments, the inhumanity of Kant's moral philosophy is undeniable. And this is so because the categorical imperative is postulated as absolute and in its absoluteness introduces into the interhuman realm—which by its nature consists of relationships—something that runs counter to its fundamental relativity. The inhumanity which is bound up with the concept of one single truth emerges with particular clarity in Kant's work precisely because he attempted to found truth on practical reason; it is as though he who had so inexorably pointed out man's cognitive limits could not bear to think that in action, too, man cannot behave like a god.

Lessing, however, rejoiced in the very thing that has ever—or at least since Parmenides and Plato—distressed philosophers: that the truth, as soon as it is uttered, is immediately transformed into one opinion among many, is contested, reformulated, reduced to one subject of discourse among others. Lessing's greatness does not merely consist in a theoretical insight that there cannot be one single truth within the human world but in his gladness that it does not exist and that, therefore, the unending discourse among men will never cease so long as there are men at all. A single absolute truth, could there have been one, would have been the death of all those disputes in which this ancestor and master of all polemicism in the German language was so much at home and always took sides with the utmost clarity and definiteness. And this would have spelled the end of humanity.

It is difficult for us today to identify with the dramatic but untragic conflict of *Nathan the Wise* as Lessing intended it. That is partly because in regard to truth it has become a matter of course for us to behave tolerantly, although for reasons that have scarcely any connection with Lessing's reasons. Nowadays someone may still occasionally put the question at least in the style of Lessing's parable of the three rings—as, for example, in Kafka's magnificent pronouncement: "It is difficult to speak the truth, for although there is only one truth, it is alive and therefore has a live and changing face." But here, too, nothing is said of the political point of Lessing's antinomy—that is, the possible antagonism between truth and humanity. Nowadays, moreover, it is rare to meet people who believe they possess the truth; instead, we are constantly confronted by those who are sure that they are right. The distinction is plain; the question of truth was in Lessing's time still a question of philosophy and of religion, whereas our problem of being right arises within the framework of science and is always decided by a mode of thought oriented toward science. In saying this I shall ignore the question of whether this change in ways of thinking has proved to be for our good or ill. The simple fact is that even men who are utterly incapable of judging the specifically scientific aspects of an argument are as fascinated by scientific rightness as men of the eighteenth century were by the question of truth. And strangely enough, modern men are not deflected from their fascination by the attitude of scientists, who as long as they are really proceeding scientifically know quite well that their "truths" are never final but are continually undergoing radical revision by living research.

In spite of the difference between the notions of possessing the truth and being right, these two points of view have one thing in common: those who take one or the other are generally not prepared to sacrifice their view to humanity or friendship in case a conflict should arise. They actually believe that to do so would be to violate a higher duty, the duty of "objectivity"; so that even if they occasionally make such a sacrifice they do not feel they are acting out of conscience but are even ashamed of their humanity and often feel distinctly guilty about it. In terms of the age in which we live, and in terms of the many dogmatic opinions that dominate our thinking, we can translate

Lessing's conflict into one closer to our experience, by showing its application to the twelve years and to the dominant ideology of the Third Reich. Let us for the moment set aside the fact that Nazi racial doctrine is in principle unprovable because it contradicts man's "nature." (By the way, it is worth remarking that these "scientific" theories were neither an invention of the Nazis nor even a specifically German invention.) But let us assume for the moment that the racial theories could have been convincingly proved. For it cannot be gainsaid that the practical political conclusions the Nazis drew from these theories were perfectly logical. Suppose that a race could indeed be shown, by indubitable scientific evidence, to be inferior; would that fact justify its extermination? But the answer to this question is still too easy, because we can invoke the "Thou shalt not kill" which in fact has become the fundamental commandment governing legal and moral thinking of the Occident ever since the victory of Christianity over antiquity. But in terms of a way of thinking governed by neither legal nor moral nor religious strictures—and Lessing's thought was as untrammeled, as "live and changing" as that—the question would have to be posed thus: *Would any such doctrine, however convincingly proved, be worth the sacrifice of so much as a single friendship between two men?*

Thus we have come back to my starting point, to the astonishing lack of "objectivity" in Lessing's polemicism, to his forever vigilant partiality, which has nothing whatsoever to do with subjectivity because it is always framed not in terms of the self but in terms of the relationship of men to their world, in terms of their positions and opinions. Lessing would not have found any difficulty in answering the question I have just posed. No insight into the nature of Islam or of Judaism or of Christianity could have kept him from entering into a friendship and the discourse of friendship with a convinced Mohammedan or a pious Jew or a believing Christian. Any doctrine that in principle barred the possibility of friendship between two human beings would have been rejected by his untrammeled and unerring conscience. He would instantly have taken the human side and given short shrift to the learned or unlearned discussion in either camp. That was Lessing's humanity.

This humanity emerged in a politically enslaved world whose foundations, moreover, were already shaken. Lessing, too, was already living in "dark times," and after his own fashion he was destroyed by their darkness. We have seen what a powerful need men have, in such times, to move closer to one another, to seek in the warmth of intimacy the substitute for that light and illumination which only the public realm can cast. But this means that they avoid disputes and try as far as possible to deal only with people with whom they cannot come into conflict. For a man of Lessing's disposition there was little room in such an age and in such a confined world; where people moved together in order to warm one another, they moved away from him. And yet he, who was polemical to the point of contentiousness, could no more endure loneliness than the excessive closeness of a brotherliness that obliterated all distinctions. He was never eager really to fall out with someone with whom he had entered into a dispute; he was concerned solely with humanizing the world by incessant and continual discourse about its affairs and the things in it. He wanted to be the friend of many men, but no man's brother.

He failed to achieve this friendship in the world with people in dispute and discourse, and indeed under the conditions then prevailing in German-speaking lands he could scarcely have succeeded. Sympathy for a man who "was worth more than all his talents" and whose greatness "lay in his individuality" (Friedrich Schlegel) could never really develop in Germany because such sympathy would have to arise out of politics in the deepest sense of the word. Because Lessing was a completely political person, he insisted that truth can exist only where it is humanized by discourse, only where each man says not what just happens to occur to him at the moment, but what he "deems truth." But such speech is virtually impossible in solitude; it belongs to an area in which there are many voices and where the announcement of what each "deems truth" both links and separates men, establishing in fact those distances between men which together comprise the world. Every truth outside this area, no matter whether it brings men good or ill, is inhuman in the literal sense of the word; but not because it might rouse men against one another and separate them. Quite the contrary, it is because it might have the result that all men would suddenly unite in a single opinion, so that out of many opinions one would emerge, as though not men in their infinite plurality but man in the singular, one species and its exemplars, were to inhabit the earth. Should that happen, the world, which can form only in the interspaces between men in all their variety, would vanish altogether. For that reason the most profound thing that has been said about the relationship between truth and humanity is to be found in a sentence of Lessing's which seems to draw from all his works wisdom's last word. The sentence is:

JEDER SAGE, WAS IHM WAHRHEIT DÜNKT,
UND DIE WAHRHEIT SELBST SEI GOTT EMPFOHLEN!

(Let each man say what he deems truth,
and let truth itself be commended unto God!)

ROSA LUXEMBURG

1871-1919

I

THE definitive biography, English-style, is among the most
admirable genres of historiography. Lengthy, thoroughly documented, heavily annotated, and generously splashed with quotations, it usually comes in two large volumes and tells more, and
more vividly, about the historical period in question than all but
the most outstanding history books. For unlike other biographies,
history is here not treated as the inevitable background of a
famous person's life span; it is rather as though the colorless
light of historical time were forced through and refracted by
the prism of a great character so that in the resulting spectrum
a complete unity of life and world is achieved. This may be why
it has become the classical genre for the lives of great statesmen
but has remained rather unsuitable for those in which the main
interest lies in the life story, or for the lives of artists, writers, and,
generally, men or women whose genius forced them to keep the
world at a certain distance and whose significance lies chiefly
in their works, the artifacts they added to the world, not in the
role they played in it.[1]

[1]Another limitation has become more obvious in recent years when Hitler
and Stalin, because of their importance for contemporary history, were

It was a stroke of genius on the part of J. P. Nettl to choose the life of Rosa Luxemburg,[2] the most unlikely candidate, as a proper subject for a genre that seems suitable only for the lives of great statesmen and other persons of the world. She certainly was nothing of the kind. Even in her own world of the European socialist movement she was a rather marginal figure, with relatively brief moments of splendor and great brilliance, whose influence in deed and written word can hardly be compared to that of her contemporaries—to Plekhanov, Trotsky, and Lenin, to Bebel and Kautsky, to Jaurès and Millerand. If success in the world is a prerequisite for success in the genre, how could Mr. Nettl succeed with this woman who when very young had been swept into the German Social Democratic Party from her native Poland; who continued to play a key role in the little-known and neglected history of Polish socialism; and who then for about two decades, although never officially recognized, became the most controversial and least understood figure in the German Left movement? For it was precisely success—success even in her own world of revolutionaries—which was withheld from Rosa Luxemburg in life, death, and after death. Can it be that the failure of all her efforts as far as official recognition is concerned is somehow connected with the dismal failure of revolution in our century? Will history look different if seen through the prism of her life and work?

However that may be, I know no book that sheds more light on the crucial period of European socialism from the last decades of the nineteenth century to the fateful day in January 1919 when Rosa Luxemburg and Karl Liebknecht, the two leaders of the

---

treated to the undeserved honor of definitive biographies. No matter how scrupulously Alan Bullock in his book on Hitler and Isaac Deutscher in his biography of Stalin followed the methodological technicalities prescribed by the genre, to see history in the light of these non-persons could only result in their falsifying promotion to respectability and in a more subtle distortion of the events. When we want to see both events and persons in right proportion we still have to go to the much less well documented and factually incomplete biographies of Hitler and Stalin by Konrad Heiden and Boris Souvarine respectively.

[2] *Rosa Luxemburg*, 2 vols., Oxford University Press, 1966.

Spartakusbund, the precursor of the German Communist Party, were murdered in Berlin—under the eyes and probably with the connivance of the Socialist regime then in power. The murderers were members of the ultra-nationalist and officially illegal *Freikorps,* a paramilitary organization from which Hitler's storm troopers were soon to recruit their most promising killers. That the government at the time was practically in the hands of the *Freikorps* because they enjoyed "the full support of Noske," the Socialists' expert on national defense, then in charge of military affairs, was confirmed only recently by Captain Pabst, the last surviving participant in the assassination. The Bonn government —in this as in other respects only too eager to revive the more sinister traits of the Weimar Republic—let it be known that it was thanks to the *Freikorps* that Moscow had failed to incorporate all of Germany into a red Empire after the First World War and that the murder of Liebknecht and Luxemburg was entirely legal "an execution in accordance with martial law." [3] This was considerably more than even the Weimar Republic had ever pretended, for it had never admitted publicly that the *Freikorps* actually were an arm of the government and it had "punished" the murderers by meting out a sentence of two years and two weeks to the soldier Runge for "*attempted* manslaughter" (he had hit Rosa Luxemburg over the head in the corridors of the Hotel Eden), and four months to Lieutenant Vogel (he was the officer in charge when she was shot in the head inside a car and thrown into the Landwehr Canal) for "failing to report a corpse and illegally disposing of it." During the trial, a photograph showing Runge and his comrades celebrating the assassination in the same hotel on the following day was introduced as evidence, which caused the defendant great merriment. "Accused Runge, you must behave properly. This is no laughing matter," said the presiding judge. Forty-five years later, during the Auschwitz trial in Frankfurt, a similar scene took place; the same words were spoken.

[3] See the *Bulletin des Presse- und Informationsamtes der Bundesregierung,* of February 8, 1962, p. 224.

With the murder of Rosa Luxemburg and Liebknecht, the split of the European Left into Socialist and Communist parties became irrevocable; "the abyss which the Communists had pictured in theory had become . . . the abyss of the grave." And since this early crime had been aided and abetted by the government, it initiated the death dance in postwar Germany: The assassins of the extreme Right started by liquidating prominent leaders of the extreme Left—Hugo Haase and Gustav Landauer, Leo Jogiches and Eugene Leviné—and quickly moved to the center and the right-of-center—to Walther Rathenau and Matthias Erzberger, both members of the government at the time of their murder. Thus Rosa Luxemburg's death became the watershed between two eras in Germany; and it became the point of no return for the German Left. All those who had drifted to the Communists out of bitter disappointment with the Socialist Party were even more disappointed with the swift moral decline and political disintegration of the Communist Party, and yet they felt that to return to the ranks of the Socialists would mean to condone the murder of Rosa. Such personal reactions, which are seldom publicly admitted, are among the small, mosaic-like pieces that fall into place in the large riddle of history. In the case of Rosa Luxemburg they are part of the legend which soon surrounded her name. Legends have a truth of their own, but Mr. Nettl is entirely right to have paid almost no attention to the Rosa myth. It was his task, difficult enough, to restore her to historical life.

Shortly after her death, when all persuasions of the Left had already decided that she had always been "mistaken" (a "really hopeless case," as George Lichtheim, the last in this long line, put it in *Encounter*), a curious shift in her reputation took place. Two small volumes of her letters were published, and these, entirely personal and of a simple, touchingly humane, and often poetic beauty, were enough to destroy the propaganda image of bloodthirsty "Red Rosa," at least in all but the most obstinately anti-Semitic and reactionary circles. However, what then grew up was another legend—the sentimentalized image of the bird watcher and lover of flowers, a woman whose guards said good-by to her with tears in their eyes when she left prison—as if they couldn't go on living without being entertained by this strange prisoner who had insisted on treating them as human beings. Nettl does not mention this story, faithfully handed down to me when I was a child and later confirmed by Kurt Rosenfeld, her friend and lawyer, who claimed to have witnessed the scene. It is probably true enough, and its slightly embarrassing features are somehow offset by the survival of another anecdote, this one mentioned by Nettl. In 1907, she and her friend Clara Zetkin (later the "grand old woman" of German Communism) had gone for a walk, lost count of time, and arrived late for an appointment with August Bebel, who had feared they were lost. Rosa then proposed their epitaph: "Here lie the last two men of German Social Democracy." Seven years later, in February 1914, she had occasion to prove the truth of this cruel joke in a splendid address to the judges of the Criminal Court which had indicted her for "inciting" the masses to civil disobedience in case of war. (Not bad, incidentally, for the woman who "was always wrong" to stand trial on this charge five months before the outbreak of the First World War, which few "serious" people had thought possible.) Mr. Nettl with good sense has reprinted the address in its entirety; its "manliness" is unparalleled in the history of German socialism.

It took a few more years and a few more catastrophes for the legend to turn into a symbol of nostalgia for the good old times of the movement, when hopes were green, the revolution around the corner, and, most important, the faith in the capacities of the masses and in the moral integrity of the Socialist or Communist leadership was still intact. It speaks not only for the person of Rosa Luxemburg, but also for the qualities of this older generation of the Left, that the legend—vague, confused, inaccurate in nearly all details—could spread throughout the world and come to life whenever a "New Left" sprang into being. But side by side with this glamorized image, there survived also the old clichés of the "quarrelsome female," a "romantic" who was neither "realistic" nor scientific (it is true that she was always out of step), and whose works, especially her great book on imperialism (*The Accumulation of Capital*, 1913), were shrugged off. Every New Left movement, when its moment came to change into the Old Left—usually when its members reached the age of forty—promptly buried its early enthusiasm for Rosa Luxemburg together with the dreams of youth; and since they had usually not bothered to read, let alone to understand, what she had to say they found it easy to dismiss her with all the patronizing philistinism of their newly acquired status. "Luxemburgism," invented posthumously by Party hacks for polemical reasons, has never even achieved the honor of being denounced as "treason"; it was treated as a harmless, infantile disease. Nothing Rosa Luxemburg wrote or said survived except her surprisingly accurate criticism of Bolshevik politics during the early stages of the Russian Revolution, and this only because those whom a "god had failed" could use it as a convenient though wholly inadequate weapon against Stalin. ("There is something indecent in the use of Rosa's name and writings as a cold war missile," as the reviewer of Nettl's book pointed out in the *Times Literary Supplement*.) Her new admirers had no more in common with her than her detractors. Her highly developed sense for theoretical differences and her infallible judgment of people, her personal likes and dislikes, would have prevented her lumping Lenin and Stalin together under all circumstances, quite apart from the fact that she had never been a "believer," had never used politics as a substitute for religion, and had been careful, as Mr. Nettl notes, not to attack religion when she opposed the church. In short, while "revolution was as close and real to her as to Lenin," it was no more an article of faith with her than Marxism. Lenin was primarily a man of action and would have gone into politics in any event, but she, who in her half-serious self-estimate was born "to mind the geese," might just as well have buried herself in botany and zoology or history and economics or mathematics, had not the circumstances of the world offended her sense of justice and freedom.

This is of course to admit that she was not an orthodox Marxist, so little orthodox indeed that it might be doubted that she was a Marxist at all. Mr. Nettl rightly states that to her Marx was no more than "the best interpreter of reality of them all," and it is revealing of her lack of personal commitment that she could write, "I now have a horror of the much praised first volume of Marx's *Capital* because of its elaborate rococo ornaments à la Hegel." [4] What mattered most in her view was reality, in all its wonderful and all its frightful aspects, even more than revolution itself. Her unorthodoxy was innocent, non-polemical; she "recommended her friends to read Marx for 'the daring of his thoughts, the refusal to take anything for granted,' rather than for the value of his conclusions. His mistakes . . . were self-evident . . . ; that was why [she] never bothered to engage in any lengthy critique." All this is most obvious in *The Accumulation of Capital*, which only Franz Mehring was unprejudiced enough to call a "truly magnificent, fascinating achievement without its equal since Marx's death." [5] The central thesis of this "curious work of genius" is simple enough. Since capitalism didn't show any signs of collapse "under the weight of its economic contradictions," she began to look for an outside cause to explain its continued existence and growth. She found it in the so-called third-man theory, that is, in the fact that the process of growth was not merely the consequence of innate laws ruling capitalist production but of the continued existence of pre-capitalist sectors in the country which "capitalism" captured and brought into its sphere of influence. Once this process had spread to the whole national territory, capitalists were forced to look to other parts of the earth, to pre-capitalist lands, to draw them into the process of capital accumulation, which, as it were, fed on whatever was outside itself. In other words, Marx's "original accumulation of capital" was not, like original sin, a single event, a unique deed of expropriation by the nascent bourgeoisie, setting off a process of accumulation that would then follow "with iron necessity" its own inherent law up to the final collapse. On the contrary, expropriation had to be repeated time and again to keep the system in motion. Hence, capitalism was not a closed system that generated its own con-

[4] In a letter to Hans Diefenbach, March 8, 1917, in *Briefe an Freunde*, Zürich, 1950.
[5] *Ibid.*, p. 84.

tradictions and was "pregnant with revolution"; it fed on outside factors, and its *automatic* collapse could occur, if at all, only when the whole surface of the earth was conquered and had been devoured.

Lenin was quick to see that this description, whatever its merits or flaws, was essentially non-Marxist. It contradicted the very foundations of Marxian and Hegelian dialectics, which hold that every thesis must create its own anti-thesis—bourgeois society creates the proletariat—so that the movement of the whole process remains bound to the initial factor that caused it. Lenin pointed out that from the viewpoint of materialist dialectics "her thesis that enlarged capitalist reproduction was impossible within a closed economy and needed to cannibalize economies in order to function at all . . . [was] a 'fundamental error.'" The trouble was only that what was an error in abstract Marxian theory was an eminently faithful description of things as they really were. Her careful "description of the torture of Negroes in South Africa" also was clearly "non-Marxist," but who would deny today that it belonged in a book on imperialism?

II

Historically, Mr. Nettl's greatest and most original achievement is the discovery of the Polish-Jewish "peer group" and Rosa Luxemburg's lifelong, close, and carefully hidden attachment to the Polish party which sprang from it. This is indeed a highly significant and totally neglected source, not of the revolutions, but of the revolutionary spirit in the twentieth century. This milieu, which even in the twenties had lost all public relevance, has now completely disappeared. Its nucleus consisted of assimilated Jews from middle-class families whose cultural background was German (Rosa Luxemburg knew Goethe and Mörike by heart, and her literary taste was impeccable, far superior to that of her German friends), whose political formation was Russian, and whose moral standards in both private and public life were uniquely their own. These Jews, an extremely small minority in the East, an even smaller percentage of assimilated Jewry in the West, stood outside all social ranks, Jewish or non-Jewish, hence had no conventional prejudices whatsoever, and had developed, in this truly splendid isolation, their own code of honor —which then attracted a number of non-Jews, among them Julian Marchlewski and Feliks Dzerzhynski, both of whom later joined the Bolsheviks. It was precisely because of this unique background that Lenin appointed Dzerzhynski as first head of the Cheka, someone, he hoped, no power could corrupt; hadn't he begged to be charged with the department of Children's Education and Welfare?

Nettl rightly stresses Rosa Luxemburg's excellent relations with her family, her parents, brothers, sister, and niece, none of whom ever showed the slightest inclination to socialist convictions or revolutionary activities, yet who did everything they could for her when she had to hide from the police or was in prison. The point is worth making, for it gives us a glimpse of this unique Jewish family background without which the emergence of the ethical code of the peer group would be nearly incomprehensible. The hidden equalizer of those who always treated one another as equals—and hardly anybody else—was the essentially simple experience of a childhood world in which mutual respect and unconditional trust, a universal humanity and a genuine, almost naïve contempt for social and ethnic distinctions were taken for granted. What the members of the peer group had in common was what can only be called moral taste, which is so different from "moral principles"; the authenticity of their morality they owed to having grown up in a world that was not out of joint. This gave them their "rare self-confidence," so unsettling to the world into which they then came, and so bitterly resented as arrogance and conceit. This milieu, and never the German Party, was and remained Rosa Luxemburg's home. The home was movable up to a point, and since it was predominantly Jewish it did not coincide with any "fatherland."

It is of course highly suggestive that the SDKPiL (Social Democracy of the Kingdom of Poland and Lithuania, formerly called SDPK, Social Democracy of the Kingdom of Poland), the party of this predominantly Jewish group, split from the official Socialist

Polish Party, the PPS, because of the latter's stand for Polish independence (Pilsudski, the Fascist dictator of Poland after World
War I, was its most famous and successful offspring), and that,
after the split, the members of the group became ardent defenders
of an often doctrinaire internationalism. It is even more suggestive
that the national question is the only issue on which one could
accuse Rosa Luxemburg of self-deception and unwillingness to
face reality. That this had something to do with her Jewishness
is undeniable, although it is of course "lamentably absurd" to
discover in her anti-nationalism "a peculiarly Jewish quality." Mr.
Nettl, while hiding nothing, is rather careful to avoid the "Jewish
question," and in view of the usually low level of debates on this
issue one can only applaud his decision. Unfortunately, his un-
derstandable distaste has blinded him to the few important facts
in this matter, which is all the more to be regretted since these
facts, though of a simple, elementary nature, also escaped the
otherwise so sensitive and alert mind of Rosa Luxemburg.

The first of these is what only Nietzsche, as far as I know, has
ever pointed out, namely, that the position and functions of the
Jewish people in Europe predestined them to become the "good
Europeans" *par excellence.* The Jewish middle classes of Paris
and London, Berlin and Vienna, Warsaw and Moscow, were in
fact neither cosmopolitan nor international, though the intellectuals among them thought of themselves in these terms. They were
European, something that could be said of no other group. And
this was not a matter of conviction; it was an objective fact. In
other words, while the self-deception of assimilated Jews usually
consisted in the mistaken belief that they were just as German
as the Germans, just as French as the French, the self-deception
of the intellectual Jews consisted in thinking that they had no
"fatherland," for their fatherland actually was Europe. There is,
second, the fact that at least the East-European intelligentsia
was multilingual—Rosa Luxemburg herself spoke Polish, Russian,
German, and French fluently and knew English and Italian very
well. They never quite understood the importance of language
barriers and why the slogan, "The fatherland of the working
class is the Socialist movement," should be so disastrously wrong

precisely for the working classes. It is indeed more than a little disturbing that Rosa Luxemburg herself, with her acute sense of reality and strict avoidance of clichés, should not have *heard* what was wrong with the slogan on principle. A fatherland, after all, is first of all a "land"; an organization is not a country, not even metaphorically. There is indeed grim justice in the later transformation of the slogan, "The fatherland of the working class is Soviet Russia"—Russia was at least a "land"—which put an end to the utopian internationalism of this generation.

One could adduce more such facts, and it still would be difficult to claim that Rosa Luxemburg was entirely wrong on the national question. What, after all, has contributed more to the catastrophic decline of Europe than the insane nationalism which accompanied the decline of the nation state in the era of imperialism? Those whom Nietzsche had called the "good Europeans"—a very small minority even among Jews—might well have been the only ones to have a presentiment of the disastrous consequences ahead, although they were unable to gauge correctly the enormous force of nationalist feeling in a decaying body politic.

III

Closely connected with the discovery of the Polish "peer group" and its continued importance for Rosa Luxemburg's public and private life is Mr. Nettl's disclosure of hitherto inaccessible sources, which enabled him to piece together the facts of her life —"the exquisite business of love and living." It is now clear that we knew next to nothing about her private life for the simple reason that she had so carefully protected herself from notoriety. This is no mere matter of sources. It was fortunate indeed that the new material fell into Mr. Nettl's hands, and he has every right to dismiss his few predecessors who were less hampered by lack of access to the facts than by their inability to move, think, and feel on the same level as their subject. The ease with which Nettl handles his biographical material is astounding. His treatment is more than perceptive. His is the first plausible portrait of this extraordinary woman, drawn *con amore*, with tact and great delicacy. It is as though she had found her last admirer, and it is for this reason that one feels like quarreling with some of his judgments.

He is certainly wrong in emphasizing her ambition, and sense of career. Does he think that her violent contempt for the careerists and status seekers in the German Party—their delight in being admitted to the Reichstag—is mere cant? Does he believe that a really "ambitious" person could have afforded to be as generous as she was? (Once, at an international congress, Jaurès finished an eloquent speech in which he "ridiculed the misguided passions of Rosa Luxemburg, [but] there was suddenly no one to translate him. Rosa jumped up and reproduced the moving oratory: from French into equally telling German.") And how can he reconcile this, except by assuming dishonesty or self-deception, with her telling phrase in one of her letters to Jogiches: "I have a cursed longing for happiness and am ready to haggle for my daily portion of happiness with all the stubbornness of a mule." What he mistakes for ambition is the natural force of a temperament capable, in her own laughing words, of "setting a prairie on fire," which propelled her almost willy-nilly into public affairs, and even ruled over most of her purely intellectual enterprises. While he stresses repeatedly the high moral standards of the "peer group," he still seems not to understand that such things as ambition, career, status, and even mere success were under the strictest taboo.

There is another aspect of her personality which Nettl stresses but whose implications he seems not to understand: that she was so "self-consciously a woman." This in itself put certain limitations on whatever her ambitions otherwise might have been—for Nettl does not ascribe to her more than what would have been natural in a man with her gifts and opportunities. Her distaste for the women's emancipation movement, to which all other women of her generation and political convictions were irresistibly drawn, was significant; in the face of suffragette equality, she might have been tempted to reply, *Vive la petite différence*. She was an outsider, not only because she was and remained a Polish

Jew in a country she disliked and a party she came soon to despise, but also because she was a woman. Mr. Nettl must, of course, be pardoned for his masculine prejudices; they would not matter much if they had not prevented him from understanding fully the role Leo Jogiches, her husband for all practical purposes and her first, perhaps her only, lover, played in her life. Their deadly serious quarrel, caused by Jogiches's brief affair with another woman and endlessly complicated by Rosa's furious reaction, was typical of their time and milieu, as was the aftermath, his jealousy and her refusal for years to forgive him. This generation still believed firmly that love strikes only once, and its carelessness with marriage certificates should not be mistaken for any belief in free love. Mr. Nettl's evidence shows that she had friends and admirers, and that she enjoyed this, but it hardly indicates that there was ever another man in her life. To believe in the Party gossip about marriage plans with "Hänschen" Diefenbach, whom she addressed as *Sie* and never dreamed of treating as an equal, strikes me as downright silly. Nettl calls the story of Leo Jogiches and Rosa Luxemburg "one of the great and tragic love stories of Socialism," and there is no need to quarrel with this verdict if one understands that it was not "blind and self-destructive jealousy" which caused the ultimate tragedy in their relations but war and the years in prison, the doomed German revolution and the bloody end.

Leo Jogiches, whose name Nettl also has rescued from oblivion, was a very remarkable and yet typical figure among the professional revolutionists. To Rosa Luxemburg, he was definitely *masculini generis*, which was of considerable importance to her: She preferred Graf Westarp (the leader of the German Conservative Party) to all the German Socialist luminaries "because," she said, "he is a *man*." There were few people she respected, and Jogiches headed a list on which only the names of Lenin and Franz Mehring could be inscribed with certainty. He definitely was a man of action and passion, he knew how to do and how to suffer. It is tempting to compare him with Lenin, whom he somewhat resembles, except in his passion for anonymity and for pulling strings behind the scenes, and his love of conspiracy and danger, which must have given him an additional erotic charm. He was indeed a Lenin *manqué*, even in his inability to write, "total" in his case (as she observed in a shrewd and actually very loving portrait in one of her letters), and his mediocrity as a public speaker. Both men had great talent for organization and leadership, but for nothing else, so that they felt impotent and superfluous when there was nothing to do and they were left to themselves. This is less noticeable in Lenin's case because he was never completely isolated, but Jogiches had early fallen out with the Russian Party because of a quarrel with Plekhanov—the Pope of the Russian emigration in Switzerland during the nineties— who regarded the self-assured Jewish youth newly arrived from Poland as "a miniature version of Nechaieff." The consequence was that he, according to Rosa Luxemburg, "completely rootless, vegetated" for many years, until the revolution of 1905 gave him his first opportunity: "Quite suddenly he not only achieved the position of leader of the Polish movement, but even in the Russian." (The SDKPiL came into prominence during the Revolution and became more important in the years following. Jogiches, though he himself didn't "write a single line," remained "none the less the very soul" of its publications.) He had his last brief moment when, "completely unknown in the SPD," he organized a clandestine opposition in the German army during the First World War. "Without him there would have been no *Spartakusbund*," which, unlike any other organized Leftist group in Germany, for a short time became a kind of "ideal peer group." (This, of course, is not to say that Jogiches made the German revolution; like all revolutions, it was made by no one. *Spartakusbund* too was "following rather than making events," and the official notion that the "Spartakus uprising" in January 1918 was caused or in- spired by its leaders—Rosa Luxemburg, Liebknecht, Jogiches—is a myth.)

We shall never know how many of Rosa Luxemburg's political ideas derived from Jogiches; in marriage, it is not always easy to tell the partners' thoughts apart. But that he failed where Lenin succeeded was at least as much a consequence of circum- stances—he was a Jew and a Pole—as of lesser stature. In any event, Rosa Luxemburg would have been the last to hold this against him. The members of the peer group did not judge one another in these categories. Jogiches himself might have agreed with Eugene Leviné, also a Russian Jew though a younger man, "We are dead men on furlough." This mood is what set him apart from the others; for neither Lenin nor Trotsky nor Rosa Luxemburg herself is likely to have thought along such lines. After her death he refused to leave Berlin for safety: "Somebody has to stay to write all our epitaphs." He was arrested two months after the murder of Liebknecht and Luxemburg and shot in the back in the police station. The name of the murderer was known, but "no attempt to punish him was ever made"; he killed another man in the same way, and then continued his "career with promotion in the Prussian Police." Such were the *mores* of the Weimar Republic.

Reading and remembering these old stories, one becomes painfully aware of the difference between the German comrades and the members of the peer group. During the Russian revolution of 1905 Rosa Luxemburg was arrested in Warsaw, and her friends collected the money for bail (probably provided by the German Party). The payment was supplemented "with an unofficial threat of reprisal; if anything happened to Rosa they would retaliate with action against prominent officials." No such notion of "action" ever entered her German friends' minds either before or after the wave of political murders when the impunity of such deeds had become notorious.

IV

More troubling in retrospect, certainly more painful for herself, than her alleged "errors" are the few crucial instances in which Rosa Luxemburg was not out of step, but appeared instead to be in agreement with the official powers in the German Social Democratic Party. These were her real mistakes, and there was none she did not finally recognize and bitterly regret.

The least harmful among them concerned the national question. She had arrived in Germany in 1898 from Zürich, where she had passed her doctorate "with a first-class dissertation about the industrial development of Poland" (according to Professor Julius Wolf, who in his autobiography still remembered fondly "the ablest of my pupils"), which achieved the unusual "distinction of instant commercial publication" and is still used by students of Polish history. Her thesis was that the economic growth of Poland depended entirely upon the Russian market and that any attempt "to form a national or linguistic state was a negation of all development and progress for the last fifty years." (That she was economically right was more than demonstrated by the chronic malaise of Poland between the wars.) She then became the expert on Poland for the German Party, its propagandist among the Polish population in the Eastern German provinces, and entered an uneasy alliance with people who wished to "Germanize" the Poles out of existence and would "gladly make you a present of all and every Pole including Polish Socialism," as an SPD secretary told her. Surely, "the glow of official approval was for Rosa a false glow."

Much more serious was her deceptive agreement with Party authorities in the revisionist controversy in which she played a leading part. This famous debate had been touched off by Eduard Bernstein[6] and has gone down in history as the alternative of reform against revolution. But this battle cry is misleading for two reasons: it makes it appear as though the SPD at the turn of the century still was committed to revolution, which was not the case; and it conceals the objective soundness of much of what Bernstein had to say. His criticism of Marx's economic theories was indeed, as he claimed, in full "agreement with reality." He pointed out that the "enormous increase of social wealth [was] not accompanied by a decreasing number of large capitalists but by an increasing number of capitalists of all degrees," that an "increasing narrowing of the circle of the well-to-do and an increasing misery of the poor" had failed to materialize, that "the modern proletarian [was] indeed poor but that he [was] no

[6] His most important book is now available in English under the title *Evolutionary Socialism* (Schocken Paperback), unfortunately lacking much-needed annotations and an introduction for the American reader.

pauper," and that Marx's slogan, "The proletarian has no fatherland," was not true. Universal suffrage had given him political
rights, the trade unions a place in society, and the new imperial-
ist development a clear stake in the nation's foreign policy. No
doubt the reaction of the German Party to these unwelcome
truths was chiefly inspired by a deep-seated reluctance to re-
examine critically its theoretical foundation, but this reluctance
was greatly sharpened by the Party's vested interest in the status
quo threatened by Bernstein's analysis. What was at stake was the
status of the SPD as a "state within a state": the Party had in fact
become a huge and well-organized bureaucracy that stood outside society and had every interest in things as they were. Revisionism à la Bernstein would have led the Party back into
German society, and such "integration" was felt to be as dangerous to the Party's interests as a revolution.

Mr. Nettl holds an interesting theory about the "pariah position" of the SPD within German society and its failure to partici-
pate in government.[7] It seemed to its members that the Party
could "provide within itself a superior alternative to corrupt
capitalism." In fact, by keeping the "defenses against society on
all fronts intact," it generated that spurious feeling of "together-
ness" (as Nettl puts it) which the French Socialists treated with
great contempt.[8] In any event, it was obvious that the more the
Party increased in numbers, the more surely was its radical élan
"organized out of existence." One could live very comfortably in
this "state within a state" by avoiding friction with society at
large, by enjoying feelings of moral superiority without any consequences. It was not even necessary to pay the price of serious
alienation since this pariah society was in fact but a mirror image,

[7] See "The German Social Democratic Party, 1890–1914, as a Political
Model," in *Past and Present*, April 1965.
[8] The situation bore very similar traits to the position of the French army
during the Dreyfus crisis in France which Rosa Luxemburg so brilliantly
analyzed for *Die Neue Zeit* in "Die Soziale Krise in Frankreich" (vol. 1,
1901). "The reason the army was reluctant to make a move was that it
wanted to show its opposition to the civil power of the republic, without at
the same time losing the force of that opposition by committing itself,"
through a serious *coup d'état,* to another form of government.

a "miniature reflection" of German society at large. This blind alley of the German Socialist movement could be analyzed correctly from opposing points of view—either from the view of Bernstein's revisionism, which recognized the emancipation of the working classes within capitalist society as an accomplished fact and demanded a stop to the talk about a revolution nobody thought of anyhow; or from the viewpoint of those who were not merely "alienated" from bourgeois society but actually wanted to change the world.

The latter was the standpoint of the revolutionists from the East who led the attack against Bernstein—Plekhanov, Parvus, and Rosa Luxemburg—and whom Karl Kautsky, the German Party's most eminent theoretician, supported, although he probably felt much more at ease with Bernstein than in the company of his new allies from abroad. The victory they won was Pyrrhic; it "merely strengthened alienation by pushing reality away." For the real issue was not theoretical and not economic. At stake was Bernstein's conviction, shamefully hidden in a footnote, that "the middle class—not excepting the German—in their bulk [was] still fairly healthy, not only economically but also *morally*" (my italics). This was the reason that Plekhanov called him a "philistine" and that Parvus and Rosa Luxemburg thought the fight so decisive for the future of the Party. For the truth of the matter was that Bernstein and Kautsky had in common their aversion to revolution; the "iron law of necessity" was for Kautsky the best possible excuse for doing nothing. The guests from Eastern Europe were the only ones who not merely "believed" in revolution as a theoretical necessity but wished to do something about it, precisely because they considered society as it was to be unbearable on *moral* grounds, on the grounds of justice. Bernstein and Rosa Luxemburg, on the other hand, had in common that they were both honest (which may explain Bernstein's "secret tenderness" for her), analyzed what they saw, were loyal to reality and critical of Marx; Bernstein was aware of this and shrewdly remarks in his reply to Rosa Luxemburg's attacks that she too had questioned "the whole Marxist predictions of the coming social evolution, so far as this is based on the theory of crises."

Rosa Luxemburg's early triumphs in the German Party rested on a double misunderstanding. At the turn of the century the SPD was "the envy and admiration of Socialists throughout the world." August Bebel, its "grand old man," who from Bismarck's foundation of the German Reich to the outbreak of the First World War "dominated [its] policy and spirit," had always proclaimed, "I am and always will be the mortal enemy of existing society." Didn't that sound like the spirit of the Polish peer group? Couldn't one assume from such proud defiance that the great German Party was somehow the SDKPIL writ large? It took Rosa Luxemburg almost a decade—until she returned from the first Russian revolution—to discover that the secret of this defiance was willful noninvolvement with the world at large and single-minded preoccupation with the growth of the Party organization. Out of this experience she developed, after 1910, her program of constant "friction" with society without which, as she then realized, the very source of the revolutionary spirit was doomed to dry up. She did not intend to spend her life in a sect, no matter how large; her commitment to revolution was primarily a moral matter, and this meant that she remained passionately engaged in public life and civil affairs, in the destinies of the world. Her involvement with European politics outside the immediate interests of the working class, and hence completely beyond the horizon of all Marxists, appears most convincingly in her repeated insistence on a "republican program" for the German and Russian Parties.

This was one of the main points of her famous *Juniusbroschüre*, written in prison during the war and then used as the platform for the *Spartakusbund*. Lenin, who was unaware of its authorship, immediately declared that to proclaim "the program of a republic . . . [means] in practice to proclaim the revolution—with an *incorrect* revolutionary program." Well, a year later the Russian Revolution broke out without any "program" whatsoever, and its first achievement was the abolition of the monarchy and the establishment of a republic, and the same was to happen in Germany and Austria. Which, of course, has never prevented the Russian, Polish, or German comrades from violently disagreeing with her on this point. It is indeed the republican question rather than the national one which separated her most decisively from all others. Here she was completely alone, as she was alone, though less obviously so, in her stress on the absolute necessity of not only individual but public freedom under all circumstances.

A second misunderstanding is directly connected with the revisionist debate. Rosa Luxemburg mistook Kautsky's reluctance to accept Bernstein's analyses for an authentic commitment to revolution. After the first Russian revolution in 1905, for which she had hurried back to Warsaw with false papers, she could no longer deceive herself. To her, these months constituted not only a crucial experience, they were also "the happiest of my life." Upon her return, she tried to discuss the events with her friends in the German Party. She learned quickly that the word "revolution" "had only to come into contact with a real revolutionary situation to break down" into meaningless syllables. The German Socialists were convinced that such things could happen only in distant barbarian lands. This was the first shock, from which she never recovered. The second came in 1914 and brought her near to suicide.

Naturally, her first contact with a real revolution taught her more and better things than disillusion and the fine arts of disdain and mistrust. Out of it came her insight into the nature of political action, which Mr. Nettl rightly calls her most important contribution to political theory. The main point is that she had learned from the revolutionary workers' councils (the latter *soviets*) that "good organization does not precede action but is the product of it," that "the organization of revolutionary action can and must be learnt in revolution itself, as one can only learn swimming in the water," that revolutions are "made" by nobody but break out "spontaneously," and that "the pressure for action" always comes "from below." A revolution is "great and strong as long as the Social Democrats [at the time still the only revolutionary party] don't smash it up."

There were, however, two aspects of the 1905 prelude which entirely escaped her. There was, after all, the surprising fact that the revolution had broken out not only in a non-industrialized, backward country, but in a territory where no strong socialist movement with mass support existed at all. And there was, second, the equally undeniable fact that the revolution had been the consequence of the Russian defeat in the Russo-Japanese War. These were the two facts Lenin never forgot and from which he drew two conclusions. First, one did not need a large organization; a small, tightly organized group with a leader who knew what he wanted was enough to pick up the power once the authority of the old regime had been swept away. Large revolutionary organizations were only a nuisance. And, second, since revolutions were not "made" but were the result of circumstances and events beyond anybody's power, wars were welcome.[9] The second point was the source of her disagreements with Lenin during the First World War; the first of her criticism of Lenin's tactics in the Russian Revolution of 1918. For she refused categorically, from beginning to end, to see in the war anything but the most terrible disaster, no matter what its eventual outcome; the price in human lives, especially in proletarian lives, was too high in any event. Moreover, it would have gone against her grain to look upon revolution as the profiteer of war and massacre—something which didn't bother Lenin in the least. And with respect to the issue of organization, she did not believe in a victory in which the people at large had no part and no voice; so little, indeed, did she believe in holding power at any price that she "was far more afraid of a deformed revolution than an unsuccessful one"—this was, in fact, "the major difference between her" and the Bolsheviks.

And haven't events proved her right? Isn't the history of the Soviet Union one long demonstration of the frightful dangers of "deformed revolutions"? Hasn't the "moral collapse" which she

---

[9] Lenin read Clausewitz' *Vom Kriege* (1832) during the First World War; his excerpts and annotations were published in East Berlin during the fifties. According to Werner Hahlberg—"Lenin und Clausewitz" in the *Archiv für Kulturgeschichte*, vol. 36, Berlin, 1954—Lenin was under the influence of Clausewitz when he began to consider the possibility that war, the collapse of the European system of nation states, might replace the economic collapse of capitalist economy as predicted by Marx.

foresaw—without, of course, foreseeing the open criminality of Lenin's successor—done more harm to the cause of revolution as she understood it than "any and every political defeat . . . in honest struggle against superior forces and in the teeth of the historical situation" could possibly have done? Wasn't it true that Lenin was "completely mistaken" in the means he employed, that the only way to salvation was the "school of public life itself, the most unlimited, the broadest democracy and public opinion," and that terror "demoralized" everybody and destroyed everything?

She did not live long enough to see how right she had been and to watch the terrible and terribly swift moral deterioration of the Communist parties, the direct offspring of the Russian Revolution, throughout the world. Nor for that matter did Lenin, who despite all his mistakes still had more in common with the original peer group than with anybody who came after him. This became manifest when Paul Levi, the successor of Leo Jogiches in the leadership of the *Spartakusbund*, three years after Rosa Luxemburg's death, published her remarks on the Russian Revolution just quoted, which she had written in 1918 "only for you" —that is, without intending publication.[10] "It was a moment of considerable embarrassment" for both the German and Russian parties, and Lenin could be forgiven had he answered sharply and immoderately. Instead, he wrote: "We answer with . . . a good old Russian fable: an eagle can sometimes fly lower than a chicken, but a chicken can never rise to the same heights as an eagle. Rosa Luxemburg . . . in spite of [her] mistakes . . . was

---

[10] It is not without irony that this pamphlet is the only work of hers which is still read and quoted today. The following items are available in English: *The Accumulation of Capital,* London and Yale, 1951; the responses to Bernstein (1899) in an edition published by the Three Arrows Press, New York, 1937; the *Juniusbroschüre* (1918) under the title *The Crisis in the German Social Democracy* by the Lanka Sama Samaja Publications of Colombo, Ceylon, in 1955, apparently in mimeographed form, and originally published in 1918 by the Socialist Publication Society, New York. In 1953, the same publishing house in Ceylon brought out her *The Mass Strike, the Political Party, and the Trade Unions* (1906).

and is an eagle." He then went on to demand publication of "her biography and the *complete* edition of her works," unpurged of "error," and chided the German comrades for their "incredible" negligence in this duty. This was in 1922. Three years later, Lenin's successors had decided to "Bolshevize" the German Communist Party and therefore ordered a "specific onslaught on Rosa Luxemburg's whole legacy." The task was accepted with joy by a young member named Ruth Fischer, who had just arrived from Vienna. She told the German comrades that Rosa Luxemburg and her influence "were nothing less than a syphilis bacillus."

The gutter had opened, and out of it emerged what Rosa Luxemburg would have called "another zoological species." No "agents of the bourgeoisie" and no "Socialist traitors" were needed any longer to destroy the few survivors of the peer group and to bury in oblivion the last remnants of their spirit. No complete edition of her works, needless to say, was ever published. After World War II, a two-volume edition of selections "with careful annotations underlining her errors" came out in East Berlin and was followed by a "full-length analysis of the Luxemburgist system of errors" by Fred Oelssner, which quickly "lapsed into obscurity" because it became "too 'Stalinist.'" This most certainly was not what Lenin had demanded, nor could it, as he had hoped, serve "in the education of many generations of Communists."

After Stalin's death, things began to change, though not in East Germany, where, characteristically, revision of Stalinist history took the form of a "Bebel cult." (The only one to protest this new nonsense was poor old Hermann Duncker, the last distinguished survivor who still could "recall the most wonderful period of my life, when as a young man I knew and worked with Rosa Luxemburg, Karl Liebknecht, and Franz Mehring.") The Poles, however, although their own two-volume edition of selected works in 1959 is "partly overlapping with the German" one, "took out her reputation almost unaltered from the casket in which it had been stored" ever since Lenin's death, and after 1956 a "flood of Polish publications" on the subject appeared on the market. One would like to believe that there is still hope for a belated recognition of who she was and what she did, as one would like to hope that she will finally find her place in the education of political scientists in the countries of the West. For Mr. Nettl is right: "Her ideas belong wherever the history of political ideas is seriously taught."

ANGELO GIUSEPPE RONCALLI:

A Christian on St. Peter's Chair
from 1958 to 1963

Journal of a Soul (New York, 1965), the spiritual diaries of Angelo Giuseppe Roncalli, who took the name John XXIII when he became Pope, is a strangely disappointing and strangely fascinating book. Written for the most part in periods of retreat, it consists of endlessly repetitive devout outpourings and self-exhortations, "examinations of conscience" and notations of "spiritual progress," with only the rarest references to actual happenings, so that for pages and pages it reads like an elementary textbook on how to be good and avoid evil. And yet in its own strange and unfamiliar way, it succeeds in giving a clear answer to two questions which were in the minds of many people when, in late May and early June 1963, he lay dying in the Vatican. They were very simply and unequivocally brought to my own attention by a Roman chambermaid: "Madam," she said, "this Pope was a real Christian. How could that be? And how could it happen that a true Christian would sit on St. Peter's chair? Didn't he first have to be appointed Bishop, and Archbishop, and Cardinal, until he finally was elected to be Pope? Had nobody been aware of who he was?" Well, the answer to the last of her three questions seems to be "No." He did not belong to the *papabile* when he entered the Conclave; no garment fitting his size had been prepared by the Vatican tailors. He was elected because the Cardinals could not agree and were convinced, as he wrote himself, that he "would be a provisional and transitional Pope" without much consequence. "Yet here I am," he continued, "already on the eve of the fourth year of my pontificate, with an immense program of work in front of me to be carried out before the eyes of the whole world, which is watching and waiting." What is astounding is not that he was not among the *papabile* but that nobody was aware of who he was, and that he had been elected because everybody thought of him as a figure without consequence.

However, this is astounding only in retrospect. To be sure, the Church has preached the *imitatio Christi* for nearly two thousand years, and no one can say how many parish priests and monks there may have been, living in obscurity throughout the centuries, who said as the young Roncalli did: "Here then is my model: Jesus Christ," knowing perfectly well even at the age of eighteen that to be "similar to the good Jesus" meant to be "treated as a madman": "They say and believe that I am a fool. Perhaps I am, but my pride will not allow me to think so. This is the funny side to it all." But the Church, being an institution and, especially since the Counter Reformation, more concerned with maintaining dogmatic beliefs than with the simplicity of faith, did not open the ecclesiastical career to men who had taken literally the invitation, "Follow me." Not that they were consciously afraid of the clearly anarchic elements in an undiluted, authentically Christian way of life; they simply would have thought that "To suffer and be despised for Christ and with Christ" was wrong policy. And this was what Roncalli wanted passionately and enthusiastically, quoting these words of St. John of the Cross over and over again. He wanted it to the point of "bearing with me a clear impression of resemblance . . . with Christ crucified" from the ceremony of his episcopal consecration, deploring that "until now I have suffered too little," hoping and expecting that "the Lord will send me trials of a particularly painful nature," "some great suffering and affliction of body and spirit." He welcomed his painful and premature death as confirmation of his vocation: the "sacrifice" that was needed for the great enterprise he had to leave undone.

The reluctance of the Church to appoint to high office those few whose sole ambition was to imitate Jesus of Nazareth is not difficult to understand. There might have been a time when people in the ecclesiastical hierarchy thought along the lines of Dostoevsky's Grand Inquisitor, fearing that, in Luther's words, "the most permanent fate of God's word is that for its sake the world is put into uproar. For the sermon of God comes in order to change and revive the whole earth to the extent that it reaches it." But such times were long past. They had forgotten that "to be gentle and humble . . . is not the same thing as being weak and easygoing," as Roncalli once jotted down. This is precisely what they were going to find out, that humility before God and meekness before men are not the same, and great as the hostility against this unique Pope was in certain ecclesiastical quarters, it speaks for the Church and the hierarchy that it was not greater, and that so many of the high dignitaries, the Princes of the Church, could be won over by him.

From the beginning of his pontificate in the fall of 1958 it was the whole world, and not just Catholics, that had been watching him for the reasons he enumerates himself: first, for having "accepted with simplicity the honor and the burden," after having always been "most careful . . . to avoid anything that might direct attention to myself." Second, for having "been able to . . . immediately put into effect certain ideas which were . . . perfectly simple, but far-reaching in their effects and full of responsibilities for the future." But while, according to his own testimony, "the idea of an Ecumenical Council, a Diocesan Synod, and the revision of the Code of Canon Law" had come to him "without any forethought," being even "quite contrary to any previous supposition . . . [of his] on this subject," it appeared to those who were watching him the almost logical or, at any rate, natural manifestation of the man and his astounding faith.

Every page in this book gives testimony to this faith, and yet none of them, and certainly not all of them together, is so convincing as the countless tales and anecdotes that were circulating through Rome during the long four days of his final agony. It was a time when the city was trembling, as usual, under the invasion of tourists, who, because of his death which came earlier than expected, were joined by legions of seminarists, monks, nuns, and priests of all colors and from all lands. Everybody you met, from cab driver to writer and editor, from waiter to shopkeeper, believers and unbelievers of all confessions, had a story to tell of what Roncalli had done and said, of how he had behaved on such or such an occasion. A number of them have by now been collected by Kurt Klinger under the title *A Pope Laughs*, and others have been published in the growing literature about "good Pope John," all of which bear the *nihil obstat* and the *imprimatur*.[1] But this kind of hagiography is of little help in understanding why the whole world had its eyes focused on the man, because, presumably in order to avoid "offense," it carefully avoids telling to what degree the ordinary standards of the world, including the world of the Church, contradict the rules of judgment and behavior contained in the preachings of Jesus. In the midst of our century this man had decided to take literally, and not symbolically, every article of faith he had ever been taught. He really wanted "to be crushed, despised, neglected for the love of Jesus." He had disciplined himself and his ambition until he really cared "nothing for the judgments of the world, even the ecclesiastical world." At the age of twenty-one he had made up his mind: "Even if I were to be Pope . . . I should still have to stand before the divine judge, and what should I be worth then? Not much." And at the end of his life, in the Spiritual Testament to his family, he could confidently write that "the Angel of Death will . . . take me, as I trust, to paradise." The enormous strength of this faith was nowhere more manifest than in the "scandals" it

<hr />

[1] Jean Chelini, *Jean XXIII, pasteur des hommes de bonne volonté*, Paris, 1963; Augustin Pradel, *Le "Bon Pape" Jean XXIII*, Paris, 1963; Leone Algisi, *John the Twenty-third*, transl. from the Italian by P. Ryde, London, 1963; Loris Capovilla, *The Heart and Mind of John XXIII, His Secretary's Intimate Recollection*, transl. from the Italian, New York, 1964; Alden Hatch, *A Man Named John*, Image Books, 1965.

innocently caused, and the stature of this man can be leveled down only if the element of scandal is omitted.

Thus, the greatest and most daring stories which then went from mouth to mouth have remained untold and, needless to say, cannot be verified. I remember some of them, and I hope they are authentic; but even if their authenticity were denied, their very invention would be characteristic enough for the man and for what people thought of him to make them worth telling. The first, the least offending story, supports the not very numerous passages in the *Journal* about his easy, non-patronizing familiarity with the workers and peasants from whom, to be sure, he himself came but whose milieu he had left when, at the age of eleven, he was admitted to the seminary of Bergamo. (His first direct contact with the world came when he faced military service. He found it "ugly, filthy, and loathsome" in the extreme: "Shall I be sent to hell with the devils? I know what life in a barracks is like —I shudder at the very thought of it.") The story tells that the plumbers had arrived for repairs in the Vatican. The Pope heard how one of them started swearing in the name of the whole Holy Family. He came out and asked politely: "Must you do this? Can't you say *merde* as we do too?"

My next three stories concern a much more serious matter. There are a few, very few, passages in his book which tell of rather strained relationships between Bishop Roncalli and Rome. The trouble, it seems, started in 1925 when he was appointed Apostolic Visitor in Bulgaria, a post of "semi-obscurity" where he was kept for ten years. His unhappiness there he never forgot —twenty-five years later he still writes about "the monotony of that life which was one long sequence of daily pricks and scratches." At the time, he became almost immediately aware of "many trials . . . [which] are not caused by the Bulgarians . . . but by the central organs of ecclesiastical administration. This is a form of mortification and humiliation that I did not expect and which hurts me deeply." And it is as early as 1926 that he began to write about this conflict as his "cross." Things began to brighten when, in 1935, he was transferred to the Apostolic Delegation in Istanbul, where he was to stay another ten years, until, in 1944, he received his first important appointment as Apostolic Nuncio to Paris. But there again, "the difference between my way of seeing situations on the spot and certain ways of judging the same things in Rome hurts me considerably; it is my only real cross." No such complaints are heard from the years in France, but not because he had changed his mind; it seems he had only got used to the ways of the ecclesiastical world. In this vein he notes in 1948 how "any kind of distrust or discourtesy shown to . . . the humble, poor, or socially inferior [by these colleagues of mine, good ecclesiastics] . . . makes me writhe with pain" and that "all the wiseacres of this world, and all the cunning minds, including those in Vatican diplomacy, cut such a poor figure in the light of the simplicity and grace shed by . . . Jesus and his Saints!"

It is with respect to his work in Turkey, where, during the war, he came into contact with Jewish organizations (and, in one instance, prevented the Turkish government from shipping back to Germany some hundred Jewish children who had escaped from Nazi-occupied Europe), that he later raised one of the very rare serious reproaches against himself—for all "examinations of conscience" notwithstanding, he was not at all given to self-criticism. "Could I not," he wrote, "should I not, have done more, have made a more decided effort and gone against the inclinations of my nature? Did the search for calm and peace, which I considered to be more in harmony with the Lord's spirit, not perhaps mask a certain unwillingness to take up the sword?" At this time, however, he had permitted himself but one outburst. Upon the outbreak of the war with Russia, he was approached by the German Ambassador, Franz von Papen, who asked him to use his influence in Rome for outspoken support of Germany by the Pope. "And what shall I say about the millions of Jews your countrymen are murdering in Poland and in Germany?" This was in 1941, when the great massacre had just begun.

It is on matters of this kind that the following stories touch. And since, so far as I know, none of the existing biographies of Pope John ever mentions the conflict with Rome, even a denial of their authenticity would not stand altogether convincing. There is first the anecdote of his audience with Pius XII before his departure for Paris in 1944. Pius XII began the audience by telling his newly appointed Nuncio that he had but seven minutes to spare, whereupon Roncalli took his leave with the words: "In that case, the remaining six minutes are superfluous." There is, second, the delightful story of the young priest from abroad who busied himself in the Vatican, trying to make a good impression on the high dignitaries to further his career. The Pope is said to have told him: "My dear son, stop worrying so much. You may rest assured that on the day of judgment Jesus is not going to ask you: And how did you get along with the Holy Office?" And there is finally the report that in the months preceding his death he was given Hochhuth's play *The Deputy* to read and then was asked what one could do against it. Whereupon he allegedly replied: "Do against it? What can you do against the truth?"

So much for the stories which were never published. There are still enough to be found in the literature about him, though some of them are strangely changed. (According to the "oral tradition," if that is what it was, the Pope had received the first Jewish delegation with the greeting: "I am your brother Joseph," the words with which Joseph in Egypt made himself known to his brothers. They are now reported to have been uttered when he first received the cardinals after his election. I am afraid that this version sounds more plausible; but while the first one would have been very great indeed, the latter is hardly more than very nice.) All of them show the complete independence which comes from a true detachment from the things of this world, the splendid freedom from prejudice and convention which quite frequently could result in an almost Voltairean wit, an astounding quickness in turning the tables. Thus, when he protested against closing the Vatican gardens during his daily walks and was told that it was not fitting his station to be exposed to the sight of ordinary mortals, he asked: "Why should people not see me? I don't misbehave, do I?" The same witty presence of mind, which the French call *esprit*, is borne out by another unpublished story. At a banquet of the Diplomatic Corps, while he was Apostolic Nuncio in France, one of the gentlemen wanted to embarrass him, and circulated a photograph of a nude woman around the table. Roncalli looked at the picture and returned it to Mr. N. with the remark, "Mrs. N., I suppose."

When he was young he had loved to talk, to linger in the kitchen and discuss things, and he accused himself of "a natural inclination to pronounce judgment like a Solomon," to tell "Tom, Dick and Harry . . . how to behave in certain circumstances," of meddling "in matters concerning newspapers, Bishops, topics of the day," and taking "up the cudgels in defense of anything which I think is being unjustly attacked and which I think fit to champion." Whether or not he ever succeeded in suppressing these qualities, he certainly never lost them, and they blossomed forth when, after a long life of "mortifications" and "humiliations" (which he thought very necessary for the sanctification of his soul), he suddenly reached the only position in the Catholic hierarchy where no voice of superiors could tell him the "will of God." He knew, he writes in his *Journal*, that he had "accepted this service in pure obedience to the Lord's will, conveyed to me through the voice of the Sacred College of Cardinals"; that is, he never thought that the cardinals had elected him but always that "the Lord chose me"—a conviction which must have been greatly strengthened by his knowledge of the purely accidental way his election had come to pass. Thus it was precisely because he knew it was all a kind of misunderstanding, humanly speaking, that he could write, not uttering some dogmatic generality, but pointing clearly to himself: "The Vicar of Christ knows what Christ wants from him." The editor of the *Journal*, Pope John's former secretary, Mgr. Loris Capovilla, mentions in his Introduction what must have been highly irritating to many and puzzling to most: "his habitual humility before God and his clear consciousness of his own worth before men—so clear as to be disconcerting." But though absolutely sure of himself and seeking the advice of no one, he did not make the mistake of pretending to know the future or the ultimate consequences of what he was trying to do. He had always been content to "live from day to day," even "from hour to hour" like the lilies in the field, and he now set down the "basic rule of conduct" for his new state—to "have no concern for the future," to make no "human provision for it," and to take care "not to speak of it confidently and casually to anyone." It was faith and not theory, theological or political, that guarded him against "in any way conniving with evil in the hope that by so doing [he] may be useful to someone."

This complete freedom from cares and worries was his form of humility; what set him free was that he could say without any reservation, mental or emotional: "Thy will be done." In the *Journal*, it is not easy to discover, under the layers and layers of pious language which has become for us, but never for him, platitudinous, this simple basic chord to which his life was tuned. Even less would we expect from it the laughing wit he derived from it. But what else except humility did he preach when he told his friends how the new awesome responsibilities of the pontificate had at first worried him greatly and even caused him sleepless nights—until one morning he said to himself: "Giovanni, don't take yourself that seriously!" and slept well ever after.

However, no one should believe it was humility that made it so easy for him to keep company with everybody, enjoying himself equally with the inmates of prisons, the "sinners," the workers in his garden, the nuns in his kitchen, Mrs. Kennedy, and the daughter and son-in-law of Khrushchev. It was rather his enormous self-confidence that enabled him to treat everybody, high or low, as his equal. And he went to considerable lengths where he felt that this equality needed to be established. He thus addressed the burglars and murderers in jail as "Sons and Brothers," and in order to make sure that this would not remain an empty word, he told them how he had stolen an apple as a child without being caught, and how one of his brothers had gone hunting without a license and had got caught. And when they led him "to the cell block where the incorrigibles were confined" he ordered "in his most commanding voice, 'Open the gates. Do not bar them from me. They are all children of our Lord.'" To be sure, all this is no more than sound and long-established Christian doctrine, but it had remained doctrine for a long time, and not even *Rerum Novarum*, the Encyclical of Leo XIII, "the great Pope of the working people," had prevented the Vatican from paying starvation wages to its employees. The new Pope's disconcerting habit of talking with everybody brought this scandal almost immediately to his attention. "How are things going?" he asked one of the workers, according to Alden Hatch. "Badly, badly, Your Eminence," said the man, and told him what he earned and how many mouths he had to feed. "We'll have to do something about this. For just between you and me, I'm not Your Eminence; I'm the Pope," by which he meant: forget the titles, I'm the boss here, I can change things. When later told that the new expenses could be met only by cutting down on charities, he remained unperturbed: "Then we'll have to cut them. For . . . justice comes before charity." What makes these stories so enjoyable is the consistent refusal to bow to the common belief "that even the everyday language of the Pope should be full of mystery and awe," which according to Pope John was in clear contradiction to "the example of Jesus." And it is indeed heartwarming to hear that it was quite in accord with Jesus' "example" to conclude the highly controversial audience with the representatives of Communist Russia by announcing: "And now the time has come with your permission for a little blessing. A little blessing can't do harm after all. Take it as it is given." [2]

The single-mindedness of this faith, never troubled by doubt, never shaken by experience, never distorted by fanaticism— "which, even if innocent, is always harmful"—is splendid in deed and living word, but becomes monotonous and lame, a dead letter on the printed page. This is even true for the few letters which are added to this edition, and the only exception is the "Spiritual Testament 'to the Roncalli family'" in which he explains to his brothers and their children and grandchildren why he, contrary to all custom, had refused to give them titles, why now as before he refused to lift "them out of their respected and contented poverty," though he had "sometimes come to their aid, as a poor man to the poor," why he had never asked "for anything—position, money or favors—never, either for myself or my relations and friends." For "Born poor, . . . I am particularly happy to die

[2] For these stories, see A. Hatch, *op. cit.*

poor, having distributed . . . whatever came into my hands—
and it was very little—during the years of my priesthood and
episcopate." There is a slightly apologetic tone in these passages
as though he knew that his family's poverty was not quite so
"contented" as he made it out to be. Much earlier, he had noted
that the constant "worries and suffering" that beset them "seemed
to serve no good purpose, but rather do them harm," and this is
one of the few instances where one can at least guess what kind
of experiences he felt necessary to discard. Just as one can guess,
more comfortably, at the enormous pride of the poor boy who
throughout his life was to stress that he had never asked a favor
of anybody, and who had found comfort in the thought that whatever he received ("Who is poorer than I? Since I became a semi-
narist I have never worn a garment that was not given me out of
charity") was provided by God so that his poverty became for
him an evident sign of his vocation: "I am of the same family as
Christ—what more can I want?"

Generations of modern intellectuals, insofar as they were not
atheists—that is, fools who pretended to know what no man can
know—have been taught by Kierkegaard, Dostoevski, Nietzsche,
and their countless followers inside and outside the existentialist
camp, to find religion and theological questions "interesting." No
doubt they will have difficulties in understanding a man who, at a
very young age, had "vowed fidelity" not merely to "material
poverty" but to "the poverty of spirit" as well. Whatever or whoever Pope John XXIII was, he was neither interesting nor brilliant, and this quite apart from the fact that he had been a rather
mediocre student and, in his later life, was without any marked
intellectual or scholarly interest whatsoever. (Apart from newspapers, which he loved, he seems to have read almost no secular
writings.) If a small boy tells himself, Alyosha-like, "As it is written: 'If thou wilt be perfect go and sell that thou hast, and give
to the poor and follow me,' how can I give just two rubles instead
of my possessions and go to early mass instead of the 'follow me'?"
And if the grown man sticks to the small boy's ambition to become "perfect" and keeps asking himself "Am I making any
progress?" setting up timetables for himself and noting with

meticulous care how far he has progressed—incidentally treating
himself quite gently in the process, cautious not to promise too
much, tackling his failings "one at a time," and not once in despair—it is not likely that the result will be of particular "interest." So little is a timetable for perfection a substitute for a story
—what remains to be told if there were no "temptation and failure, never, never," no "mortal or venial sins"?—that even the few
instances of an intellectual development in the *Journal* remained
strangely unnoticed by its author, who reread and prepared it for
posthumous publication during the last months of his life. He
never tells when he ceased to see in Protestants the "poor unfortunates outside the Church" and came to the conviction that
"all, whether baptized or not, belong by right to Jesus," nor was
he aware of how odd it was that he who felt in his "heart and
soul a love of [the Church's] rules, precepts and regulation,"
should make, as Alden Hatch says, "the first change in the Canon
of the Mass in a thousand years," and generally put his whole
strength immediately into the "efforts to straighten, to reform,
and . . . to make improvements in everything," trusting that his
Ecumenical Council "will surely be . . . a real and new Epiph-
any."

No doubt it was the "poverty of spirit" that preserved him
"from anxieties and tiresome perplexities" and gave him the
"strength of daring simplicity." It also contains the answer to
the question of how it could have happened that the most daring
man was chosen when an easygoing and compliant one had been
wanted. He had succeeded in his desire, recommended by
Thomas à Kempis's *The Imitation of Christ,* one of his favorite
books, "to be unknown and little esteemed," words which, as
early as 1903, he had adopted as his "motto." He probably was
thought by many—he lived in a milieu of intellectuals, after all—
to be a bit stupid, not simple but simple-minded. And it is unlikely that those who had observed for decades that he really
seemed "never [to have] felt any temptation against obedience,"
understood the tremendous pride and self-confidence of this man
who never for a moment relinquished his judgment when he
obeyed what for him was not the will of his superiors but the

will of God. His faith was: "Thy will be done," and it is true, though he said it himself, that it was "wholly evangelical in nature," true also that it "demanded and obtained universal respect and edified many." It is the same faith that inspired his greatest words when he lay dying: "Every day is a good day to be born, every day is a good day to die." [3]

[3] *"Ogni giorno è buono per nascere; ogni giorno è buono per morire."* See his *Discorsi, Messagi, Colloqui,* vol. V, Rome, 1964, p. 310.

KARL JASPERS:
A Laudatio[1]

WE HAVE assembled here for the presentation of the Peace Prize. That prize, if I may recall a phrase used by the President of the Federal Republic, is awarded not only for "excellent literary work," but also for "having proved oneself in life." It is awarded, therefore, to a person, and awarded for the work insofar as it still remains the spoken word, which has not yet broken free from the speaker to begin its uncertain, always adventurous course through history. For this reason, the award of this prize must be accompanied by the *laudatio*, a eulogy whose task it is to praise the man rather than his work. How to do this we can perhaps learn from the Romans, who, more experienced in matters of public significance than we are, tell us what such an enterprise should be all about: *in laudationibus . . . ad personarum dignitatem omnia referrentur*, said Cicero[2]—"in eulogies . . . the sole consideration is the greatness and dignity of the individuals con-

---

[1] Address delivered when the German Book Trade's Peace Prize was awarded to Karl Jaspers.

[2] *De Oratore* I, 141.

cerned." In other words, a eulogy concerns the dignity that pertains to a man insofar as he is more than everything he does or creates. To recognize and to celebrate this dignity is not the business of experts and colleagues in a profession; it is the public that must judge a life which has been exposed to the public view and proved itself in the public realm. The award only confirms what this public has long known.

The *laudatio,* therefore, can only attempt to express what you all know. But to say in public what many know in the seclusion of privacy is not superfluous. The very fact that something is being heard by all confers upon it an illuminating power that confirms its real existence. Still, I must confess that I have taken upon myself this "venture into the public realm" (Jaspers) and its limelight with hesitation and timidity. I feel as I presume the great majority of you do. We are all modern people who move mistrustfully and awkwardly in public. Caught up in our modern prejudices, we think that only the "objective work," separate from the person, belongs to the public; that the person behind it and his life are private matters, and that the feelings related to these "subjective" things stop being genuine and become sentimental as soon as they are exposed to the public eye. When the German Book Trade decided that there had to be a *laudatio* at the awarding of the prize, it was really harking back to an older and more proper sense of the public realm, a sense that it is precisely the human person in all his subjectivity who needs to appear in public in order to achieve full reality. If we accept this new-old sense, we must change our views and forsake our habit of equating personal with subjective, objective with factual or impersonal. Those equations come from the scientific disciplines, where they are meaningful. They are obviously meaningless in politics, in which realm people on the whole appear as acting and speaking persons and where, therefore, personality is anything but a private affair. But these equations also lose their validity in public intellectual life, which of course includes and goes considerably beyond the sphere of academic life.

In order to speak to the point here we must learn to distinguish not between subjectivity and objectivity, but between the

individual and the person. It is true that it is an individual subject who offers some objective work to the public, abandons it to
the public. The subjective element, let us say the creative process
that went into the work, does not concern the public at all. But
if this work is not only academic, if it is also the result of, "having
proved oneself in life," a living act and voice accompanies the
work; the person himself appears together with it. What then
emerges is unknown to the one who reveals it; he cannot control it
as he can control the work he has prepared for publication. (Anyone who consciously tries to intrude his personality into his work is
play-acting, and in so doing he throws away the real opportunity
that publication means for himself and others.) The personal element is beyond the control of the subject and is therefore the
precise opposite of mere subjectivity. But it is that very subjectivity that is "objectively" much easier to grasp and much more
readily at the disposal of the subject. (By self-control, for example, we mean simply that we are able to lay hold of this purely
subjective element in ourselves in order to use it as we like.)

Personality is an entirely different matter. It is very hard to
grasp and perhaps most closely resembles the Greek *daimon,* the
guardian spirit which accompanies every man throughout his life,
but is always only looking over his shoulder, with the result that
it is more easily recognized by everyone a man meets than by
himself. This *daimon*—which has nothing demonic about it—
this personal element in a man, can only appear where a public
space exists; that is the deeper significance of the public realm,
which extends far beyond what we ordinarily mean by political
life. To the extent that this public space is also a spiritual realm,
there is manifest in it what the Romans called *humanitas.* By that
they meant something that was the very height of humanness
because it was valid without being objective. It is precisely what
Kant and then Jaspers mean by *Humanität,* the valid personality
which, once acquired, never leaves a man, even though all other
gifts of body and mind may succumb to the destructiveness of
time. *Humanitas* is never acquired in solitude and never by giving one's work to the public. It can be achieved only by one who
has thrown his life and his person into the "venture into the public

73

realm"—in the course of which he risks revealing something which is not "subjective" and which for that very reason he can neither recognize nor control. Thus the "venture into the public realm," in which *humanitas* is acquired, becomes a gift to mankind.

When I suggest that the personal element which comes into the public realm with Jaspers is *humanitas,* I wish to imply that no one can help us as he can to overcome our distrust of this same public realm, to feel what honor and joy it is to praise one we love in the hearing of all. For Jaspers has never shared the general prejudice of cultivated people that the bright light of publicity makes all things flat and shallow, that only mediocrity shows up well in it, and that therefore the philosopher must keep his distance from it. You will recall Kant's opinion that the touchstone for determining whether the difficulty of a philosophical essay is genuine or mere "vapors of cleverness" may be found in its susceptibility to popularization. And Jaspers, who in this respect, as indeed in every other, is the only successor Kant has ever had, has like Kant more than once left the academic sphere and its conceptual language to address the general reading public. Moreover, he has three times—once shortly before the Nazis came to power in his *Man in the Modern Age* (1933),[3] then immediately after the downfall of the Third Reich in *The Question of German Guilt,* and now in *The Atom Bomb and the Future of Man*—intervened directly in political questions of the day.[4] For he knows, as the statesman does, that political questions are far too serious to be left to the politicians.

Jaspers's affirmation of the public realm is unique because it comes from a philosopher and because it springs from the fundamental conviction underlying his whole activity as a philosopher: that both philosophy and politics concern everyone. This is what they have in common; this is the reason they belong in the public realm where the human person and his ability to prove himself are what count. The philosopher—in contrast to the

[3] The German original, *Die geistige Situation der Zeit,* appeared in 1931.
[4] Jaspers's most important political publication since 1958, when this speech was written, is *The Future of Germany,* 1967.

scientist—resembles the statesman in that he must answer for his opinions, that he is held responsible. The statesman, in fact, is in the relatively fortunate position of being responsible only to his own nation, whereas Jaspers, at least in all his writings after 1933, has always written as if to answer for himself before all of mankind.

For him, responsibility is not a burden and it has nothing whatsoever to do with moral imperatives. Rather, it flows naturally out of an innate pleasure in making manifest, in clarifying the obscure, in illuminating the darkness. His affirmation of the public realm is in the final analysis only the result of his loving light and clarity. He has loved light so long that it has marked his whole personality. In the works of a great writer we can almost always find a consistent metaphor peculiar to him alone in which his whole work seems to come to a focus. One such metaphor in Jaspers's work is the word "clarity." Existence is "clarified" by reason; the "modes of encompassing"—on one hand our mind which "encompasses" everything that occurs to us, on the other hand the world which "encompasses" us, "the being-in by which we are"—are "brought to light" by reason; reason itself, finally, its affinity to truth, is verified by its "breadth and lightness." Whatever stands up to light and does not dissolve in vapors under its brightness, partakes of *humanitas;* to take it upon oneself to answer before mankind for every thought means to live in that luminosity in which oneself and everything one thinks is tested.

Long before 1933 Jaspers was what is called "famous," in the way other philosophers are too, but only in the course of the Hitler period and especially in the years afterward did he become a public figure in the full sense of the word. Nor was this, as one might imagine, due solely to the circumstances of the time which first forced him into the obscurity of the persecuted and then made him the symbol of changed times and attitudes. Insofar as the circumstances had anything to do with it, they only thrust him into the place in which he belonged by nature—into the full light of world opinion. The process was not that he first suffered something, then proved himself in his ordeal, and finally, when the worst came to the worst, represented something like "the other Germany." In this sense he represents nothing at all. He has always stood entirely alone and was independent of all groupings, including the German resistance movement. The magnificence of this position, which is sustained solely by the weight of the person, is precisely that without representing anything but his own existence he could provide assurance that even in the darkness of total domination, in which whatever goodness there may still remain becomes absolutely invisible and therefore ineffective—even then reason can be annihilated only if all reasonable men are actually, literally slaughtered.

It was self-evident that he would remain firm in the midst of catastrophe. But that the whole thing could never become even a temptation for him—this, which is less self-evident, was his inviolability, and to those who knew of him it meant far more than resistance and heroism. It meant a confidence that needed no confirmation, an assurance that in times in which everything could happen one thing could not happen. What Jaspers represented then, when he was entirely alone, was not Germany but what was left of *humanitas* in Germany. It was as if he alone in his inviolability could illuminate that space which reason creates and preserves between men, and as if the light and breadth of this space would survive even if only one man were to remain in it. Not that this was actually so or even could have been so. Jaspers has often said: "The individual by himself cannot be reasonable." In this sense he was never alone, nor did he think very highly of such solitude. The *humanitas* whose existence he guaranteed grew from the native region of his thought, and this region was never unpopulated. What distinguishes Jaspers is that he is more at home in this region of reason and freedom, knows his way about it with greater sureness, than others who may be acquainted with it but cannot endure living constantly in it. Because his existence was governed by the passion for light itself, he was able to be like a light in the darkness glowing from some hidden source of luminosity.

There is something fascinating about a man's being inviolable, untemptable, unswayable. If we wished to explain this in psychological and biographical terms, we might perhaps think of the home Jaspers came from. His father and mother were still closely linked to the high-spirited and strong-minded Frisian peasantry who possessed a sense of independence quite uncommon in Germany. Well, freedom is more than independence, and it remained for Jaspers to develop out of independence the rational consciousness of freedom in which man experiences himself as given to himself. But the sovereign naturalness—a certain cheerful recklessness (*Ubermut*) as he himself sometimes puts it—with which he loves to expose himself to the currents of public life, while at the same time remaining independent of all the trends and opinions that happen to be in vogue, is probably due also to that indigenous self-assurance, or at any rate has sprung from it. He need only dream himself, as it were, back into his personal origins and then out again into the breadth of humanity to convince himself that even in isolation he does not represent a private opinion, but a different, still hidden public view—a "footpath," as Kant put it, "which someday no doubt will widen out into a great highway."

There can be danger in such unerring certainty of judgment and sovereignty of mind. Not to be exposed to temptations can lead to inexperience, or at any rate, to lack of experience with the realities that any given period has to offer. And truly, what could be further from the experiences of our time than the high-spirited independence in which Jaspers has always been at home, the cheerful unconcern for what people say and think? This spirit is not even in rebellion against the conventions, because the conventions are always recognized as such, never taken seriously as standards of conduct. What could be further removed from our *ère du soupçon* (Nathalie Sarraute) than the confidence which deeply underlies this independence, the secret trust in man, in the *humanitas* of the human race?

And since we are already examining subjective, psychological matters: Jaspers was fifty years old when Hitler came to power. At this age the overwhelming majority of people have long since ceased to add to their experiences, and intellectuals in particular have usually become so hardened in their opinions that in all real events they can only perceive corroboration of these opinions. Jaspers reacted to the decisive events of these times (which he had no more foreseen than anyone else and for which he was possibly even less prepared than many other persons) neither by retreating into his own philosophy, nor by negating the world, nor by falling into melancholy. After 1933, that is, after the completion of his three-part *Philosophy*, and again after 1945, after completion of his book *On Truth*, he embarked on what we might call new eras of productivity. Unfortunately, this phrase suggests the renewal of vitality that sometimes occurs in men of great talent. But what is so magnificent about Jaspers is that he renews himself because he remains unchanged—as linked with the world as ever and following current events with unchanging keenness and capacity for concern.

The Great Philosophers just as much as the *Atom Bomb* lies wholly within the sphere of our most recent experience. This contemporaneity or rather this living in the present continuing into so advanced an age is like a stroke of luck which wipes out the question of just deserts. It was thanks to this same good fortune that Jaspers could be isolated in the course of his life, but could not be driven into solitude. That good fortune is based on a marriage in which a woman who is his peer has stood at his side ever since his youth. If two people do not succumb to the illusion that the ties binding them have made them one, they can create a world anew between them. Certainly for Jaspers this marriage has never been merely a private thing. It has proved that two people of different origins—Jaspers's wife is Jewish—could create between them a world of their own. And from this world in miniature he has learned, as from a model, what is essential for the whole realm of human affairs. Within this small world he unfolded and practiced his incomparable faculty for dialogue, the splendid precision of his way of listening, the constant readiness to give a candid account of himself, the patience to linger over a matter under discussion, and above all the ability to lure what is otherwise passed over in silence into the area of discourse, to make it worth talking about. Thus in speaking and

78

listening, he succeeds in changing, widening, sharpening—or, as
he himself would beautifully put it, in illuminating.

In this space forever illuminated anew by a speaking and listening thoughtfulness Jaspers is at home; this is the home of his mind
because it is a space in the literal sense of the word, just as the
ways of thinking taught by his philosophy are ways in the word's
original meaning, paths that open up a piece of otherwise un-
explored ground. Jaspers's thought is spatial because it forever
remains in reference to the world and the people in it, not because
it is bound to any existing space. In fact, the opposite is the
case, because his deepest aim is to "create a space" in which the
humanitas of man can appear pure and luminous. Thought of
this sort, always "related closely to the thoughts of others," is
bound to be political even when it deals with things that are
not in the least political; for it always confirms that Kantian "enlarged mentality" which is the political mentality *par excellence*.

In order to explore the space of *humanitas* which had become
his home, Jaspers needed the great philosophers. And he has
splendidly repaid them for their help, so to speak, by establishing
with them a "realm of the spirit" in which they once more appear as speaking persons—speaking from the realm of the shades
—who because they have escaped from temporal limitations can
become everlasting companions in the things of the mind. I wish
I could give you some conception of the freedom, the independence of thought that was required to establish this realm of the
spirit. For it was essential above all to abandon the chronological
order hallowed by tradition, in which there appeared to be a
succession, a consistent sequence with one philosopher handing
the truth on to the next. Granted, this tradition had lost the
validity of its contents for us some time ago; but the temporal
pattern of handing down, of following one upon the other, nevertheless seemed to us so compelling that without its Ariadne's
thread we felt as if we were straying helplessly about in the past,
utterly unable to orient ourselves. In this predicament, with the
whole relationship of modern man to his past at stake, Jaspers
converted the succession in time into a spatial juxtaposition, so
that nearness and distance depend no longer on the centuries

which separate us from a philosopher, but exclusively on the freely chosen point from which we enter this realm of the spirit, which will endure and expand as long as there are men on earth.

This realm, in which Jaspers is at home and to which he has opened the ways for us, does not lie in the beyond and is not utopian; it is not of yesterday nor of tomorrow; it is of the present and of this world. Reason has created it and freedom reigns in it. It is not something to locate and organize; it reaches into all the countries of the globe and into all their pasts. And although it is worldly, it is invisible. It is the realm of *humanitas*, which everyone can come to out of his own origins. Those who enter it recognize one another, for then they are "like sparks, brightening to a more luminous glow, dwindling to invisibility, alternating and in constant motion. The sparks see one another, and each flames more brightly because it sees others" and can hope to be seen by them.

I speak here in the name of those whom Jaspers once led into this realm. What was then in their hearts Adalbert Stifter has expressed more beautifully than I can: "Now there sprang forth astonishment at the man, and there rose up a great praise of him."

KARL JASPERS:
Citizen of the World?

Nobody can be a citizen of the world as he is the citizen of his country. Jaspers, in his *Origin and Goal of History* (1953), discusses extensively the implications of a world state and a world empire.[1] No matter what form a world government with centralized power over the whole globe might assume, the very notion of one sovereign force ruling the whole earth, holding the monopoly of all means of violence, unchecked and uncontrolled by other sovereign powers, is not only a forbidding nightmare of tyranny, it would be the end of all political life as we know it. Political concepts are based on plurality, diversity, and mutual limitations. A citizen is by definition a citizen among citizens of a country among countries. His rights and duties must be defined and limited, not only by those of his fellow citizens, but also by the boundaries of a territory. Philosophy may conceive of the earth as the homeland of mankind and of one unwritten law, eternal and valid for all. Politics deals with men, nationals of many countries and heirs to many pasts; its laws are the positively established fences which hedge in, protect, and limit the space in

[1] *Origin*, pp. 193ff.

which freedom is not a concept, but a living, political reality. The establishment of one sovereign world state, far from being the prerequisite for world citizenship, would be the end of all citizenship. It would not be the climax of world politics, but quite literally its end.

To say, however, that a world state conceived in the image of sovereign nation states or of a world empire in the image of the Roman Empire is dangerous (and the dominion of the Roman Empire over the civilized and barbarian parts of the world was bearable only because it stood against the dark and frightening background of unknown parts of the earth) is no solution for our present political problem. Mankind, which for all preceding generations was no more than a concept or an ideal, has become something of an urgent reality. Europe, as Kant foresaw, has prescribed its laws to all other continents; but the result, the emergence of mankind out of and side by side with the continued existence of many nations, has assumed an altogether different aspect from the one which Kant envisaged when he saw the unification of mankind "in a far-distant future." [2] Mankind owes its existence not to the dreams of the humanists nor to the reasoning of the philosophers and not even, at least not primarily, to political events, but almost exclusively to the technical development of the Western world. When Europe in all earnest began to prescribe its "laws" to all other continents, it so happened that she herself had already lost her belief in them. No less manifest than the fact that technology united the world is the other fact that Europe exported to the four corners of the earth its processes of disintegration—which had started in the Western world with the decline of the traditionally accepted metaphysical and religious beliefs and had accompanied the grandiose development of the natural sciences and the victory of the nation state over all other forms of government. The same forces which took centuries to undermine the ancient beliefs and political ways of life, and which have their place in the continuous development of the West alone, took only a few decades to break down, by working

[2] "Idea for a Universal History with Cosmopolitan Intent" (1784).

from without, beliefs and ways of life in all other parts of the world.

It is true, for the first time in history all peoples on earth have a common present: no event of any importance in the history of one country can remain a marginal accident in the history of any other. Every country has become the almost immediate neighbor of every other country, and every man feels the shock of events which take place at the other side of the globe. But this common factual present is not based on a common past and does not in the least guarantee a common future. Technology, having provided the unity of the world, can just as easily destroy it and the means of global communication were designed side by side with means of possible global destruction. It is difficult to deny that at this moment the most potent symbol of the unity of mankind is the remote possibility that atomic weapons used by one country according to the political wisdom of a few might ultimately come to be the end of all human life on earth. The solidarity of mankind in this respect is entirely negative; it rests, not only on a common interest in an agreement which prohibits the use of atomic weapons, but, perhaps also—since such agreements share with all other agreements the uncertain fate of being based on good faith—on a common desire for a world that is a little less unified.

This negative solidarity, based on the fear of global destruction, has its correspondence in a less articulate, but no less potent, apprehension that the solidarity of mankind can be meaningful in a positive sense only if it is coupled with political responsibility. Our political concepts, according to which we have to assume responsibility for all public affairs within our reach regardless of personal "guilt," because we are held responsible as citizens for everything that our government does in the name of the country, may lead us into an intolerable situation of global responsibility. The solidarity of mankind may well turn out to be an unbearable burden, and it is not surprising that the common reactions to it are political apathy, isolationist nationalism, or desperate rebellion against all powers that be rather than enthusiasm or a desire for a revival of humanism. The idealism of the humanist tradition of enlightenment and its concept of mankind look like reckless optimism in the light of present realities. These, on the other hand, insofar as they have brought us a global present without a common past, threaten to render irrelevant all traditions and all particular past histories.

It is against this background of political and spiritual realities, of which Jaspers is more aware than probably any other philosopher of our time, that one must understand his new concept of mankind and the propositions of his philosophy. Kant once called upon the historians of his time to write a history "with cosmopolitan intent." One could easily "prove" that Jaspers's whole philosophical work, from its beginnings in the *Psychology of World Views* (1919) to the world history of philosophy,[3] was conceived with "intent toward world citizenship." If the solidarity of mankind is to be based on something more solid than the justified fear of man's demonic capabilities, if the new universal neighborship of all countries is to result in something more promising than a tremendous increase in mutual hatred and a somewhat universal irritability of everybody against everybody else, then a process of mutual understanding and progressing self-clarification on a gigantic scale must take place. And just as the prerequisite for world government in Jaspers's opinion is the renunciation of sovereignty for the sake of a world-wide federated political structure, so the prerequisite for this mutual understanding would be the renunciation, not of one's own tradition and national past, but of the binding authority and universal validity which tradition and past have always claimed. It is by such a break, not with tradition but with the authority of tradition, that Jaspers entered philosophy. His *Psychology of World Views* denies the absolute character of any doctrine and puts in its stead a universal relativity, in which each specific philosophical content becomes means for individual philosophizing. The shell of traditional authority is forced open and the great contents of the past are freely and "playfully" placed in communication with each other in the test of communicating with a present living philosophizing.

[3] See now *The Great Philosophers*, vol. I, 1962, vol. II, 1966.

In this universal communication, held together by the existential experience of the present philosopher, all dogmatic metaphysical contents are dissolved into processes, trains of thought, which, because of their relevance to my present existing and philosophizing, leave their fixed historical place in the chain of chronology and enter a realm of the spirit where all are contemporaries. Whatever I think must remain in constant communication with everything that has been thought. Not only because, "in philosophy, novelty is an argument against truth," but because present philosophy cannot be more than "the natural and necessary conclusion of Western thought up to now, the candid synthesis brought about by a principle large enough to comprehend everything that in a sense is true." The principle itself is communication; truth, which can never be grasped as dogmatic content, emerges as "existential" substance clarified and articulated by reason, communicating itself and appealing to the reasonable existing of the other, comprehensible and capable of comprehending everything else. "*Existenz* only becomes clear through reason; reason only has content through *Existenz*." [4]

The pertinence of these considerations for a philosophical foundation of the unity of mankind is manifest: "limitless communication," [5] which at the same time signifies the faith in the comprehensibility of all truths *and* the good will to reveal and to listen as the primary condition for all human intercourse, is one, if not the central, idea of Jaspers's philosophy. The point is that here for the first time communication is not conceived as "expressing" thoughts and therefore being secondary to thought itself. Truth itself is communicative, it disappears and cannot be conceived outside communication; within the "existential" realm, truth and communication are the same. "Truth is what binds us together." [6] Only in communication—between contemporaries as well as between the living and the dead—does truth reveal itself.

[4] *Reason and Existence,* New York, 1955, p. 67.
[5] "*Grenzenlose Kommunikation*" is a term which appears in almost all of Jaspers's works.
[6] Cf. "Vom lebendigen Geist der Universität" (1946) in: *Rechenschaft und Ausblick* (Munich, 1951), p. 185.

A philosophy that conceives of truth and communication as one and the same has left the proverbial ivory tower of mere contemplation. Thinking becomes practical, though not pragmatic; it is a kind of practice between men, not a performance of one individual in his self-chosen solitude. Jaspers is, as far as I know, the first and the only philosopher who has ever protested against solitude, to whom solitude has appeared "pernicious" and who has dared to question "all thoughts, all experiences, all contents" under this one aspect: "What do they signify for communication? Are they such that they may help or such that they will prevent communication? Do they seduce to solitude or arouse to communication?" [7] Philosophy has lost both its humility before theology and its arrogance toward the common life of man. It has become *ancilla vitae*.[8]

This attitude is of special relevance within the German philosophical tradition. Kant seems to have been the last great philosopher who was still quite confident of being understood and of being able to dispel misunderstandings. Hegel's remark on his deathbed—*se non è vero, è bene trovato*—has become famous, "Nobody has understood me except one; and he misunderstood me." Since then, the growing loneliness of philosophers in a world that does not care about philosophy because it has become entirely fascinated by science has resulted in the well-known and often denounced ambiguity and obscurity which to many appear to be typical of German philosophy and which certainly are the hallmark of all strictly solitary, uncommunicative thought. On the level of common opinion, this means that clarity and greatness are seen as opposites. Jaspers's numerous utterances after the war, his articles, lectures, radio broadcasts, have all been guided by a deliberate attempt at popularization, at talking philosophy without using technical terminology,

---

[7] Cf. "Über meine Philosophie" (1941) in *op. cit.*, pp. 350, 352.

[8] Jaspers does not use this term. He mentions often that philosophizing is "inner action," practice, etc. The relationship between thinking and living cannot be discussed here. But the following sentence may show in which sense my interpretative use of *ancilla vitae* could be justified: "*Was im denkenden Leben getan werden muss, dem soll ein Philosophieren dienen, das erinnernd und vorausgreifend die Wahrheit offenbar macht.*" *Ibid.*, p. 356.

that is, by the conviction that one can appeal to reason and to the "existential" concern in all men. Philosophically this has been possible only because truth and communication are conceived to be the same.

From a philosophical viewpoint, the danger inherent in the new reality of mankind seems to be that this unity, based on the technical means of communication and violence, destroys all national traditions and buries the authentic origins of all human existence. This destructive process can even be considered a necessary prerequisite for ultimate understanding between men of all cultures, civilizations, races, and nations. Its result would be a shallowness that would transform man, as we have known him in five thousand years of recorded history, beyond recognition. It would be more than mere superficiality; it would be as though the whole dimension of depth, without which human thought, even on the mere level of technical invention, could not exist, would simply disappear. This leveling down would be much more radical than the leveling to the lowest common denominator; it would ultimately arrive at a denominator of which we have hardly any notion today.

As long as one conceives of truth as separate and distinct from its expression, as something which by itself is uncommunicative and neither communicates itself to reason nor appeals to "existential" experience, it is almost impossible not to believe that this destructive process will inevitably be triggered off by the sheer automatism of technology which made the world one and, in a sense, united mankind. It looks as though the historical pasts of the nations, in their utter diversity and disparity, in their confusing variety and bewildering strangeness for each other, are nothing but obstacles on the road to a horridly shallow unity. This, of course, is a delusion; if the dimension of depth out of which modern science and technology have developed ever were destroyed, the probability is that the new unity of mankind could not even technically survive. Everything then seems to depend upon the possibility of bringing the national pasts, in their original disparateness, into communication with each other as the only way to catch up with the global system of communication which covers the surface of the earth.

It is in the light of such reflections that Jaspers made the great historical discovery which became the cornerstone of his philosophy of history, its origin and its goal. The Biblical notion that all men descend from Adam and share the same origin and that they all travel to the same goal of salvation and final judgment is beyond knowledge and beyond proof. Christian philosophy of history, from Augustine to Hegel, saw in the appearance of Christ the turning point and the center of world history. As such, it is valid only for Christian believers; and if it claims authority over all, it is no less in the way of a unity of mankind than another myth which may teach a plurality of beginnings and ends.

Against this and similar philosophies of history which harbor a concept of one world history on the basis of the historical experience of one people or one particular part of the world, Jaspers has discovered an empirically given historical axis which gives all nations "a common framework of historical self-understanding. The axis of world history seems to pass through the fifth century B.C., in the midst of the spiritual process between 800 and 200 B.C."—Confucius and Lao-tse in China, the Upanishads and Buddha in India, Zarathustra in Persia, the prophets in Palestine, Homer, the philosophers, the tragedians in Greece.[9] It is characteristic of the events which took place during this era that they were completely unconnected, that they became the origins of the great historical world civilizations, and that these origins, in their very differentiation, had something uniquely in common. This peculiar sameness can be approached and defined in many ways: it is the time when mythologies were being discarded or used for the foundation of the great world religions with their concept of One transcendent God; when philosophy makes its appearance everywhere: man discovers Being as a whole and himself as radically different from all other beings; when, for the first time, man becomes (in the words of Augustine) a question for himself, becomes conscious of consciousness, begins to think

[9] *Origin*, pp. 1f.

about thinking; when great personalities appear everywhere who will no longer accept or be accepted as mere members of their respective communities but think of themselves as individuals and design new individual ways of life—the life of the wise man, the life of the prophet, the life of the hermit who retreats from all society into an entirely new inwardness and spirituality. All basic categories of our thought and all basic tenets of our beliefs were created during this period. It was the time when mankind first discovered the human condition on earth, so that from then on the mere chronological sequence of events could become a story and the stories be worked into a history, a significant object of reflection and understanding. The historical axis of mankind then is "an era around the middle of the last millennium B.C., for which everything that preceded it would appear to have been a preparation, and to which everything subsequent actually, and often in clear consciousness, relates back. The world history of humanity derives its structure from this period. It is not an axis of which we might assert the permanent absoluteness and uniqueness. But it is the axis of the short world history that has taken place up till now, that which, in the consciousness of all men, might represent the basis of the historical unity they recognize in solidarity. This real axis would then be the incarnation of an ideal axis, around which mankind in its movement is drawn together." [10]

In this perspective, the new unity of mankind might acquire a past of its own through a communication system, so to speak, in which the different origins of mankind would reveal themselves in their very sameness. But this sameness is far from being uniformity; just as man and woman can be the same, namely human, only by being absolutely different from each other, so the national of every country can enter this world history of humanity only by remaining and clinging stubbornly to what he is. A world citizen, living under the tyranny of a world empire, and speaking and thinking in a kind of glorified Esperanto, would be no less a monster than a hermaphrodite. The bond between men is, subjectively, the "will to limitless communication" and, objectively,

[10] *Ibid.*, pp. 262f.

the fact of universal comprehensibility. The unity of mankind and its solidarity cannot consist in a universal agreement upon one religion, or one philosophy, or one form of government, but in the faith that the manifold points to a Oneness which diversity conceals and reveals at the same time.

The pivotal age began the development of the great world civilizations which together constitute what we usually call world history, and it ended a period which because of this subsequent development we call pre-historic. If we think of our own era in terms of this historical design, then we may well come to the conclusion that the emergence of mankind as a tangible political reality marks the end of that period of world history which began in the pivotal age. Jaspers, in a way, agrees with the widespread feeling that our time somehow has come to an end, but he disagrees with the emphasis on doom that usually accompanies such diagnoses. "We live as though we stand knocking at doors which are still closed to us." [11] What so clearly appears as an end is better understood as a beginning whose innermost meaning we cannot yet grasp. Our present is emphatically, and not merely logically, the suspense between a no-longer and a not-yet. What begins now, after the end of world history, is the history of mankind. What this will eventually be, we do not know. We can prepare ourselves for it through a philosophy of mankind whose central concept would be Jaspers's concept of communication. This philosophy will not abolish, not even criticize, the great philosophical systems of the past in India, China, and the Occident, but will strip them of their dogmatic metaphysical claims, dissolve them, as it were, into trains of thought which meet and cross each other, communicate with each other and eventually retain only what is universally communicative. A philosophy of mankind is distinguished from a philosophy of man by its insistence on the fact that not Man, talking to himself in the dialogue of solitude, but men talking and communicating with each other, inhabit the earth. Of course, the philosophy of mankind cannot

[11] "Vom Europäischen Geist" (1946), in *Rechenschaft und Ausblick*, p. 260.

prescribe any particular political action, but it may comprehend politics as one of the great human realms of life as against all former philosophies which, since Plato, thought of the *bios politikos* as an inferior way of life and of politics as a necessary evil or, in the words of Madison, "the greatest of all reflections on human nature." [12]

In order to grasp the philosophical relevance of Jaspers's concept of mankind and world citizenship, it may be well to remember Kant's concept of mankind and Hegel's notion of world history, since these two are its proper traditional background. Kant viewed mankind as a possible ultimate result of history. History, he says, would offer nothing but the view of "melancholy haphazardness" (*"trostloses Ungefähr"*) if there were not a justified hope that the unconnected and unpredictable actions of men might in the end bring about mankind as a politically united community together with the fully developed humanity of man. What one sees of "men's actions on the great world stage . . . in the large [seems] woven together from folly, childish vanity, often from childish malice and destructiveness," and it can acquire meaning only if we assume that there exists a secret "intent of nature in this nonsensical course of human affairs," [13] which works behind the backs of men. It is interesting to note, and characteristic of our tradition of political thought, that it was Kant, not Hegel, who was the first to conceive of a cunning secret force in order to find meaning in political history at all. The experience behind this is no other than Hamlet's: "Our thoughts are ours, their ends none of our own," except that this experience was particularly humiliating for a philosophy whose center was the dignity and the autonomy of man. Mankind, for Kant, was that ideal state in "a far-distant future" where the dignity of man would coincide with the human condition of earth. But this ideal state would necessarily put an end to politics and political action as we know it today and whose follies and vanities are recorded by history. Kant foresees a far-distant future when past history

---

[12] *The Federalist*, No. 51.
[13] "Idea for a Universal History," *op. cit.*, Introduction.

will indeed have become "the education of mankind" in the words of Lessing. Human history would then be of no more interest than natural history, where we consider the present state of each species as the *telos* inherent in all previous development, its end in the double sense of aim and conclusion.

Mankind for Hegel manifests itself in the "world spirit"; in its quintessence it is always there in one of its historical stages of development, but it can never become a political reality. It is also brought about by a secret cunning force; but the "ruse of reason" is different from Kant's "cunning of nature," insofar as it can be perceived only by the contemplative glance of the philosopher, to whom alone the chain of meaningless and seemingly arbitrary events makes sense. The climax of world history is not the factual emergence of mankind, but the moment when the world spirit acquires self-consciousness in a philosophy, when the Absolute finally reveals itself to thought. World history, world spirit, and mankind have hardly any political connotations in Hegel's work, despite the strong political impulses of the young Hegel. They became immediately, and quite properly, leading ideas in the historical sciences, but remained without notable influence on political science. It was in Marx, who decided to "put Hegel back on his feet," that is, to change the *interpretation* of history into the *making* of history, that these concepts showed their political relevance. And this is an altogether different story. It is obvious that no matter how far distant or how close at hand the realization of mankind may be, one can be a world citizen only within the framework of Kant's categories. The best that can happen to any individual in the Hegelian system of historical revelation of the world spirit is to have the good fortune to be born among the right people at the right historical moment, so that one's birth will coincide with the revelation of the world spirit in this particular period. For Hegel to be a member of historical mankind meant to be a Greek and not a barbarian in the fifth century B.C., a Roman citizen and not a Greek in the first centuries of our era, to be a Christian and not a Jew in the Middle Ages, etc.

Compared with Kant, Jaspers's concept of mankind and world citizenship is historical; compared with Hegel, it is political. It somehow combines the depth of Hegel's historical experience with Kant's great political wisdom. Yet, what distinguishes Jaspers from both is decisive. He believes neither in the "melancholy haphazardness" of political action and the follies of recorded history nor in the existence of a secret cunning force that manipulates man into wisdom. He has abandoned Kant's concept of a "good will" which, because it is grounded in reason, is incapable of action.[14] He has broken with both the despair and the consolation of German idealism in philosophy. If philosophy is to become *ancilla vitae,* then there is no doubt what function it has to fulfill: in Kant's words, it will rather have to "carry the torch in front of her gracious lady than the train of her dress behind." [15]

The history of mankind which Jaspers foresees is not Hegel's world history, where the world spirit uses and consumes country after country, people after people, in the stages of its gradual realization. And the unity of mankind in its present reality is far from being the consolation or recompense for all past history as Kant hoped it to be. Politically, the new fragile unity brought about by technical mastery over the earth can be guaranteed only within a framework of universal mutual agreements, which eventually would lead into a world-wide federated structure. For this, political philosophy can hardly do more than describe and prescribe the new principle of political action. Just as, according to Kant, nothing should ever happen in war which would make a future peace and reconciliation impossible, so nothing, according to the implications of Jaspers's philosophy, should happen today in politics which would be contrary to the actually existing solidarity of mankind. This in the long run may mean that war must be ruled out of the arsenal of political means, not only because the possibility of an atomic war may endanger the existence of all mankind, but because each war, no matter how limited in the use of means and in territory, immediately and directly affects all mankind. The abolition of war, like the abol-

---

[14] ". . . the revered, but practically ineffectual general will which is founded in reason," "To Eternal Peace" (1795), translation quoted from Carl Joachim Friedrich, Modern Library edition.

[15] *Ibid.*

ishment of a plurality of sovereign states, would harbor its own peculiar dangers; the various armies with their old traditions and more or less respected codes of honor would be replaced by federated police forces, and our experiences with modern police states and totalitarian governments, where the old power of the army is eclipsed by the rising omnipotence of the police, are not apt to make us overoptimistic about this prospect. All this, however, still lies in a far-distant future.

ISAK DINESEN

1885-1963

Les grandes passions sont rares
comme les chefs-d'oeuvre. —BALZAC

THE Baroness Karen Blixen née Karen Christentze Dinesen—called Tanne by her family and Tania first by her lover and then by her friends—was the Danish woman author of rare distinction who wrote in English out of loyalty to her dead lover's language and, in the spirit of good old-fashioned coquetry, half hid, half showed her authorship by prefixing to her maiden name the male pseudonym "Isak," the one who laughs. Laughter was supposed to take care of several rather troublesome problems, the least serious of which, perhaps, was her firm conviction that it was not very becoming for a woman to be an author, hence a public figure; the light that illuminates the public domain is much too harsh to be flattering. She had had her experiences in this matter since her mother had been a suffragette, active in the fight for women's franchise in Denmark, and probably one of those excellent women who will never tempt a man to seduce them. When she was twenty she had written and published some short stories and been encouraged to go on but immediately decided not to. She "never once wanted to be a writer," she "had an

95

intuitive fear of being trapped," and every profession, because it invariably assigns a definite role in life, would have been a trap, shielding her against the infinite possibilities of life itself. She was in her late forties when she began to write professionally and close to fifty when her first book, *Seven Gothic Tales*, appeared. At that time, she had discovered (as we know from "The Dreamers") that the chief trap in life is one's own identity—"I will not be one person again. . . . Never again will I have my heart and my whole life bound up with one woman"—and that the best advice to give one's friends (for instance, Marcus Cocoza in the story) was not to worry "too much about Marcus Cocoza," for this means to be "really his slave and his prisoner." Hence, the trap was not so much writing or professional writing as taking oneself seriously and identifying the woman with the author who has his identity confirmed, inescapably, in public. That grief over having lost her life and her lover in Africa should have made her a writer and given her a sort of second life was best understood as a joke, and "God loves a joke" became her maxim in the latter part of her life. (She loved such mottoes to live by and had started with *navigare necesse est, vivere non necesse est,* to adopt later Denys Finch-Hatton's *Je responderay,* I shall answer and give account.)

But there was more than the fear of being trapped that caused her, in interview upon interview, to defend herself emphatically against the common notion of her being a born writer and a "creative artist." The truth was that she never had felt any ambition or particular urge to write, let alone *be* a writer; the little writing she had done in Africa could be dismissed, as it had only served "in times of drought" in every sense to disperse her worries about the farm and relieve her boredom when no other work could be done. Only once had she "created some fiction to make money," and though *The Angelic Avengers* did make some money, it turned out "terrible." No, she had started writing simply "because she had to make a living" and "could do only two things, cook and . . . perhaps, write." How to cook she had learned in Paris and later in Africa in order to please her friends, and in order to entertain friends and natives alike, she had taught herself how to tell stories. "Had she been able to stay in Africa, she would never have become a writer." For, *"Moi, je suis une conteuse, et rien qu'une conteuse. C'est l'histoire elle-même qui m'intéresse, et la façon de la raconter."* ("I, I am a storyteller and nothing else. What interests me is the story and the way to tell it.") All she needed to begin with was life and the world, almost any kind of world or milieu; for the world is full of stories, of events and occurrences and strange happenings, which wait only to be told, and the reason why they usually remain untold is, according to Isak Dinesen, lack of imagination —for only if you can imagine what has happened anyhow, repeat it in imagination, will you see the stories, and only if you have the patience to tell and retell them (*"Je me les raconte et re-raconte"*) will you be able to tell them well. This, of course, she had done all her life, but not in order to become an artist, not even to become one of the wise and old professional storytellers we find in her books. Without repeating life in imagination you can never be fully alive, "lack of imagination" prevents people from "existing." "Be loyal to the story," as one of her storytellers admonishes the young, "be eternally and unswervingly loyal to the story," means no less than, Be loyal to life, don't create fiction but accept what life is giving you, show yourself worthy of whatever it may be by recollecting and pondering over it, thus repeating it in imagination; this is the way to remain alive. And to live in the sense of being fully alive had early been and remained to the end her only aim and desire. "My life, I will not let you go except you bless me, but then I will let you go." The reward of storytelling is to be able to let go: "When the storyteller is loyal . . . to the story, there, in the end, silence will speak. Where the story has been betrayed, silence is but emptiness. But we, the faithful, when we have spoken our last word, will hear the voice of silence."

This, to be sure, needs skill, and in this sense storytelling is not only part of living but can become an art in its own right. To become an artist also needs time and a certain detachment from the heady, intoxicating business of sheer living that, perhaps, only the born artist can manage in the midst of living. In her case, anyhow, there is a sharp line dividing her life from her afterlife as an author. Only when she had lost what had constituted her life, her home in Africa and her lover, when she had returned home to Rungstedlund a complete "failure" with nothing in her hands except grief and sorrow and memories, did she become the artist and the "success" she never would have become otherwise—"God loves a joke," and divine jokes, as the Greeks knew so well, are often cruel ones. What she then did was unique in contemporary literature though it could be matched by certain nineteenth-century writers—Heinrich Kleist's anecdotes and short stories and some tales of Johann Peter Hebel, especially *Unverhofftes Wiedersehen* come to mind. Eudora Welty has defined it definitively in one short sentence of utter precision: "Of a story she made an essence; of the essence she made an elixir; and of the elixir she began once more to compound the story."

The connection of an artist's life with his work has always raised embarrassing problems, and our eagerness to see recorded, displayed, and discussed in public what once were strictly private affairs and nobody's business is probably less legitimate than our curiosity is ready to admit. Unfortunately, the questions one is bound to raise about Parmenia Migel's biography (*Titania. A Biography of Isak Dinesen*, Random House, 1967) are not of this order. To say that the writing is nondescript is putting it kindly, and although five years spent in research supposedly yielded "enough material . . . for a monumental work," we hardly ever get more than quotations from previously published material drawn either from books and interviews of the subject or from *Isak Dinesen: A Memorial*, which Random House published in 1965. The few facts revealed here for the first time are treated with a sloppy non-workmanship which any copy editor should have been able to spot. (A man who is about to commit suicide [her father] cannot very well be said to have "some premonition . . . of his approaching death"; on p. 36 we are instructed that her first love should "remain nameless," but he doesn't, on p. 210 we learn who he was; we are informed in passing that her father "had sympathized with the Communards and had leftist leanings" and are told, through the voice of an aunt, that "he was profoundly saddened by the horrors he had witnessed during the Paris Commune." A disabused man, we would conclude, if we did not know from the above-mentioned memorial volume, that he had later written a book of memoirs "in which . . . he rendered justice to the patriotism and idealism of the 'communards.'" His son confirms the sympathies with the Commune and adds that "in parliament his party was the Left.") Worse than the sloppiness is the wrong-headed *délicatesse* applied to the by far most relevant new fact the book contains, the venereal infection—the husband from whom she was divorced but whose name and title she kept (for "the satisfaction of being addressed as Baroness," as her biographer suggests?) had "left her a legacy of illness"— from whose consequences she had suffered all her life. Her medical history would indeed have been of considerable interest; her secretary relates to what an extent her later life was consumed by a "heroic fight against the overwhelming odds of illness . . . like one human being trying to stem an avalanche." And worst of all is the occasional, rather innocent impertinence, so typical of the professional adorers to be found in the surroundings of most celebrities; Hemingway, who quite generously had said in his acceptance speech for the Nobel Prize that it should have been given to "that beautiful writer Isak Dinesen," "could not help envying [Tania's] poise and sophistication" and "needed to kill in order to prove his manhood, to extirpate the insecurity which he never did really conquer." All this would not need saying and the whole enterprise would best be passed over in silence, if it were not for the unhappy fact that it was Isak Dinesen herself (or was it the Baroness Karen Blixen?) who had commissioned, as it were, this biography, had spent hours and days with Mrs. Migel to instruct her, and, shortly before her death, reminded her once more of "*my* book," exacting a promise that it would be finished "as soon as I die." Well, neither vanity nor the need for adoration —the sad substitute for the supreme confirmation of one's existence which only love, mutual love, can give—belongs among the mortal sins; but they are unsurpassed prompters when we need suggestions for making fools of ourselves.

No one, obviously, could have told the story of her life as she herself might have told it, and the question why she did not write an autobiography is as fascinating as it is unanswered. (What a pity that her biographer apparently never asked her this obvious question.) For *Out of Africa*, which is often called autobiographical, is singularly reticent, silent on almost all the issues her biographer would be bound to raise. It tells us nothing of the unhappy marriage and the divorce, and only the careful reader will learn from it that Denys Finch-Hatton was more than a regular visitor and friend. The book is indeed, as Robert Langbaum, by far her best critic, has pointed out, "an authentic pastoral, perhaps the best prose pastoral of our time," and because it is a pastoral and not dramatic in the least, not even in the narration of Denys Finch-Hatton's death in an airplane crash and of the last desolate weeks in empty rooms on packed cases, it can incorporate many stories but only hint, by the most tenuous, rarefied allusions, at the underlying story of a *grande passion* which was then, and apparently remained to the end, the source of her storytelling. Neither in Africa nor at any other time of her life did she ever hide anything; she must have been proud, one gathers, to be the mistress of this man who in her descriptions remains curiously lifeless. But in *Out of Africa*, she admits her relation only by implication—he "had no other home in Africa than the farm, he lived in my house between his Safaris," and when he came back the house "gave out what was in it; it spoke—as the coffee-plantations speak, when with the first showers of the rainy season they flower"; then "the things of the farm were all telling what they really were." And she, having "made up many [stories] while he had been away," would be "sitting on the floor, crosslegged like Scheherazade herself."

When she called herself Scheherazade in this setting she meant more than the literary critics who later followed her lead, more than mere storytelling, the *"Moi, je suis une conteuse and rien qu'une conteuse."* The Thousand and One Nights—whose "stories she placed above everything else"—were not merely whiled away with telling tales; they produced three male children. And her lover, who "when he came to the farm would ask: 'Have you got a story?'," was not unlike the Arabian King who "being restless was pleased with the idea of listening to the story." Denys Finch-Hatton and his friend, Berkeley Cole, belonged to the generation of young men whom the First World War had made forever unfit to bear the conventions and fulfill the duties of everyday life, to pursue their careers and play their roles in a society that bored them to distraction. Some of them became revolutionists and lived in the dreamland of the future; others, on the contrary, chose the dreamland of the past and lived as though "theirs was . . . a world which no longer existed." They belonged together in the fundamental conviction that "they did not belong to their century." (In political parlance, one would say that they were antiliberal insofar as liberalism meant the acceptance of the world as it was together with the hope for its "progress"; historians know to what an extent conservative criticism and revolutionary criticism of the world of the bourgeoisie coincide.) In either case, they wished to be "outcasts" and "deserters," quite ready "to pay for their wilfulness" rather than settle down and found a family. At any rate, Denys Finch-Hatton came and went as he wished, and nothing was obviously further from his mind than to be bound by marriage. Nothing could bind him and lure him back but the flame of passion, and the surest way of preventing the flame from being extinguished by time and inevitable repetition, by knowing each other too well and having already heard all the stories, was to become inexhaustible in making up new ones. Surely, she was no less anxious to entertain than Scheherazade, no less conscious that failing to please would be her death.

Hence *la grande passion*, with Africa, still wild, not yet domesticated, the perfect setting. There one could draw the line "between respectability and decency, and [divide] up our acquaintances, human and animal, in accordance with the doctrine. We put down domestic animals as respectable and wild animals as decent, and held that, while the existence and prestige of the first were decided by their relation to the community, the others stood in direct contact with God. Pigs and poultry, we agreed, were worthy of our respect, inasmuch as they loyally returned what was invested in them, and . . . behaved as was expected of them. . . . We registered ourselves with the wild animals, sadly admitting the inadequacy of our return to the community —and to our mortgages—but realizing that we could not possibly, not even in order to obtain the highest approval of our surroundings, give up that direct contact with God which we shared with the hippo and the flamingo." Among the emotions, *la grande passion* is just as destructive of what is socially acceptable, just as contemptuous of what is deemed "worthy of our respect," as the outcasts and deserters were of the civilized society they had come from. But life is lived in society, and love, therefore—not romantic love, to be sure, that sets the stage for marital bliss—is destructive of life too, as we know from the famous pairs of lovers in history and literature who all came to grief. To escape society—couldn't that mean to be granted not just passion but a passionate life? Hadn't that been the reason why she left Denmark, to expose herself to a life unprotected by society? "What business had I had to set my heart on Africa?" she asked, and the answer came in the song of the "Master" whose "word has been a lamp unto my feet and a light unto my path"—

Who doth ambition shun
And loves to live i' the sun,
Seeking the food he eats,
And pleas'd with what he gets,
Come hither, come hither, come
    hither:
    Here shall he see
    No enemy
But winter and rough weather.

If it do come to pass
That any man turn ass
Leaving his wealth and ease,
A stubborn will to please,
Ducdame, ducdame, ducdame:
    Here shall he see
    Gross fools as he,
And if he will come to me.

Scheherazade, with everything the name implies, living among Shakespeare's "gross fools" who shun ambition and love to live in the sun, having found a place "nine thousand feet up" from where to laugh down "at the ambition of the new arrivals, of the Missions, the business people and the Government itself, to make the continent of Africa respectable," intent upon nothing except preserving the natives, the wild animals, and the wilder outcasts and deserters from Europe, the adventurers turned guides and safari hunters, in "their innocence of the period before the Fall"—that is what she wanted to be, how she wanted to live, and how she appeared to herself. It was not necessarily how she appeared to others, and particularly to her lover. Tania he had called her, and then he had added Titania. ("There is such magic in the people and the land here," she had said to him; and Denys had "smiled at her with affectionate condescension. 'The magic is not in the people and the land, but in the eye of the beholder. . . . You bring your own magic to it, Tania . . . Titania.'") Parmenia Migel has chosen the name as title for her biography, and it wouldn't have been a bad title if she had remembered that the name implies more than the Queen of fairies and her "magic." The two lovers between whom the name first fell, forever quoting Shakespeare to each other, knew of course better; they knew that the Queen of fairies was quite capable of falling in love with Bottom and that she had a rather unrealistic estimate of her own magical powers:

> "And I will purge thy mortal grossness so
> That thou shalt like an airy spirit go."

Well, Bottom did not transform into an airy spirit, and Puck tells us what is the truth of the matter for all practical purposes:

> "My mistress with a monster is in love. . . .
> Titania wak'd and straightway lov'd an ass."

The trouble was that magic once more proved utterly ineffective. The catastrophe that finally befell her she had brought about herself, when she decided to stay on the farm even when she must have known that coffee growing "at an altitude so high . . . was decidedly unprofitable," and, to make matters worse, she "did not know or learn much about coffee but persisted in the unshakable conviction that her intuitive power would tell her what to do"—as her brother, in sensible and tender reminiscences, remarked after her death. Only when she had been expelled from the land that for seventeen long years, supported by the money of her family, had permitted her to be Queen, Queen of fairies, did the truth dawn upon her. Remembering from afar her African cook, Kamante, she wrote, "Where the great Chef walked in deep thought, full of knowledge, nobody sees anything but a little bandy-legged Kikuyu, a dwarf with a flat, still face." Yes, nobody except herself, forever repeating everything in the magic of imagination out of which the stories grew. However, the point of the matter is that even this dispro-portion, once it has been discovered, can become the stuff for a story. Thus, we meet Titania again in "The Dreamers," only now she is called "Donna Quixota de la Mancha" and reminds the wise old Jew, who in the story plays the role of Puck, of "dancing snakes" he once saw in India, snakes that have "no poison what-ever" and kill, if they kill, by sheer force of embrace. "In fact, the sight of you, unfolding your great coils to revolve around, impress yourself upon, and finally crush a meadow mouse is enough to split one's side with laughter." In a way, that is how one feels when one reads on page after page about her "suc-cesses" in later life and how she enjoyed them, magnifying them out of all proportion—that so much intensity, such bold passion-ateness should be wasted on Book-of-the-Month-Club selections and honorary memberships in prestigious societies, that the early clear-headed insight that sorrow is better than nothing, that "be-tween grief and nothing I will take grief" (Faulkner), should finally be rewarded by the small change of prizes, awards, and honors might be sad in retrospect; the spectacle itself must have been very close to comedy.

Stories had saved her love, and stories saved her life after disaster had struck. "All sorrows can be borne if you put them into a story or tell a story about them." The story reveals the meaning of what otherwise would remain an unbearable se-quence of sheer happenings. "The silent, all-embracing genius of consent" that also is the genius of true faith—when her Arab servant hears of Denys Finch-Hatton's death, he replies "God is great," just as the Hebrew Kaddish, the death prayer said by the closest relative, says nothing but "Holy be His name"—rises out of the story because in the repetition of imagination the happen-ings have become what she would call a "destiny." To be so at one with one's own destiny that no one will be able to tell the dancer from the dance, that the answer to the question, Who are you? will be the Cardinal's answer, "Allow me . . . to answer you in the classic manner, and to tell you a story," is the only aspiration worthy of the fact that life has been given us. This is also called pride, and the true dividing line between people is whether they are capable of being "in love with [their] destiny" or whether they "accept as success what others warrant to be so . . . at the quotation of the day. They tremble, with reason, before their fate." All her stories are actually "Anecdotes of Destiny," they tell again and again how at the end we shall be privileged to judge; or, to put it differently, how to pursue one of the "two courses of thought at all seemly to a person of any intelligence . . . : What did God mean by creating the world, the sea, and the desert, the horse, the winds, woman, amber, fishes, wine?"

It is true that storytelling reveals meaning without committing the error of defining it, that it brings about consent and reconciliation with things as they really are, and that we may even trust it to contain eventually by implication that last word which we expect from the "day of judgment." And yet, if we listen to Isak Dinesen's "philosophy" of storytelling and think of her life in the light of it, we cannot help becoming aware of how the slightest misunderstanding, the slightest shift of emphasis in the wrong direction, will inevitably ruin everything. If it is true, as her "philosophy" suggests, that no one has a life worth thinking about whose life story cannot be told, does it not then follow that life could be, even ought to be, lived as a story, that what one has to do in life is to make the story come true? "Pride," she once wrote in her notebook, "is faith in the idea that God had, when he made us. A proud man is conscious of the idea, and aspires to realize it." From what we now know of her early life it seems quite clear that this is what she herself had tried to do when she was a young girl, to "realize" an "idea" and to anticipate her life's destiny by making an old story come true. The idea came to her as a legacy of her father, whom she had greatly loved—his death, when she was ten years old, was the first great grief, the fact that he had committed suicide, as she later learned, the first great shock from which she refused to be parted—and the story she had planned to act out in her life was actually meant to be the sequence of her father's story. The latter had concerned *"une princesse de conte de fées* whom everybody adored," whom he had known and loved before his marriage, and who had died suddenly at the age of twenty. Her father had mentioned it to her and an aunt had later suggested that he had never been able to recover from losing the girl, that his suicide was the result of his incurable grief. The girl, it turned out, had been a cousin of her father, and the daughter's greatest ambition became to belong to this side of her father's family, Danish high nobility to boot, "a race totally different" from her own milieu, as her brother relates it. It was only natural that one of its members, who would have been the dead girl's niece, became her best friend, and when "she fell in love 'for the first time and really forever,' [as] she used to say," it was with another second cousin of hers, Hans Bror Blixen, who would have been the dead girl's nephew. And since this one took no notice of her, she decided, even at the age of twenty-seven, old enough to know better—to the distress and the amazement of everybody around her—to marry the twin brother and leave with him for Africa, shortly before the outbreak of the First World War. What then came was petty and sordid, not at all the stuff you could safely put into a story or tell a story about. (She was separated immediately after the war and received her divorce in 1923.)

Or was it? As far as I know, she never wrote a story about this absurd marriage affair, but she did write some tales about what must have been for her the obvious lesson of her youthful follies, namely, about the "sin" of making a story come true, of interfering with life according to a preconceived pattern, instead of waiting patiently for the story to emerge, of repeating in imagination as distinguished from creating a fiction and then trying to live up to it. The earliest of these tales is "The Poet" (in *Seven Gothic Tales*); two others were written nearly twenty-five years later (Parmenia Migel's biography unfortunately contains no chronological table), "The Immortal Story" (in *Anecdotes of Destiny*) and "Echoes" (in *Last Tales*). The first tells of the encounter between a young poet of peasant stock and his high-placed benefactor, an elderly gentleman who in his youth had fallen under the spell of Weimar and "the great Geheimerat Goethe," with the result that "outside of poetry there was to him no real ideal in life." Alas, no such high ambition has ever made a man a poet, and when he realized "that the poetry of his life would have to come from somewhere else" he decided on the part "of a Maecenas," began to look for "a great poet" worthy of his consideration, and found him conveniently at hand in the town he lived in. But a real Maecenas, one who knew so much about poetry, could not very well be content with shelling out the money; he had also to provide the great tragedies and sorrows out of which he knew great poetry draws its best inspirations. Thus, he acquired a young wife and arranged it so that the two young people under his protection should fall in love with each other without any prospect of marriage. Well, the end is pretty bloody; the young poet shoots at his benefactor, and while the old man in his death agony dreams of Goethe and Weimar, the young woman, seeing as in a vision her lover "with the halter around his neck," finishes him off. "Just because it suited him that the world should be lovely, he meant to conjure it into being so," she said to herself. " 'You!,' she cried at him, 'You poet!' "

The perfect irony of "The Poet" is perhaps best realized by those who know German *Bildung* and its unfortunate connection with Goethe as well as its author did herself. (The story contains several allusions to German poems by Goethe and Heine as well as to Voss's translation of Homer. It could also be read as a story about the vices of *Bildung*.) "The Immortal Story," on the contrary, is conceived and written in the manner of a folk story. Its hero is an "immensely rich tea-trader" in Canton with very down-to-earth reasons for having "faith in his own omnipotence," who only at the end of his life came into contact with books. He then was bothered that they told of things that had never happened, and he got positively outraged when told that the only story he knew—about the sailor who had come ashore, met an old gentleman, "the richest man" in town, was asked by him to "do your best" in the bed of his young wife that he might still have a son, and was given a five-guinea piece for his service—"never has happened, and . . . never will happen, and that is why it is told." So the old man goes in pursuit of a sailor to make the old story, told in all harbor towns the world over, come true. And all seems to go well—except that the young sailor in the morning refuses to recognize the slightest similarity between the story and what had happened to him during the night, refuses the five guineas, and leaves for the lady in question the only treasure he possesses, "one big shining pink shell" of which he thinks "that perhaps there is not another one just like it in all the world."

"Echoes," the last one in this category, is a belated sequel to "The Dreamers" in *Gothic Tales*, the story about Pellegrina Leoni. "The diva who had lost her voice" in her wanderings hears it again from the boy Emanuele, whom she now proceeds to make into her own image so that her dream, her best and least selfish dream, should come true—that the voice which gave so much pleasure should be resurrected. Robert Langbaum, whom I mentioned before, noticed that here "Isak Dinesen pointed the finger of accusation against herself" and that the story, as the first pages suggest anyhow, is "about cannibalism," but nothing in it bears out that the singer had "been feeding on [the boy] in order to restore her own youth and to resurrect the Pellegrina Leoni whom she buried in Milan twelve years ago." (The very choice of a male successor precludes this interpretation.) The singer's own conclusion is, "And the voice of Pellegrina Leoni will not be heard again." The boy, before starting to throw stones at her, had accused her, "You are a witch. You are a vampire. . . . Now I know that I should die if I went back to you"—for the next singing lesson. The same accusations, the young poet could have hurled at his Maecenas, the young sailor at his benefactor, and generally all people who, under the pretext of being helped, are used for making another person's dream come true. (Thus, she herself had thought she could marry without love because her cousin "needed her and was perhaps the only human being who did," while she actually used him to start a new life in East Africa and to live among natives as her father had done when he had lived like a hermit among the Chippeway Indians. "The

Indians are better than our civilized people of Europe," he had told his small daughter, whose greatest gift was never to forget. "Their eyes see more than ours, and they are wiser.")

Thus, the earlier part of her life had taught her that, while you can tell stories or write poems about life, you cannot make life poetic, live it as though it were a work of art (as Goethe had done) or use it for the realization of an "idea." Life may contain the "essence" (what else could?); recollection, the repetition in imagination, may decipher the essence and deliver to you the "elixir"; and eventually you may even be privileged to "make" something out of it, "to compound the story." But life itself is neither essence nor elixir, and if you treat it as such it will only play its tricks on you. It was perhaps the bitter experience of life's tricks that prepared her (rather late, she was in her middle thirties when she met Finch-Hatton) for being seized by the *grande passion* which indeed is no less rare than a chef-d'oeuvre. Storytelling, at any rate, is what in the end made her wise—and, incidentally, not a "witch," "siren," or "sibyl," as her entourage admiringly thought. Wisdom is a virtue of old age, and it seems to come only to those who, when young, were neither wise nor prudent.

HERMANN BROCH

1886-1951

I. THE RELUCTANT POET [1]

Hermann Broch was a poet in spite of himself. That he was born a poet and did not want to be one was the fundamental trait of his nature, inspired the dramatic action of his greatest book, and became the basic conflict of his life. Of his life, not his psyche; for this was not a psychological conflict that could have been expressed in psychic struggles, with no other consequences than what Broch himself half ironically, half disgustedly called "soul clamor." Nor was it a conflict between gifts—between, say, the gift for science and mathematics and the imaginative, poetic gift. Such a conflict could have been solved, or if insoluble could at best have produced belles-lettres but never real creative work. Moreover, a psychological conflict or a struggle among various talents can never be the fundamental trait of a man's nature, since this always lies at a deeper level, as it were, than all gifts and talents, than all psychologically describable peculiarities and qualities. The latter grow out of his nature, develop according to its laws, or are destroyed by it. The circuit of Broch's life and

---

[1] "Poet" is used throughout this essay in the sense of the German *Dichter*. (Translator's note.)

creativity, the horizon in which his work moved, was not actually a circle; rather, it resembled a triangle whose sides can be accurately labeled: Literature—Knowledge—Action. Only this man in his uniqueness could fill the area of that triangle.

We assign entirely different talents to these three fundamentally different activities of men: artistic, scientific, and political work. But Broch approached the world with the demand, never quite openly expressed but always latent and insistent, that in his life on earth man must make the three coincide and become one. He demanded of literature that it possess the same compelling validity as science, that science summon into being the "totality of the world" [2] as does the work of art whose "task is the constant recreation of the world," [3] and that both together, art impregnated with knowledge and knowledge that has acquired vision, should comprehend and include all the practical, everyday activities of man.

This was the fundamental trait of his nature, and as such without conflict. But within a life, and above all within the limited span that is meted out to human life, such a demand must necessarily lead to conflicts. For within the structure of contemporary attitudes and occupations it places an excessive burden upon art, upon science, and upon politics. And these conflicts were manifest in Broch's attitude toward the fact that he was a poet; he became one in spite of himself and by his reluctance gave personally valid and adequate expression to both the fundamental trait of his nature and the fundamental conflict of his life.

In terms of Broch's biography, the phrase "reluctant poet," insofar as it expresses a conflict, probably applies primarily to the period after *The Death of Virgil*. In this book the dubiousness of art in general became the thematic content of a work of art itself; and since the completion of the work coincided with the greatest shock of the age, revelation of massacres in the death camps, Broch henceforth forbade himself to continue creative writing,

[2] "Gedanken zum Problem der Erkenntnis in der Musik," in *Essays* (Zürich, 1955), II, 100.

[3] "Hofmannsthal und seine Zeit," *op. cit.*, I, 140.

and thus cut himself off from his accustomed mode of resolving all conflicts. In regard to life, he conceded absolute primacy to action, and in regard to creativity, to knowledge. Thus the tension between literature, knowledge, and action assailed him daily and almost hourly, permanently affecting his everyday life and his everyday work. (We shall come back to the objective basis of this tension, which sprang from Broch's regarding action in terms of goal-oriented work and thinking in terms of result-producing knowledge.)

This had certain remarkable practical consequences. Whenever an acquaintance—not just a friend, which would have kept things within reasonable limits, but any acquaintance—was in distress, was sick or had no money or was dying, it was Broch who took care of everything. (And distress, of course, was ubiquitous in a circle of friends and acquaintances consisting largely of refugees.) It seemed to be assumed that all help would come from Broch, who had neither money nor time. He was exempt from such responsibilities—which inevitably widened his circle of acquaintance and thus imposed fresh demands on his time—only when he himself landed in the hospital (not without a measure of spiteful glee) and there obtained some repose, which cannot very well be refused to a broken arm or leg.

But this, of course, was only the most innocent phase of the conflict that determined his life in America. It was incomparably more burdensome to him that his past as a poet and novelist trailed after him, and since he was in fact one, he could not withdraw from this obligation. This began with *Die Schuldlosen* ("The Guiltless"), which had to be written when, after the war, a German publisher wanted to reprint some old, half-forgotten stories by Broch in their old form. To forestall this he wrote the book, that is, he revised the stories until they would fit into the "frame" narrative, and added some new stories, including the story of the servant-girl Zerline, perhaps the finest love story in German literature. Undoubtedly it turned into a very fine book, but it was hardly written of his own free will.

The novel he was working on at the time of his death belongs in this same category. It now appears in his collected works under the title of *Der Versucher* ("The Tempter").[4] In this case Alfred A. Knopf wanted to publish a book of Broch's, and Broch could not refuse if only because he needed money. It was well known that he had brought a virtually finished novel with him from Austria and kept it in his desk drawer. He needed only to turn the manuscript over to the American publisher for translation. But instead he set to work revising it for the third time—and on this occasion he did something that is probably unique in the history of literature. The novel belonged to an entirely different era of his life—had come out of what was probably his most confused period, the first years of Hitlerism. Its contents had in a good many respects become alien to him. But he recast it in the very "style of old age" which he himself had described and hailed in his essay on "The Style of the Mythical Age."[5] If we compare the two hundred typewritten pages of the last version with the chapters of the second version from which they grew, we see that his labors consisted in nothing but deletions, in other words, in that process of "abstracting" characteristic of the style of old age. This abstracting has resulted in a spare, purified prose of inviolable beauty and vitality, and in a perfect interweaving of man and landscape, such as we otherwise have only from the hands of old masters—masters who have grown old.

To be sure, we would not need the late unfinished literary works to realize that Broch never ceased to be a poet and novelist, for all that he wanted less and less to be one. Every one of his published essays is essentially the statement of a writer. This is particularly true of the Hofmannsthal study, that splendid essay, saturated with historical insights, in which Broch dealt with all

[4] Unfortunately, it became apparent too late, from the posthumous papers, that Broch had meant to call it *Der Wanderer* ("The Wanderer"), a fact not without significance, since it provides evidence that in the course of his final revision Broch thought of the character of the doctor, not that of Marius Ratti, as the hero of the book.

[5] This miracle of reshaping can no longer be detected in the present edition, in which the second and third versions (the third being the last) have been integrated for reasons of readability.

This essay, an introduction to Rachel Bespaloff's *On the Iliad* (New York, 1947), was written and published in English.

the premises of his own literary existence: Jewish origin and assimilation, the splendors and miseries of declining Austria, the respectable middle-class milieu that he found so detestable, and the even more detestable literary cliquishness of Vienna, that "metropolis of the ethical vacuum." [6] All his great historical perceptions: the co-ordination of the baroque and the drama and his analysis of the theater as the last refuge of the grand style in a styleless age;[7] the discovery that it is "a novelty in the history of art that posthumous fame has become more important than fame" and the connection of this phenomenon with the bourgeois age;[8] finally the unforgettable sketch of the last Emperor and his loneliness[9]—all this, of course, struck fire because he was a writer, and although it was all seen with the eyes of Hofmannsthal (especially the portrait of the Emperor), it was still seen through the eyes, the poet's eyes, of Broch.

His last novel, had it been completed, would probably have been another work to rank with *The Death of Virgil*, though written in a completely different style, epic rather than lyric. Nevertheless, it too was written consciously in spite of himself. For while he may have submitted with some reluctance and half-heartedness to the primacy of action in life, he was, where creativity and work were at question, during the last years of his life completely convinced of the primacy of knowledge over literature, of science over art. And at the end of his life he was persuaded that there was even a kind of priority, if not primacy, of a general theory of knowledge to science and politics. (He had notions about such a theory, which was to place both science and politics on a new basis; it existed in his mind under the title of *Mass Psychology*.) Thus, a mixture of external and internal circumstances produced the peculiar frenzy in which the fundamental trait of his nature, which had been really without conflict, resulted in almost nothing but conflicts. Behind the novel on which he was working, and which he regarded as wholly superfluous

---

[6] "Hofmannsthal . . . ," *op. cit.,* I, 105.
[7] *Ibid.,* p. 49.
[8] *Ibid.,* p. 55.
[9] *Ibid.,* pp. 96ff.

(wrongly, to be sure, but what did that matter?), stood the torso of the *Mass Psychology*, the burden of work already invested in it and the greater burden of work that had not even been started yet. But behind both, even more pressing, even more depressing, was his anxiety about the theory of knowledge. He had initially intended to set forth his ideas on epistemology only in a series of appendices to the theory of mass psychology. But in the course of the work he had come to see it as his proper subject, in fact the only essential one.

Behind the novel, in which against his will he completed his evolution as a writer reaching the style of old age, and behind the results of his scholarly researches in psychology and history, there remained to the last his wearisome and unwearied search for an absolute. That search had probably started him on his course to begin with, as, in the end, it gave him the notion of an "earthly absolute" as the solution to satisfy his head and to console his heart.

What Broch had to say objectively about the fate of being a poet in spite of oneself may be found in almost every one of his essays. For an ultimate understanding of him, however, the decisive thing is how he solved the resultant conflicts and problems in his fiction, and what roles he assigned there to literature, knowledge, and action. To this end we must turn to *The Death of Virgil*, where the *Aeneid* is to be burned for the sake of knowledge, this knowledge being then sacrificed to the friendship between Virgil and the Emperor and to highly practical political requirements of the age which this particular friendship contains. That "literature is only impatience on the part of knowledge";[10] that the maxim, "Confession is nothing, knowledge is everything," [11] is especially valid for poetry; that the time, however, calls not for knowledge but for action, not for a "scientific" but

_____

[10] "Die mythische Erbschaft der Dichtung," *op. cit.*, I, 237.

[11] A reference to Goethe's "all my works are but fragments of a great confession." See Hugo von Hofmannsthal, *Selected Prose*, trans. by Mary Hottinger, Tania and James Stern, introd. by Hermann Broch (New York, 1952), p. xi.

an "ethical work of art," [12] although art because of its cognitive function can never break with the "spirit of the age," [13] least of all with its science; that, finally, it is the "extraordinary mission" of contemporary literature, which "has had first to pass through all the hells of *l'art pour l'art*," to "cast everything aesthetic into the power of the ethical" [14]—all these were principles he never doubted from the very beginning of his creative work to the very end. He never questioned the absolute, inviolable primacy of ethics, the primacy of action. Nor did he ever doubt the specific modernity—we may call it the limitation of contemporaneity, if we will—which compelled him to express the fundamental attitude and the fundamental requirements of his nature only in a life determined by conflicts and problems.

This last, to be sure, was something he never directly spoke of, probably because of his peculiar, highly characteristic reserve about all things which too plainly pertained to the personal realm. "Man as such is the problem of our time; the problems of individuals are fading away and are even forbidden, morally forbidden. The personal problem of the individual has become a subject of laughter for the gods, and they are right in their lack of pity." [15] Broch seems never to have kept a diary; not even notebooks have been found among his papers; and it is almost touching to see that the only time he spoke directly of his most personal problems, and not indirectly in their poetic transformation, he talked not about himself but about Kafka, thus once again saying in disguise what he had wanted to say in *The Death of Virgil* but could not for the simple reason that the literary force of the book was too great for its "message," the attack on literature as such, to have its full impact. Therefore, writing in English about Kafka but actually engaged in hidden self-interpretation, he stated what might with greater justice have been said of himself, but which no one did say: "He has reached the point of the Either-Or: either poetry is able to proceed to myth, or it goes bankrupt.

[12] "James Joyce und die Gegenwart," *Essays*, I, 207.
[13] "Die mythische Erbschaft . . . ," *op. cit.*, I, 246.
[14] "James Joyce . . . ," *op. cit.*, I, 208.
[15] "Die mythische Erbschaft . . . ," *op. cit.*, I, 263.

Kafka, in his presentiment of the new cosmogony, the new theogony that he had to achieve, *struggling with his love for literature, his disgust for literature, feeling the ultimate insufficiency of any artistic approach,* decided (as did Tolstoy, faced with a similar decision) to quit the realm of literature and asked that his work be destroyed; he asked this for the sake of the universe whose new mythical concept had been bestowed upon him." [16] (My italics.)

What Broch says in this essay goes far beyond hatred of the literary pose and its cheap aestheticism, even beyond his embittered criticism of *l'art pour l'art,* which occupies a central place in his topical critical work as well as his philosophizing about art and his early reflections on ethics and the theory of value. Works of art as such are regarded as questionable. Literature as such is "ultimately insufficient." A puzzling sort of reticence, which should not be equated with modesty, kept him from propounding his own work as the model of what he was talking about; but of course he was referring just as much to *The Death of Virgil* here as, ten years earlier in the essay on Joyce, he concealed his criticism of *The Sleepwalkers* behind a remark on Gide to the effect that modernity is hardly attained when "a novel is used as a framework for psychoanalytical or other scientific digressions." [17] But then, in the early essays as in his early self-criticism, he was concerned only with liberating the novel from its "literariness," its subjection to bourgeois society whose leisure and craving for culture had to be fed with "entertainment and instruction." [18] Undoubtedly he succeeded, in *The Death of Virgil,* in transforming the novel form, in spite of its inherently specious or naturalistic tendencies, into authentic poetry—and therefore had demonstrated by this example the insufficiency of poetry as such.

The mention of Tolstoy suggests why Broch thought literature insufficient. Literature imposes no binding edicts. Its insights do not have the compelling character of the *mythos* which it serves

[16] *Ibid.*
[17] "James Joyce . . . ," *op. cit.,* I, 195.
[18] "Hofmannsthal . . . ," *op. cit.,* I, 206.

in an intact religious view of the world—this service being the real justification of art. (For Broch, the great prototype and example of such service was always the hierarchically ordered system of life and thought that prevailed during the Catholic Middle Ages.) Neither does art, and especially literature, possess the coercive forcefulness, the incontrovertibility, of logical statements; although it manifests itself in language, it lacks the cogency of *logos*. Broch probably faced the question, "What then shall we do?" for the first time in connection with the First World War. Subsequently it was posed for him, with more and more insistence, by all the further disasters of our age. Again and again this question overpowered him "like a thunderclap." And he concluded that an answer to be valid at all would have to have the same coercive force as that possessed by *mythos* on the one hand and *logos* on the other.[19]

For although the question was posed for him in the context of the twentieth century, the century "of the darkest anarchy, the darkest atavism, the darkest cruelty," [20] it was also the basic question of living and mortal man. Its answer, therefore, must be compatible not only with the times, but also with the phenomenon of death itself. The question of what to do may have been kindled by the tasks of the age; but for Broch it was also an inquiry into the possibility of an earthly conquest of death. Its answer, therefore, must possess the same inescapable necessity as death itself.

For Broch this initial formulation of the problem, one which he held to all his life, was governed by the alternatives of *mythos* and *logos*. In his last years, however, he probably no longer had any faith in the "new *mythos*" [21] which had been his entire hope from *The Sleepwalkers* to *The Death of Virgil*. In the course of his work on *Mass Psychology*, at any rate, the weight of his results shifted more and more away from *mythos* toward *logos*, away from literature toward science. More and more he searched for a strictly logical, verifiable mode of knowing.

But even if he had not lost this faith, his attitude toward litera-

[19] "Das Böse in Wertsystem der Kunst," *op. cit.*, I, 313.
[20] "Hofmannsthal . . . ," *op. cit.*, I, 59.
[21] "James Joyce . . . ," *op. cit.*, I, 210.

ture after *The Death of Virgil,* which means of course his attitude toward himself as a poet, could scarcely have assumed any other form. For relevant though the shift in Broch's thinking from *mythos* to *logos* was, productive though its effects upon his episte-mology proved to be (indeed, it was the actual origin of the epistemology), it had no bearing on the basic question of his being a poet and not wanting to be one. That was, rather, a question of social criticism and of the artist's position in his times, a question which Broch posed on many planes and almost always answered negatively. Since Broch's philosophy of art held that the real cognitive function of a work of art must be to represent the otherwise unattainable totality of an era, we may well ask whether a world in "valuational disintegration" can still be represented as a totality. So, for example, the question is put in the essay on Joyce. But in that essay literature is still regarded as "mythic task and mythic action," [22] whereas in the study on Hofmannsthal, written twelve years later, even Dante's poetry can "scarcely be characterized any longer as properly mythic." [23] The Joyce essay was written in the same mood that so powerfully erupts from the surging lyric rhythms of *The Death of Virgil* and closes with the hope of a "new *mythos,*" a "world ordering itself anew" as a culmination of the total literary effort of the times. But in the Hofmannsthal study we hear only of the "urge of all art, all great art . . . to be allowed to become *mythos* once more, to represent once again the totality of the universe." [24] And already this urge is perilously close to an illusion.

This disillusionment was decisive in the development of Broch as a writer, since for him writing itself must undoubtedly have been a kind of ecstasy. But aside from all disillusionment he always knew one thing: that no poem can become the cornerstone of a religion and above all that no poet has the right to try. That was why he had so high a regard for Hofmannsthal (and why Rilke's "poetic religious statements" [25] seemed extremely suspect

[22] *Ibid.,* p. 184.
[23] "Hofmannsthal . . . ," *op. cit.,* I, 65.
[24] *Ibid.,* p. 60.
[25] *Ibid.,* p. 125.

to him, although he of course knew that Rilke was the greater poet), who never confounded religion and literature, never surrounded beauty with "the nimbus of religiousness." [26] And when, continuing and going far beyond Hofmannsthal, he said that art "can never be raised to an absolute and therefore must remain cognitively mute," [27] he was making a statement which he might not have formulated so sharply and categorically in his earlier years, but which had always been part of his thinking.

II. THE THEORY OF VALUE

At its lowest, earliest, and most plausible stage, Broch's criticism of himself as writer and of literature as such begins with the criticism of *l'art pour l'art*. This was also the starting point for his theory of value. (Broch, in contrast to the much more innocuous and insignificant academic "value philosophers," was well aware that he owed his concept of value to Nietzsche, as is apparent from the one place in which he comments on Nietzsche.[28]) The disintegration of the world or the dissolution of values was, for Broch, the result of the secularization of the West. In the course of that process belief in God was lost. What is more, secularization shattered the Platonic world view which postulated a supreme, absolute, and therefore non-earthly "value" which confers upon all of man's actions a relative "value" set within a hierarchy of values. Every remaining fragment of the religious and Platonic world view now raised claims to absoluteness. Thus there arose the "anarchy of values" in which everyone could shift as he pleased from one closed and consonant value system into another. Moreover, each of these systems necessarily became the relentless foe of all others, since each claimed absoluteness and there was no longer any true absolute against which these claims could have been measured. In other words, the anarchy of the world, and man's desperate flounderings within it, is primarily due to the loss of the standard of measurement and the resultant excessiveness,

[26] Hugo von Hofmannsthal, *op. cit.*, p. xv.
[27] *Ibid.*
[28] "Das Böse . . . ," *Essays*, I, 313. (First published in 1933.)

a cancerlike growth of each of the areas that had thus been rendered independent. For example, the philosophy of art for art's
sake ends, if it has the courage to pursue its tenets to their logical
conclusions, in the idolization of beauty. Should we happen to
conceive of the beautiful in terms of burning torches we will be
prepared, like Nero, to set living human bodies aflame.

What Broch understood by kitsch (and who else before him
had even looked into the question with the keenness and profundity it demands?) was by no means a simple matter of de-
generacy. Nor did he think of the relation between kitsch and
true art as comparable to that of superstition to religion in a
religious age, or of pseudo-science to science in the modern mass
age. Rather, for him kitsch is art, or art at once becomes kitsch
as soon as it breaks out of the controlling value system. *L'art
pour l'art* in particular, appearing though it did in aristocratic
and haughty guise and furnishing us—as Broch of course knew—
with such convincing works of literature, is actually already
kitsch, just as in the commercial realm the slogan "Business is
business" already contains within itself the dishonesty of the un-
scrupulous profiteer, and just as in the First World War the
obtrusive maxim "War is war" had already transformed the war
into mass slaughter.

There are several characteristic elements in this value philosophy of Broch's. It is not only that he defined kitsch as "evil in
the value system of art." It is that he saw the criminal element
and the element of radical evil as personified in the figure of the
aestheticizing literary man (in which category, for instance, he
placed Nero and even Hitler), and as one and the same with
kitsch. Nor was this because evil revealed itself to the writer
understandably first of all in his own "value system." Rather, it
was because of his insight into the peculiar character of art and
its enormous attraction for man. As he saw it, the real seductive-
ness of evil, the quality of seduction in the figure of the devil, is
primarily an aesthetic phenomenon. Aesthetic in the broadest
sense; the businessmen whose credo is "Business is business" and
the statesmen who hold with "War is war" are aestheticizing
literati in the "value vacuum." They are aesthetes insofar as they

are enchanted by the consonance of their own system, and they become murderers because they are prepared to sacrifice everything to this consonance, this "beautiful" consistency. From such trains of thought, which are to be found in many a variation in his earlier essays, Broch quite naturally, or at any rate with no visible break, evolved the later distinction between "open and closed systems" and the identification of dogmatism with evil itself.

We have spoken above of Broch's Platonism. In the early period of his creative work, which extended from *The Sleepwalkers* to *The Death of Virgil,* that is from the end of the twenties to the beginning or middle of the forties, Broch frequently called himself a Platonist. But if we wish to understand both the meaning and the motivation of his later turn to an earthly absolute and to a logical-positivist epistemology, we must realize that Broch was never an unconditional Platonist. It is not of crucial importance that he interpreted Plato's theory of ideas exclusively in the sense of a theory of standards, that is, that he transformed the originally by no means absolute, but rather distinctly earth-bound transcendence of ideas (in the parable of the cave in *The Republic* the heaven of ideas arches over the earth and is by no means absolutely transcendent to it) into the logically necessary, absolute transcendence of a standard; standards like yardsticks after all can measure nothing unless they are of a totally different order and are applied from outside to the objects to be measured. That would not be crucial if only because this transformation of the ideas into standards and yardsticks with which to "measure" human conduct can already be found in Plato, so that the misunderstanding, if such it is, might be laid to Plato's having misunderstood himself. What is crucial is that for Broch the absolute yardstick which applies to all "areas of value," of any sort whatever, is always an ethical standard. That alone explains why with the disappearance of the standard all areas of value are at one fell swoop transformed into areas of non-value, all good into evil: the absolute and absolutely transcendent standard is an ethical absolute which alone confers "value" upon the life of man in its various aspects. And this would simply not apply to Plato, if only because the concept of ethics such as we find it in Broch is inseparably connected with Christianity.

Let us stay with Broch's own examples. According to him, the "value" inherent in the businessman's vocation, the value by which everything is to be measured and which should also be the sole aim of commercial activity, is honesty. The wealth which can arise from commercial activity must be a by-product, an effect never intended as such, just as beauty is a by-product for the artist, who should aim only at "good," not "beautiful," work. Desiring wealth, desiring beauty, is, morally speaking, playing to the gallery; aesthetically speaking it is kitsch, and in the sense of the value theory it is a dogmatic absolutizing of a special area.[29] If Plato had ever chosen this example (which he could not have done since in keeping with Greek views he regarded commerce solely in terms of acquisitiveness and therefore considered it an altogether senseless occupation), he would have seen the inherent goal of the vocation as exchange of goods among men and nations. The notion of honesty would probably never have occurred to him in this context. Or let us reverse the case and choose a Platonic example which is only hinted at in Broch's own work. Plato defines the real goal of all medical art as the preservation or restoration of health. For health, Broch would substitute *help*. The physician as one concerned with health and the physician as helper—the two views are incompatible. Plato himself permits no doubts about the matter, for he explains, as if it were a self-evident truth, that one of the duties of the physician is to allow those he cannot heal to die, and not to prolong the lives of the sick by unwarranted medical arts. Human life, that is, is not of decisive importance. The affairs of men are subordinate to an extrahuman standard. Man is "not the measure of all things"; moreover, life itself may not be the measure of all human things. These tenets stand in the center of Platonic political philosophy. But all Christian and post-Christian philosophy assumes, tacitly at first and since the seventeenth century with increasing explicit-

[29] "Das Weltbild des Romans," *op. cit.*, I, 216.

ness, that life is the highest good, or the value in itself, and that the absolute non-value is death. So does Broch.

This fundamental estimate of death and life is the unchanging constant in Broch's work from first to last. It also forms the axis around which all his social criticism, philosophy of art, epistemology, ethics, and politics revolve. For a long stretch of his life this view brought him very close to Christianity in an entirely undogmatic manner that was independent of any church affiliations. For it had been Christianity, after all, which brought into the dying world of classical antiquity the "good tidings" of the conquest of death. Whatever the preaching of Jesus of Nazareth meant originally, and however primitive Christianity may originally have understood his words, in the pagan world those tidings could mean only one thing: Your fears for the world, which you had thought eternal and for whose sake you had been able to reconcile yourselves to dying, are justified; the world is doomed, and its end is actually much closer than you think; but in recompense what you always thought of as the most transitory of all things, human life in its individual, personal particularity, will have no end. The world will die, but you will live. That is how the "good tidings" must have sounded to the death-menaced world of antiquity, and that is how Broch, his hearing sharpened by poetic insight, heard them again in the dying world of the twentieth century. What he once called the "crime" of the Renaissance, and what he repeatedly diagnosed as the peculiar murderousness of the process of secularization, the "shattering of the stable Catholic world view," [30] is that in modern times human life is sacrificed for the world's sake, in other words for something earthly which is in any case destined to die. By sacrifice of human life, he meant loss of the absolute certainty of the eternity of life as such.

This view of Christianity and of secularization ceases to be important for the understanding of Broch's later writings. But what is important, what alone opens the way to understanding

[30] See "Politik. Ein Kondensat (Fragment)," *op. cit.*, II, 227.

the most abstract and the seemingly, but only seemingly, most specialized of Broch's arguments, is his original view of life and death. All his life he clung to the thought that "death is non-value in itself," that we "experience the meaning of value only from the negative pole, from the viewpoint of death. Value signifies the overcoming of death or, more precisely, the saving illusion that dispels consciousness of death." [31] It is unnecessary here to raise the objection that at first intrudes: that this is but a new variation of that confusion, so crucial for the history of Occidental morality, between wickedness and evil, between the radically bad and the *summum malum*; to Broch their profound identity is rather the guarantee that an absolute ethical norm exists. Because we know that death is the absolute evil, the *summum malum*, we can say that murder is absolutely evil. If wickedness were not anchored in evil, there would be simply no standard by which to measure it.

It is obvious that this thesis is based on the conviction that the worst thing that man can do to man is killing, and that there can therefore be no penalty harsher than the death penalty. [32] (Here we have the concrete basis for the limit of absoluteness set forth in the two posthumous chapters of his *Politics*.) This view of death and murder suggests an empirical limitation peculiar not only to Broch but to his whole generation. It was characteristic of the war generation and the philosophy of the twenties in Germany that the experience of death attained to a hitherto unknown philosophical dignity, a dignity it had had only once before, in Hobbes's political philosophy, and then only seemingly. For although the fear of death plays a central part in Hobbes, it is not fear of inevitable mortality, but of "violent death." Undoubtedly the war experience was bound up with fear of violent death; but it was precisely characteristic of the war generation that this fear was transposed into the general anxiety about death, or that this fear became the pretext for display of the far more general and more central phenomenon of anxiety. But whatever we may think of the philosophical dignity of the death experience,

[31] *Ibid.*, pp. 232f.
[32] *Ibid.*, p. 248.

it is plain that Broch remained limited to this, his generation's, horizon of experience; and it is decisive that this horizon was broken through by the generation for whom not war but totalitarian forms of rule were the basic, the crucial experience. For we know today that killing is far from the worst that man can inflict on man, and that on the other hand death is by no means what man most fears. Death is not "the quintessence of everything terrifying," and unfortunately there can be far harsher punishments than the death penalty. The sentence: "If there were no death there would be no fear on earth"[33] must be amended to make room for unbearable pain alongside of death. Moreover, were it not for death, such pain would be even more unbearable for man. Precisely that is the direness of the eternal punishments of hell, which would never have been invented had they not been a greater threat than eternal death. In the light of our experiences the time may have come to investigate the philosophical dignity of the experience of pain, which present-day philosophy looks down upon with the same secret contempt as the academic philosophy of thirty or forty years ago did upon the experience of death.

Within his horizon, however, Broch drew the most sweeping and radical conclusion from the experience of death. Not, to be sure, in the early value theory, in which death appears only as *summum malum* or, in anticipation of the earthly absolute, as the metaphysical reality as such: there is "no phenomenon which, measured by its vital content, can be further removed from this world and more metaphysical than death."[34] This radical conclusion appears in the epistemology, according to which "all true knowledge is turned toward death"[35] and not toward the world, so that the value of knowledge, like the value of all human action, is to be measured by whether and to what degree it serves to overcome death. Finally—and this marks the last period of his creative life—he arrived at the absolute primacy of knowledge.

[33] *Ibid.*, p. 243.
[34] See "Das Weltbild . . . ," *op. cit.*, I, 231.
[35] See "Gedanken zum Problem der Erkenntnis in der Musik," *op. cit.*, II, 100.

He had already formulated this principle in jottings for his *Mass Psychology:* "He who succeeds in knowing everything has abolished time and therefore death as well."

III. THE THEORY OF KNOWLEDGE

How could knowledge succeed in abolishing death? How could a man succeed in "knowing everything"? In posing these questions we step squarely into the middle of Broch's theory of knowledge. Broch's answer will give us some notion of its scope. Thus, he answers the first question in this wise: From all-embracing knowledge there necessarily results simultaneity, which abolishes the successiveness of time and, therefore, death; a kind of eternity, an image of eternity, is established in human life. As for the second question, the key to it lies in the sentence: "What is needed is a general theory of empiricism," [36] that is, a system which will take into account all possible future experiences. ("If the sum total of all human potentialities could really be fathomed, such a model would provide us with an outline of all possible future experiences," Broch writes in the "Preliminary Table of Contents" for the *Mass Psychology*.) Through such a theory man, "by virtue of the absolute that functions in him, by virtue of the logic of his thinking, which is imposed on him," [37] secures an "imageness" which is "an imageness in itself" [38] and would exist even if there were no God for him to be an image of. In Broch's own words, this would be an attempt to see whether epistemology might not succeed in "reaching behind God's back, so to speak, in order to regard him from there." [39] And both together—the abolition of time in the simultaneity of knowledge and the establishment of an all-embracing theory of experience in which the outrageous haphazardness of individual experiences and empirical data is transformed into the self-evident, axiomatic (and therefore always tautological) certainty and necessity of logical propositions—

[36] "Über syntaktische und kognitive Einheiten," *op. cit.*, II, 194.
[37] "Politik . . . ," *op. cit.*, II, 204.
[38] *Ibid.*, p. 217.
[39] *Ibid.*, p. 255.

can be attained by discovering an "epistemological subject" which like the scientific subject in the field of observation represents "the human personality in extremest abstraction." [40] But while the scientific subject in the field of observation represents only the "act of seeing itself, observing itself," the "epistemological subject" would be able to represent the whole man, the human personality in general, because knowing is the highest of all human functions.[41]

Let us anticipate the most likely misunderstanding. This theory of knowledge, which we shall discuss in more detail in a moment, is not a philosophy in the proper sense, and the words "knowing" and "thinking" cannot be taken as equivalents here any more than they can elsewhere. Strictly speaking, only knowing can have a goal, and Broch was always primarily concerned with a highly practical goal, whether ethical, religious, or political. Thinking does not have a real goal, and unless thinking finds its meaning in itself, it has no meaning at all. (This, of course, applies only to the activity of thinking itself, not to writing down thoughts, an act that has far more to do with artistic and creative processes than with thinking in itself. The writing down of thoughts has in fact both goal and purpose; like all producing activities, it has a beginning and an end.) Thinking has neither beginning nor end; we think as long as we live, because we cannot do otherwise. This is why, ultimately, Kant's "I think" must accompany not only all "notions" but all human activities and passivities.

Precisely what Broch would call the "cognitive value" of thinking is of a rather dubious nature, and what philosophy calls truth is utterly different from the correct determination of objectively given facts in the world or of data of consciousness; but also provably and demonstrably correct propositions do not yet constitute truth—whether they are governed by the Aristotelian axiom of noncontradiction or by Hegelian dialectics or, as in the case of Broch's logic, exclusively by whether their content appears as compellingly necessary, that is self-evident, and therefore absolutely valid. That such self-evidence can only be ex-

[40] *Ibid.*, p. 248.
[41] "James Joyce . . . ," *op. cit.*, I, 197.

pressed in tautological propositions is, as Broch repeatedly emphasizes, in no way to its discredit: the "cognitive value" of the tautology resides in the fact that it presents directly the compelling quality which is the attribute of all valid propositions. The problem is only how the tautology can be rescued from its formality and from the circle in which it turns; and Broch thought he had solved this problem by his discovery of the earthly absolute, which possesses both tautological, self-evident force and a demonstrably given content. But cognition, whether in the form of discovery or of logic, is distinct from thinking (as manifest in literature and philosophy) in that it alone is compelling, that it alone can lead to a necessity and a compelling absolute, and that consequently it alone may give rise to a theory of (political or ethical) action which can hope to ascend, as it were, above the unpredictability and unforeseeability of human action.

Broch was always conscious of this difference between philosophy and cognition. In his early writings he revealed this awareness by ascribing to art greater potential for knowledge than philosophy. The latter, he said, "since its expulsion from its theological association" was no longer capable of "a knowledge embracing totality," which now had to be left to art.[42] And in the Hofmannsthal study he declared that Hofmannsthal had learned from Goethe "that poetry, if it is to lead to the purification and self-identification of man, has to plunge into the depths of man's antinomies, quite in contrast to philosophy, which remains on the brink of the abyss and, without venturing the leap, rests content with mere analysis of what it has seen."[43] In the early writings it was not only philosophy which he relegated to a subordinate place compared with literature in regard to the value and content of knowledge but also science. In those days Broch could still say that "the cognitive system of science never attains that absoluteness [which art achieves] of world totality which after all is what matters," whereas every "individual work of art is the mirror of totality."[44] But this is the very view that changed

[42] *Ibid.*, pp. 203–204.
[43] Hugo von Hofmannsthal, *op. cit.*, p. xl.
[44] "Das Böse . . . ," *op. cit.*, I, 330.

in his later writings, most strikingly in the opposition he posed between value and truth. Once thought had fallen away from the theological association, truth had "been robbed of its real ground for proof." [45] Truth had thenceforth to be transformed into knowledge. Only then could value arise. In fact, value is "truth that has been transformed into knowledge." [46] The original objection to philosophy remains: that "thinking (rejecting extralogical, mystic approaches of the Indian type) purely out of itself and its logic of cognition can yield no final result." Where it attempts to do so it becomes "only contentless verbal fantasy." [47] But now Broch no longer regards literature as able to take up the task from philosophy's impotent hands. Rather, science has become the rescuer. Thus "the problem of impermissible tautology is, to be sure, a philosophical problem, but the decision on its solubility lies in the hands of mathematical practice," and the theory of relativity has shown that what philosophy regarded as insoluble antinomies can become "soluble equations." [48]

All these objections on Broch's part are quite correct. Given Broch's demands—victory over the ego's mortality, over contingency, over the "anarchy" of the world, which the Catholic world view had accomplished by its *mythos* of the dead and resurrected son of man and son of God—given these demands, philosophy could only demonstrate its inadequacy. Philosophy only asks the questions which *mythos* once answered in religion and in poetry and which today science must answer in research and epistemology. *Mythos* and *logos,* or to put it in standard terms, religion and logic, belong together insofar as both "are born out of the fundamental structure of man." They "dominate" the externality of the universe and therefore "represent timelessness itself" to man.[49] But this task of overcoming death is not imposed upon and assigned to human cognition simply by the passionate desire to remain alive, from the naked vital impulse that man shares with

[45] "James Joyce . . . ," *op. cit.,* I, 203.
[46] "Werttheoretische Bemerkungen zur Psychoanalyse," *op. cit.,* II, 70.
[47] "Über syntaktische . . . ," *op. cit.,* II, 168.
[48] *Ibid.,* pp. 201f.
[49] "Die mythische Erbschaft . . . ," *op. cit.,* I, 239.

animals. Rather, it emerges from the ground of the cognitive and as it were bodiless ego itself. For insofar as the ego is the subject of cognition it is "completely incapable of imagining its own death." [50]

Since the ego is incapable of conceiving its own beginning or its own end, the first fundamental experience of man, which he derives entirely from the empirically given world, is the experience of time, of transitoriness, and of death. Thus the external world presents itself to the "ego nucleus" not only as utterly alien, but also as utterly threatening. It is not really recognized by the ego as "world" but as "non-ego." The "epistemological ego nucleus," since it knows nothing of transitoriness, also knows nothing about the external world, and in that alien world nothing is "so utterly alien to it as time." [51] Thus Broch arrives at his view of time, which is very characteristic of him and, as far as I know, entirely original. While all Western speculations about time, from Augustine's *Confessions* to Kant's *Critique of Pure Reason*, see time as an "inner sense," for Broch, on the contrary, time assumes the function that is ordinarily ascribed to space. Time is the "innermost external world," [52] that is, the sense by which the external world is given to us internally. But this externality which manifests itself so inwardly does not belong to the real structure of the ego nucleus any more than death, located though death is within life, hollowing out life from the inside, and belonging to it as such. The category of space, on the other hand, is for him not the category of the outside world, for it is immediately present within man in his "ego nucleus." Whether man wishes to dominate the hostile "non-ego" by *mythos* or *logos*, he can do so only by "annihilating" and abrogating time, "and this abrogation is called space." [53] Thus for Broch music, which is normally regarded as the most time-bound of the arts, is on the contrary "the transformation of time into space"; it is "abrogation of time," and that, of course,

---

[50] "Werttheoretische Bemerkungen . . . ," *op. cit.*, II, 74.
[51] *Ibid.*, p. 73.
[52] *Ibid.*, p. 74.
[53] "Der Zerfall der Werte. Diskurse, Exkurse und ein Epilog," *op. cit.*, II, 10.

always means "abrogation of time hastening toward death," metamorphosis of sequence into coexistence, which he calls the "architecturization of the passage of time" and in which is accomplished "the direct abrogation of death in the consciousness of mankind." [54]

What is involved here, evidently, is achieving a simultaneity which transforms all sequence into coexistence and in which the temporally structured course of the world with its empirical richness is presented as it would be seen by the eye of a god, who would take it all in simultaneously. Man is bound to feel akin to this god because of the human ego's alienation from world and time (to Broch both are the same). The structure of the ego nucleus, which is timeless, indicates that man is really destined to live in such absoluteness. That this is so is apparent in all specifically human modes of behavior. It is apparent above all in the structure of language, which for Broch is never a means of communication, nor has anything to do with the fact that a plurality of men, not Man, inhabit the earth and must communicate with one another. He does not say so, but it is as if he held that for purposes of communication among human beings mere animal sounds would have sufficed. For him what is essential about language is that it syntactically indicates an abrogation of time "within the sentence" because it necessarily "places subject and object in a relationship of simultaneity." [55] The "assignment" which is imposed on the speaker is "to make cognitive units audible and visible," and this is "the sole task of language." [56] Whatever is frozen into the simultaneity of the sentence—to wit, thought, which "in a single moment can comprehend wholes of extraordinary extent"—is wrenched out of the passages of time. Surely it need scarcely be mentioned that these considerations provide, *inter alia*, a commentary on Broch's lyrical style, which is only seemingly lyrical, on his extraordinarily long sentences and the extraordinarily precise repetitions within them.

These linguistic speculations date from the last years of Broch's

[54] "Gedanken zum Problem . . . ," *op. cit.*, II, 99.
[55] "Über syntaktische . . . ," *op. cit.*, II, 158.
[56] *Ibid.*, p. 153.

life, when he was trying to solve the problem of simultaneity in the realm of the *logos*. But the conviction that the simultaneity of linguistic expression provides a glimpse of eternity, that in it the "*logos* and life" can become "one once more," [57] and indeed that "the requirement of simultaneity is the real goal of all epic, all poetry" [58]—all this is already to be found in the much earlier essay on Joyce. Then, as well as later, he was concerned with "bringing into unity the sequence impressions and experience, *forcing* successiveness back into the unity of the simultaneous, relegating what is time-restricted to the timelessness of the monad," which he would later call the "ego nucleus." [59] (My italics.) In the later period, however, he was no longer satisfied with "establishing the supratemporality in the work of art" but wished to impress the same supratemporality of simultaneity upon life itself. At the time of the Joyce essay he still conceded that "this striving for simultaneity . . . cannot break through the necessity that coexistence and concatenation must be expressed by a sequence, the unique by repetition," while later he would concede this only to the extent that literature and literary expression cannot do better, whereas mathematics, in making equations, and certainly the absolute logic which underlies mathematics (not in anything concrete, to be sure, but as a model of all possible cognition) are perfectly able to assume this function of transforming all temporal sequence into spatial coexistence.

It is striking how frequently Broch uses such words as "compulsion," "necessity," "compelling necessity" in these contexts, and how greatly he depended on the coercive character of logical argumentation. In the radical switch from *mythos* to *logos*, in which his theory of knowledge has its starting point, he consciously wanted to replace the coerciveness of the mythic world view with the compelling necessity of the logical argument. Compelling necessity is as it were the common denominator of the mythic and the logical world view. Only what is necessary and therefore appears to man as compulsory can raise the claim of

[57] "James Joyce . . . ," *op. cit.*, I, 209.
[58] *Ibid.*, p. 192.
[59] *Ibid.*, p. 193.

absolute validity. From this identification of necessity and the absolute flows the peculiarly ambivalent attitude that Broch took on the question of human freedom. Actually he had not much higher an opinion of freedom than of philosophy; at any rate he always looked for it solely in the realm of psychology and never accorded it the metaphysical and science-founding dignity which he always accorded to necessity.

For Broch freedom is the anarchic striving, slumbering in every ego, toward "detachment" from fellow men. That striving is already represented in the animal kingdom by the "loner." If man follows only his ego's striving for freedom, he is "the anarchic animal." [60] But since man is "incapable of getting along without his fellow men, hence incapable of fully living out his anarchic tendencies," he tries to subjugate and enslave other human beings. The rebelliously anarchic aspect of the ego, which although dependent on other men prefers to linger in total inner unrelatedness to them for the sake of independence, already appears in the early writings as one of the sources of radical evil. But in those early writings it remains overshadowed by Broch's analysis of the purely aesthetic cast of real evil. In the later writings, which are all oriented in terms of the theory of knowledge, the situation is reversed. From the theory of knowledge there follows directly the political consequence that man in his relations to his fellow men should be subjected to the selfsame compulsion to which he necessarily subjects himself in his cognition, in other words in his intercourse with himself. Broch never believed that this political sphere, in which man acts outwardly and is engaged by the machinery of the outside world, could be brought to order by categories which were political in origin. "For the world's commotion and bustle can result in scarcely anything but anarchy . . ." and "politics is the mechanics of the external bustle." [61] The world's commotion must be subjected to the same compelling evident necessity as the ego itself; and in order to validate this compulsion, it must be demonstrated that the coercion is actually a human one, that is, that it really emerges from

[60] "Politik . . . ," *op. cit.*, II, 209.
[61] *Ibid.*, p. 210.

man's humanity. The politico-ethical task of the theory of knowledge is to make this demonstration. The theory must show that the humanity of man is a compelling necessity and thus offers salvation from anarchy.

It should be apparent at this point that what we in fact have here is a system whose general outlines can be sketched with little difficulty from the fragments that have been handed down to us. The task is all the more alluring because the fundamental features of Broch's system, in spite of all the shifts in accent that it underwent over the years, remained fixed from the beginning. Within this system, the time-abrogating function of cognition and its simultaneity had to be demonstrable by its application to two sets of concrete problems: It had to be able to abolish the anarchy of the world, that is, to co-ordinate the entirely worldless ego and the entirely egoless world; and it had to replace "mythic prophecy" by "logical prophecy," so as to force the future into simultaneity with the present with the same certainty that memory redeems the past from its perishability by drawing it into the present. It had to "demonstrate the unity of memory and prophecy" [62] which *The Death of Virgil* had only conjured up poetically.

As far as the first problem is concerned, the co-ordination of ego and world, that is, the redemption of the ego from that radical subjectivism in which "everything that man 'is'" proves to "belong to the ego, everything he 'has' to lie near the ego, and all the rest, the whole rest of the world . . . alien, hostile to the ego, fraught with death" [63]—as far as this problem is concerned Broch seems to have merely taken the way that all serious subjectivism had taken before him, and whose greatest predecessor is Leibniz. It is the way of "pre-established harmony," the way of building two "houses identical in plan and also in the foundations, but because of their infinite extent a priori not susceptible to completion, houses whose visible structure has been begun for different corners, so that during its infinite building time they become more and more identical to one another, but in practice never can

[62] "Die mythische Erbschaft . . . ," *op. cit.*, I, 245.
[63] "Politik . . . ," *op. cit.*, II, 234.

achieve complete identity and, if you will, interchangeability."[64]

To the question of how man can "intuitively grasp the innermost kinship of his own nature with that of the external world" [65] Broch replied that "the pre-established harmony is a logical necessity," [66] and with this answer he certainly took a decisive step beyond the usual theories of all monadologies, not only of Leibniz's. The logical necessity of a pre-established harmony flows from the fact that Broch (quite along the lines of Husserl, to whom he owes other crucial suggestions) finds the object (which is to say the model of the world) already present in the act of thinking, insofar as no "I-think" is possible unless it is an "I-think-something." Thus the ego finds in itself a sketch of a non-ego, and "although thinking is indissolubly part of the ego, it is distinguished from the ego subject, hence it concurrently belongs to a non-ego." [67]

From this it follows that the ego belongs to the world in a different fashion from "expansion of the ego," which attains its peak in ecstasy, or "deprivation of the ego," which attains its nadir in panic. The ego belongs to the world independently of ecstasy or panic. It also follows that the world is not only experienced from outside; before all such experience it is already given in the "unconscious." This unconscious is neither alogical nor irrational. On the contrary, all real logic must necessarily include a "logic of the unconscious," must test itself against the knowledge of the "epistemological sphere of unconsciousness," [68] in which is located not concrete experience but that cognition of experience in general which precedes all experience—in other words, "experience in itself."

In that same sphere of the unconscious which is completely accessible to cognition lies the solution to the second problem: the mastering of simultaneity, the rescuing of the future as well as the past from its enslavement to sequence. But here the estab-

---

[64] Über syntaktische . . . ," *op. cit.,* II, 169.
[65] *Ibid.,* p. 151.
[66] "Das System als Welt-Bewältigung," *op. cit.,* II, 121.
[67] "Werttheoretische Bemerkungen . . . ," *op. cit.,* II, 67.
[68] "Über syntaktische . . . ," *op. cit.,* II, 166.

lishment of co-existence for future as well as past is to be accomplished by the dream aspect peculiar to the unconscious. The "thrust into the future peculiar to man and man alone [makes] it a part of the present"; a logic going beyond Aristotelian logic should someday be able to anticipate those "inspirations" out of which the newness of the future is shaped. A "formal determination of these areas, assuming that this will someday be achieved," [69] would provide no more nor less than a dependable "theory of prophecy," because it would offer us the "outline of all possible future experiences." This "logical prophecy," whose object is that unconscious out of which the impulses and "inspirations" for all newness arise, is itself a totally rational and logical discipline which will flow "in all naturalness . . . from the growth and deepening of research into foundations." [70] The prerequisite for this "theory of newness"—which is only another name for "logical prophecy"—is, of course, that although time itself is seen as "innermost external world," everything "truly new in the world, even if it appears in empirical guise, never arises out of actual experience, but always out of the ego realm alone, from the soul, from the heart, from the mind." [71] In other words, the subject of cognition, "man in uttermost abstraction," [72] is of such nature that it carries a world within itself, and the miracle of cognition results from pre-established harmony, from the harmonizing of this interior world with the empirically given world.

Specifically this harmonizing is accomplished by the "system," which as a "system of mastering" does not merely accept the world and the inexhaustible "experiential content of the world," but creates it anew by mastering it";[73] this creative "systematizing function of the *logos*" is "its essential and sole manifestation" [74] by means of which it "again and again creates the world

[69] "Die mythische Erbschaft . . . ," *op. cit.,* I, 244.
[70] *Ibid.,* pp. 245–46.
[71] "Über syntaktische . . . ," *op. cit.,* II, 187.
[72] "Politik . . . ," *op. cit.,* II, 247.
[73] "Das System . . . ," *op. cit.,* II, 111ff.
[74] "Über syntaktische . . . ," *op. cit.,* II, 200.

anew for the first time." Cognition and creation are not only identical in the divine act of *intuitus originarius* (Kant); this identity is a demonstrable fact, independent of all revelation and present in man's "duty of creation," in which he must "endlessly repeat the creation of the universe," [75] a duty which can be proven by logical-positivist arguments. This is the *logos* which will take the place of *mythos* in a "future unitary science" [76] and which will restore a world out of joint to the orderliness of a "system," will lead man lost in anarchy back to the constraints of necessity.

Thus in the mid-thirties Broch had expressed, in the form of a premonition and a hope, the idea that the *logos* will be able to redeem man by the route of science. At the end of his life this notion had become a certainty: "If all world contents could actually be brought into balance, if the world could actually be formed and re-formed into one total system, a system in which all parts mutually condition and sustain each other, if this state —which science seeks in the strictly rational realm—could actually come into being, then the ultimate pacification of Being would have come about, the redemption of the world, into which all the metaphysically religious aspirations of humanity will flow." [77]

Who can possibly read these sentences without being reminded of the first chapter of the Gospel of St. John: Ἐν ἀρχῇ ἦν ὁ λόγος . . . καὶ ὁ λόγος σὰρξ ἐγένετο (I:1 and 14). ("In the beginning was the Word . . . And the Word was made flesh. . . .") But the flesh that the *logos* became is no longer the mythic son of God; it is "man in uttermost abstraction." If it can be demonstrated, Broch thought, in positivistic and not speculatively metaphysical terms, that the word made flesh is man himself, then within the earthly realm and without any transcendental flights the demonstration has been given of "imageness in itself," and since in "imageness in itself" man has also become independent of Him whose image he is, time and death have therefore been abrogated. This would be the redemption of man on earth.

[75] "Politik . . . ," *op. cit.*, II, 208.
[76] "Über syntaktische . . . , *op. cit.*, II, 169.
[77] "Gedanken zum Problem . . . ," *op. cit.*, II, 98.

IV. THE EARTHLY ABSOLUTE

Everything that Broch thought along these lines, and that he left in fragmentary form, is contained in quintessence in the concept, or rather the discovery, of the "earthly absolute." If we would understand what is really meant by the earthly absolute, we must guard against equating Broch's early remarks about death as the absolute for human existence on earth—remarks that may be found occasionally even in the later works—with the real discovery of his late period. What bridges the two views is only—though this is certainly a great deal—that both are associated with death, both are fundamentally determined by the experience of death. Nevertheless, the difference is very clear. When death is understood as the absolute, irremovable limit of life, it is possible to state that there is "no phenomenon which can possibly be more remote from this world and more metaphysical in its significance for life" than death;[78] that from the human viewpoint *sub specie aeternitatis* always means also *sub specie mortis*;[79] that the search for an absolute value is spurred by death, that "non-value in itself"; and that "its absoluteness, which is the sole absoluteness of reality and of nature, must be countered by an absoluteness which, sustained by the human will, is capable of creating the absoluteness of the soul, the absoluteness of culture." [80] And undoubtedly Broch never abandoned his basic conviction that "where there is no genuine relationship to death and where its quality of absoluteness in the here and now is not perpetually acknowledged, there can be no true ethics." [81] This basic conviction was in fact so strong that in his *Politics*—that is, in the application of his theory of knowledge to the realm of things by nature anarchic—he again had recourse to death as the one absolute that appears in the earthly realm. That is to say, he based his entire legal and political system on the fact that the death penalty represents a natural maximum which sets an absolute

[78] "Das Weltbild . . . ," *op. cit.*, I, 231.
[79] "James Joyce . . . ," *op. cit.*, I, 186.
[80] "Das Böse . . . ," *op. cit.*, I, 317.
[81] "Hofmannsthal . . . ," *op. cit.*, I, 123.

limit to punishment. Nevertheless, Broch's concept of the earthly absolute did not refer to death alone. The absolute inherent in death is, after all, by its nature non-earthly; it obviously begins only after death, so to speak; it stands beyond death, although it manifests itself in the earthly realm only through death. Making this otherworldly, transcendent absolute finite and worldly was in fact the mortal sin of secularism, which led to the collapse of values and the disintegration of the world.

The relationship which the earthly absolute has to death is of a different nature. What is involved is abolishing in life the consciousness of death, liberating life, as long as it lives, from death, so that life goes on as if it were eternal. Just as the function of cognition is to overcome "time as innermost external world," and thus conquer the world where it is closest to the ego and therefore most alien and menacing to it, so the function of the earthly absolute is to conquer death in life, countering the "world pregnant with death" by confronting it with the ego, which in its nucleus, in its cognitive nucleus, knows itself as immortal. Even as he turns to logical positivism (though a logical positivism of a highly idiosyncratic and original sort), Broch clings to his early and basically Christian conviction that death and perishability are rooted in the world, but immortality and eternity are anchored in the ego, so that life which seems to us mortal is in truth immortal and the world which seems to us eternal is in truth the prey of death.

The shift to logical positivism, which is most markedly manifested in the concept of the earthly absolute, of course implied an unspoken revision of Broch's *Zeitkritik*, which was originally cast in terms of a plaint against the process of secularization. This revision, in turn, is most clearly expressed in the shift from the hope of a "new myth" to the conviction that a "positivistic de-deification" had become a necessity. But the question that presumably produced this shift, and which Broch set about answering in logical-positivistic terminology in the two posthumous sections of his Theory of Knowledge (the "concept of system" and the "syntactic and cognitive units")—that question can be most plausibly formulated as follows: From what does the ego derive its conviction of its own immortality? May not the ground for this conviction be in itself proof of this immortality?

If we link the same question with the earlier value theory, which was so exclusively oriented in terms of death, we might formulate the question in this way: May not the purely negative experience of death—purely negative because never foreseeable by the ego nucleus—which strikes sudden panic into man (who in his absolute world-lessness knows himself to be immortal)—may not this purely negative experience be complemented by a positive experience in which immortality and the absolute are manifested just as tangibly and factually as death? The answer, reduced to a nutshell, is to be found in the following sentence, which dates back to Broch's early period but whose full implications he did not see until his late period: "The structure of formal logic rests upon material foundations." [82]

Cognition, to summarize Broch's train of thought in deliberately simplified form, manifests itself in two types of knowledge which correspond to two fundamentally different types among the sciences. First, there are the inductive empirical sciences which grope their way forward from fact to fact, from research to research, and in principle are non-finite, uncompletable, requiring an endless succession of new facts, new finds, to make progress. Secondly, there are the deductive formal sciences which come to their axiomatic results out of themselves, as it were, and are apparently independent of all empirical facts. To Broch the most important science of the inductive type is physics (although for purposes of illustration he often used the example of archaeology because in this science the "finds" of excavation coincide with the new "findings" so indispensable to the advance of any empirical science), while the classic deductive science is, of course, mathematics. Real cognition that goes beyond mere knowledge of facts, he held, can be achieved only in the system-forming deductive sciences. Only after mathematics has deduced the formulas for the empirical facts observed by physicists is it permissible to speak of a scientific understanding of the physical facts.

This relationship between the deductive and inductive sciences

[82] "Der Zerfall der Werte . . . ," *op. cit.*, II, 14.

corresponds to Broch's distinction between "proto-system" and "absolute system." [83] The proto-system serves the direct mastering of the world, its assimilation, which is the prerequisite for the survival of all life, including animal life; whereas the absolute system, which is unattainable to man in its perfection, would contain within itself "the solution to all the problems that ever have occurred or ever can occur in the world, . . . in short would be the cognitive system of a god." [84] At first glance it looks as though man's cognitive system might perhaps be fitted in between these two systems, the system of all life and the system of a god, but that nevertheless the two remain as opposed to each other as are the inductive and deductive methods.

The next step in the reasoning is concerned with the elimination of this opposition, or, alternatively, the proof that this opposition is only ostensible. This is accomplished first by the demonstration that a bridge exists from the proto-system to the absolute system, a bridge founded on the peculiar iteration of all cognitive processes; and secondly that there is no such thing as an absolutely deductive system. Rather, the basis of every formal system is always empirical. This signifies that every system rests upon a foundation transcendent to itself, which it must posit as absolute because otherwise it cannot even begin its various chains of deductions.

The bridge from the proto-system to the absolute system, which on the one hand represents the bridge from purely inductive science to deductive cognition and on the other hand the bridge from animal through man to a god, takes place as follows: The proto-system is a system of "experiences" which are "known" but not "understood"; this knowledge, which is inherent in every experience and would not be possible without it, is actually already a "knowing about knowing," a first iteration, without which memory would not be possible, and memory belongs to all experience; Broch, identifying it with consciousness, also attributes it to animals.[85]

[83] "Das System . . . ," *op. cit.*, II, 122ff.
[84] *Ibid.*
[85] *Ibid.*, p. 134.

This knowing about knowing remains directly linked to the world. It provides for direct mastering of the things of the world in their concrete factuality; what it does not master is the worldness of the world, which Broch sees as given in the world's aboriginal "irrationality" (or, in political language, in its "anarchy"). The "cognitive system" now sets out to accomplish the mastering of this worldness, and it can succeed because it has already liberated itself from the concrete things of the world and therefore can grasp the worldness of the world, its "irrationality" as such, and thus becomes a preliminary form of the absolute system. Direct experience and the "knowing about knowing" necessary for it are no longer involved, but rather a "knowing about knowing about knowing," in other words another iteration, which however naturally flows out of the first iteration of "knowing about knowing."

Between the proto-system of knowing about knowing, in which real knowledge is not yet achieved, and in which the living being merely becomes conscious of its experiences, and the absolute system of a god, there is a continuous series of iterative stages which can be positivistically demonstrated. And although Broch explicitly warns us against "conceiving a kind of stratified arrangement of systems in which—starting with the proto-system and going on all the way up to the absolute system—they are layered one above the other according to the proportion in which their 'empirical content' diminishes and their 'cognitive content' increases," he nevertheless considers it "definite . . . that the way . . . mostly though not always lies in the direction of increasing cognitive content and diminishing expressibility." [86] The significance of these demonstrations for producing evidence of the factual existence of an earthly absolute lies in the intimate connection between those cognitive operations that presuppose its existence and the mere experiencing; it lies in the continuous sequence that links experiencing to cognitive knowing, so that it is as though some absolute arises out of the conditions of all life on earth.

[86] *Ibid.*, p. 123.

The aim of these considerations is twofold: it is to show the earthly origin of the absolute, to show that it springs objectively out of the evolution of organic life, and at the same time to demonstrate that all deductive systems rest upon an absolute empirical foundation which cannot be derived from the system itself, that is, on the contrary, to show that all form encroaches upon content.[87] In other words, the demonstration that earthliness by its very essence reaches into the absolute, grows into it, so to speak, is paralleled by the counterproof that everything absolute is attached to earthliness. This is most evident in the case of mathematics. The very thing that is mathematical about mathematics is obviously not provable or demonstrable mathematically; it remains for mathematics a "plus unknown," that is, it resides in a sphere lying outside mathematics. This is true both for the actual basis from which all mathematics arises, which Broch identifies as "number as such," and for the "problem impulses" which lead to advances in mathematical understanding. In fact, mathematics remains dependent upon physics for its advances.[88] But this is also true for the theory of knowledge, or for logic itself, which might be thought to have initially supplied mathematics with "number as such" and hence to have laid the basis for mathematical operations in the first place. For "the logician has precisely as naïvely realistic a relation toward his own investigations as the mathematician toward his; that is, on the one hand— at least as long as he does not shift his considerations to the next higher plane, that of meta-logic—he will dismiss knowledge about the logical system as a whole and about logical operability as a self-evident concomitant of research needing no special regard, and on the other hand he will be even less inclined than the mathematician to pay any attention to the subject or bearer of that knowledge." [89]

Thus there are two things that the deductive sciences, logic and mathematics, always and necessarily overlook: first, they cannot see what makes logic or mathematics precisely what it is, that is,

[87] "Politik . . . ," *op. cit.*, II, 247.
[88] "Über syntaktische . . . ," *op. cit.*, II, 178ff.
[89] *Ibid.*, p. 183.

its logicality or mathematicality, any more than a person can see the very ground on which he is standing; and secondly they cannot observe the subject of the logical and mathematical operations. They always see only their own shadows, so to speak, but not themselves. Now it is natural that the mathematicality in mathematics, in other words "number as such," should be the "absolute" for mathematics; and this very absolute is given to mathematics from outside, demonstrably existing outside its own system. This absolute is not absolutely transcendent, but empirically given, even though it must be sought outside the mathematical system. We can say that a science always receives what is absolute for itself from the "next higher" science, so that a hierarchy of sciences arises whose principle might be possible to grasp in an all-embracing, unifying, systematic way. Physics receives its absolute from mathematics, mathematics its from epistemology, epistemology its from logic, and logic is dependent on a meta-logic.

But this chain, in which the absolute is each time handed down in different form from science to science, from cognitive system to cognitive system, in each case making science and cognition possible at all, is not infinitely continuable and repeatable. In every case what functions as an absolute, as an absolute standard, and is not observed by the person who uses it precisely because he is using it, is the subject who uses the standard; it is the "act of seeing itself," the "physical person" in physics, who corresponds to the "mathematical person," the bearer of "number as such," the logical person, the subject of "logical operability" as such. Thus the absolute in these sciences is not only given "contentually"— no science could function if its contents were not brought to it from outside—but its source is altogether earthly and positive, which is to say in epistemological terms: demonstrable on a logical-positivistic basis; it is the "human personality in uttermost abstraction." The content of this abstraction can change—from the "act of seeing as such" to the act of counting as such and to logical operation as such. This does not mean that man with all the properties of body, soul, and mind has become the measure of all things, but it does mean that man, insofar as he is nothing but the cognitive subject, the bearer of acts of cognition, is the source of the absolute. The origin of the absolute, in its absolute, necessary, compelling validity, is of this world.

Broch believed that his theory of the earthly absolute could be applied directly to politics, and in the two chapters of the "condensed" *Mass Psychology* he actually, though fragmentarily, did translate his epistemology into ideas of practical politics. He thought this could be done because he construed all political action in terms of those acts which play the central part in his theory of knowledge, and which are conceived as in themselves worldless, or, as he himself puts it, "in a camera obscura." [90] In other words, he was not really concerned with political action or with action at all; what he wanted was to answer the question he had posed in his youth: "What then shall we do?"

Acting and doing are no more identical than thinking and knowing. Just as knowing, as opposed to thinking, has a goal of cognition and a cognitive task, so doing has specific aims and must be governed by specific standards in order to attain them, whereas acting always takes place wherever human beings are together, even if there is nothing to be attained. The ends-means category, to which all doing and all producing are necessarily bound, always proves to be ruinous when applied to acting. For doing, like producing, starts with the assumption that the subject of the "acts" fully knows the end to be attained and the object to be produced, so that the only problem is to find the proper means to achieve those ends. Such an assumption in turn presupposes a world in which there is only a single will, or which is so arranged that all the active ego-subjects in it are sufficiently isolated from one another so that there will be no mutual interference of their ends and aims. With action the reverse is true; there is an infinitude of intersecting and interfering intentions and purposes which, taken all together in their complex immensity, represent the world into which each man must cast his

[90] "Werttheoretische Bemerkungen . . . ," *op. cit.*, II, 71.

147

act, although in that world no end and no intention has ever been achieved as it was originally intended. Even this description, and the consequent frustrating nature of all deeds, the ostensible futility of action, is inadequate and misleading because really conceived in terms of doing, and that means in terms of the ends-means category. Within these categories we can only agree with the Gospel phrase: "For they know not what they do"; in this sense no acting person ever knows what he is doing; he cannot know and for the sake of man's freedom is not permitted to know. For freedom is dependent on the absolute unpredictability of human actions. If we would express it paradoxically—and we invariably become entangled in paradoxes as soon as we attempt to judge action by the standards of doing—we can say: Every good action for the sake of a bad end actually adds to the world a portion of goodness; every bad action for the sake of a good end actually adds to the world a portion of badness. In other words, whereas for doing and producing ends are totally dominant over means, just the opposite is true for acting: the means are always the decisive factor.

Since Broch had epistemologically placed the ego worldlessly in "the camera obscura," he naturally interpreted acting in the sense of doing, and the actor in the sense of a producing, isolated ego, the subject of specific acts. But of far more decisive importance is that, being an artist, he interpreted doing as a kind of world creation and demanded of it the sort of "re-creation of the world" which he had originally required of the work of art. If politics could ever have become what he required of it, it would in fact be an "ethical work of art." In doing, the two fundamental capacities of man coincide: the creative faculty involved in literature and the cognitive, world-mastering faculty involved in science. For Broch, therefore, politics was really art, world creation become a science and at the same time science become art. He never put it that way, it is true, but the fragmentary material we have permits us at least to guess the outlines of his fundamental conception.

This, at any rate, is what cognition aims at in the final analysis:

it desires the deed. Because literature did nothing, Broch turned away from literature, he rejected philosophy because it was limited to mere contemplation and thinking, and ended by placing all his hopes on politics. Broch's central concern is always redemption, redemption from death, and he is just as much concerned with redemption in his politics as in his epistemology or his fiction. The utopian elements of a politics oriented toward redemption cannot be overlooked. Nevertheless, we must guard against underestimating the realism which guided Broch in his concrete reflections, and which preserved him from dogmatically and ill-consideredly applying the earthly absolute he had sighted in the theory of knowledge to politics.

Broch's ultimate faith was in the earthly absolute. He was consoled by the insight that something absolute on earth can be found and demonstrated, and that even the political realm—that is, the inherently anarchic conglomeration of human beings in the conditions of life on earth—contains a limiting absolute. This meant that such a thing as "absolute justice" must exist from which to derive a new declaration of "the rights of man," which then would bear the same relationship to political actualities as mathematics to physics. Under its sovereignty a right-producing "right-creating (and therefore right-minded) subject" would correspond precisely to the "physical person," or the "act of seeing in itself." [91] Thanks to these insights, which more and more tended to center around "man in his uttermost abstraction," Broch could resign himself to the facts of the political realm just as the mathematician is prepared to resign himself to the facts of physical space. Thus perhaps the beautiful and poetic figure of speech in which he once formulated the facts and the possibilities of political life must also have seemed to him something like its mathematical formula. It is the figure of the compass card: "The compass card whose function it is to show from which of the four corners of the world the wind of history is blowing; with its inscription 'Right Makes Might' points toward Paradise, with

[91] See "Politik . . . ," *op. cit.*, II, 219 and 247f.

'Might Makes Wrong' toward Purgatory, with 'Wrong Makes Might' toward Hell, but with 'Might Makes Right' toward ordinary life on earth; and since again and again what threatens to roar over humanity is the devil's tempest, man usually rests modestly content with the earthly 'Might Makes Right,' though hoping for the paradisaical breezes—when there would no longer be any death penalty on all the vast orb of earth—but knowing nevertheless that the miracle will not come unless it is made to come. The miracle of 'Right Makes Might' requires first and foremost that Right shall be provided with Might." [92]

Behind these sentences we distinctly feel what Broch does not say and in this context probably did not intend to say. We know from *The Death of Virgil* and also from the character of the doctor in *The Tempter* that for Broch all relationships with other men are ultimately governed by the idea of "helpfulness," by the imperativeness of the claim for help. The absoluteness of the "ethical claim" ("the unity of the concept remains inviolate, inviolate the ethical requirement")[93] was something he took so much for granted that he thought it did not even need demonstrating. "The aim of the ethical claim lies in the absolute and the infinite," [94] which means that every ethical deed is performed in the sphere of the absolute and that men's claim to help from one another is never-ending and inexhaustible. Just as Broch took it for granted that he must instantly lay aside any work, any activity, in order to give help when it was needed, so he ultimately took it for granted that he must lay aside literature because he had begun to doubt that literature would ever be able to satisfy its "obligation to the absoluteness of cognition." [95] Above all he had begun to doubt whether literature and cognition would ever succeed in taking the leap from knowledge of what is needed to help for those in need. The "mission" of which Broch spoke so often, the "inescapably imposed task" he saw everywhere, was ultimately neither logical nor epistemological in nature, al-

[92] *Ibid.*, p. 253.
[93] "Der Zerfall der Werte . . . ," *op. cit.*, II, 40.
[94] "Das Weltbild des Romans," *op. cit.*, I, 212.
[95] "James Joyce . . . ," *op. cit.*, I, 204.

though he came upon it and demonstrated its presence everywhere in logic and epistemology. The mission was the ethical imperative, and the task that could not be evaded was men's claim to help.

WALTER BENJAMIN

1892-1940

I. THE HUNCHBACK

FAMA, that much-coveted goddess, has many faces, and fame comes in many sorts and sizes—from the one-week notoriety of the cover story to the splendor of an everlasting name. Posthumous fame is one of FAMA's rarer and least desired articles, although it is less arbitrary and often more solid than the other sorts, since it is only seldom bestowed upon mere merchandise. The one who stood most to profit is dead and hence it is not for sale. Such posthumous fame, uncommercial and unprofitable, has now come in Germany to the name and work of Walter Benjamin, a German-Jewish writer who was known, but not famous, as contributor to magazines and literary sections of newspapers for less than ten years prior to Hitler's seizure of power and his own emigration. There were few who still knew his name when he chose death in those early fall days of 1940 which for many of his origin and generation marked the darkest moment of the war—the fall of France, the threat to England, the still intact Hitler-Stalin pact whose most feared consequence at that moment was the close co-operation of the two most powerful secret police forces in Europe. Fifteen years later a two-volume edition of his writings was published in Germany and brought him almost immediately a *succès d'estime* that went far beyond the recognition among the few which he had known in his life. And since mere reputation, however high, as it rests on the judgment of the best, is never enough for writers and artists to make a living that only fame, the testimony of a multitude which need not be astronomical in size, can guarantee, one is doubly tempted to say (with Cicero), *Si vivi vicissent qui morte vicerunt* —how different everything would have been "if they had been victorious in life who have won victory in death."

Posthumous fame is too odd a thing to be blamed upon the blindness of the world or the corruption of a literary milieu. Nor can it be said that it is the bitter reward of those who were ahead of their time—as though history were a race track on which some contenders run so swiftly that they simply disappear from the spectator's range of vision. On the contrary, posthumous fame is usually preceded by the highest recognition among one's peers. When Kafka died in 1924, his few published books had not sold more than a couple of hundred copies, but his literary friends and the few readers who had almost accidentally stumbled on the short prose pieces (none of the novels was as yet published) knew beyond doubt that he was one of the masters of modern prose. Walter Benjamin had won such recognition early, and not only among those whose names at that time were still unknown, such as Gerhard Scholem, the friend of his youth, and Theodor Wiesengrund Adorno, his first and only disciple, who together are responsible for the posthumous edition of his works and letters.[1] Immediate, instinctive, one is tempted to say, recognition came from Hugo von Hofmannsthal, who published Benjamin's essay on Goethe's *Elective Affinities* in 1924, and from Bertolt Brecht who upon receiving the news of Benjamin's death is reported to have said that this was the first real loss Hitler had caused to German literature. We cannot know if there is such a thing as altogether unappreciated genius, or whether it is the

---

[1] Walter Benjamin, *Schriften*, Frankfurt a.M., Suhrkamp Verlag, 1955, 2 vols., and *Briefe*, Frankfurt a.M., 1966, 2 vols. The following references are to these editions.

daydream of those who are not geniuses; but we can be reasonably sure that posthumous fame will not be their lot.

Fame is a social phenomenon; *ad gloriam non est satis unius opinio* (as Seneca remarked wisely and pedantically), "for fame the opinion of one is not enough," although it is enough for friendship and love. And no society can properly function without classification, without an arrangement of things and men in classes and prescribed types. This necessary classification is the basis for all social discrimination, and discrimination, present opinion to the contrary notwithstanding, is no less a constituent element of the social realm than equality is a constituent element of the political. The point is that in society everybody must answer the question of *what* he is—as distinct from the question of *who* he is—which his role is and his function, and the answer of course can never be: I am unique, not because of the implicit arrogance but because the answer would be meaningless. In the case of Benjamin the trouble (if such it was) can be diagnosed in retrospect with great precision; when Hofmannsthal had read the long essay on Goethe by the completely unknown author, he called it *"schlechthin unvergleichlich"* ("absolutely incomparable"), and the trouble was that he was literally right, it could not be compared with anything else in existing literature. The trouble with everything Benjamin wrote was that it always turned out to be *sui generis*.

Posthumous fame seems, then, to be the lot of the unclassifiable ones, that is, those whose work neither fits the existing order nor introduces a new genre that lends itself to future classification. Innumerable attempts to write à la Kafka, all of them dismal failures, have only served to emphasize Kafka's uniqueness, that absolute originality which can be traced to no predecessor and suffers no followers. This is what society can least come to terms with and upon which it will always be very reluctant to bestow its seal of approval. To put it bluntly, it would be as misleading today to recommend Walter Benjamin as a literary critic and essayist as it would have been misleading to recommend Kafka in 1924 as a short-story writer and novelist. To describe adequately his work and him as an author within our usual framework of reference, one would have to make a great many negative statements, such as: his erudition was great, but he was no scholar; his subject matter comprised texts and their interpretation, but he was no philologist; he was greatly attracted not by religion but by theology and the theological type of interpretation for which the text itself is sacred, but he was no theologian and he was not particularly interested in the Bible; he was a born writer, but his greatest ambition was to produce a work consisting entirely of quotations; he was the first German to translate Proust (together with Franz Hessel) and St.-John Perse, and before that he had translated Baudelaire's *Tableaux Parisiens*, but he was no translator; he reviewed books and wrote a number of essays on living and dead writers, but he was no literary critic; he wrote a book about the German baroque and left behind a huge unfinished study of the French nineteenth century, but he was no historian, literary or otherwise; I shall try to show that he thought poetically, but he was neither a poet nor a philosopher.

Still, in the rare moments when he cared to define what he was doing, Benjamin thought of himself as a literary critic, and if he can be said at all to have aspired to a position in life it would have been that of "the only true critic of German literature" (as Scholem put it in one of the few, very beautiful letters to the friend that have been published), except that the very notion of thus becoming a useful member of society would have repelled him. No doubt he agreed with Baudelaire, "*Être un homme utile m'a paru toujours quelque chose de bien hideux.*" In the introductory paragraphs to the essay on *Elective Affinities*, Benjamin explained what he understood to be the task of the literary critic. He begins by distinguishing between a commentary and a critique. (Without mentioning it, perhaps without even being aware of it, he used the term *Kritik*, which in normal usage means criticism, as Kant used it when he spoke of a *Critique of Pure Reason*.)

Critique [he wrote] is concerned with the truth content of a work of art, the commentary with its subject matter. The relationship between the two is determined by that basic law of literature according

WALTER BENJAMIN

to which the work's truth content is the more relevant the more inconspicuously and intimately it is bound up with its subject matter. If therefore precisely those works turn out to endure whose truth is most deeply embedded in their subject matter, the beholder who contemplates them long after their own time finds the *realia* all the more striking in the work as they have faded away in the world. This means that subject matter and truth content, united in the work's early period, come apart during its afterlife; the subject matter becomes more striking while the truth content retains its original concealment. To an ever-increasing extent, therefore, the interpretation of the striking and the odd, that is, of the subject matter, becomes a prerequisite for any later critic. One may liken him to a paleographer in front of a parchment whose faded text is covered by the stronger outlines of a script referring to that text. Just as the paleographer would have to start with reading the script, the critic must start with commenting on his text. And out of this activity there arises immediately an inestimable criterion of critical judgment: only now can the critic ask the basic question of all criticism—namely, whether the work's shining truth content is due to its subject matter or whether the survival of the subject matter is due to the truth content. For as they come apart in the work, they decide on its immortality. In this sense the history of works of art prepares their critique, and this is why historical distance increases their power. If, to use a simile, one views the growing work as a funeral pyre, its commentator can be likened to the chemist, its critic to an alchemist. While the former is left with wood and ashes as the sole objects of his analysis, the latter is concerned only with the enigma of the flame itself: the enigma of being alive. Thus the critic inquires about the truth whose living flame goes on burning over the heavy logs of the past and the light ashes of life gone by.

The critic as an alchemist practicing the obscure art of transmuting the futile elements of the real into the shining, enduring gold of truth, or rather watching and interpreting the historical process that brings about such magical transfiguration—whatever we may think of this figure, it hardly corresponds to anything we usually have in mind when we classify a writer as a literary critic.

There is, however, another less objective element than the mere fact of being unclassifiable which is involved in the life of those who "have won victory in death." It is the element of bad luck, and this factor, very prominent in Benjamin's life,

157

cannot be ignored here because he himself, who probably never thought or dreamed about posthumous fame, was so extraordinarily aware of it. In his writing and also in conversation he used to speak about the "little hunchback," the "*bucklicht Männlein*," a German fairy-tale figure out of *Des Knaben Wunderhorn*, the famous collection of German folk poetry.

Will ich in mein' Keller gehn,
Will mein Weinlein zapfen;
Steht ein bucklicht Männlein da,
Tät mir'n Krug wegschnappen.

(When I go down to the cellar
There to draw some wine,
A little hunchback who's in there
Grabs that jug of mine.

Will ich in mein Küchel gehn,
Will mein Süpplein kochen;
Steht ein bucklicht Männlein da,
Hat mein Töpflein brochen.

When I go into my kitchen,
There my soup to make
A little hunchback who's in there
My little pot did break.)

The hunchback was an early acquaintance of Benjamin, who had first met him when, still a child, he found the poem in a children's book, and he never forgot. But only once (at the end of *A Berlin Childhood around 1900*), when anticipating death, he attempted to get hold of "his 'entire life' . . . as it is said to pass before the eyes of the dying," and clearly stated who and what it was that had terrified him so early in life and was to accompany him until his death. His mother, like millions of other mothers in Germany, used to say, "Mr. Bungle sends his regards" (*Ungeschickt lässt grüssen*) whenever one of the countless little catastrophes of childhood had taken place. And the child knew of course what this strange bungling was all about. The mother referred to the "little hunchback," who caused the objects to play their mischievous tricks upon children; it was he who had tripped you up when you fell and knocked the thing out of your hand when it went to pieces. And after the child came the grown-up man who knew what the child was still ignorant of, namely, that it was not he who had provoked "the little one" by looking at him—as though he had been the boy who wished to learn what fear was—but that the hunchback had looked at him and that bungling was a misfortune. For "anyone whom the little man looks at pays no attention; not to himself and not to the

little man. In consternation he stands before a pile of debris"
(*Schriften I, 650–52*).

Thanks to the recent publication of his letters, the story of
Benjamin's life may now be sketched in broad outline; and it
would be tempting indeed to tell it as a sequence of such piles
of debris since there is hardly any question that he himself
viewed it in that way. But the point of the matter is that he knew
very well of the mysterious interplay, the place "at which weak-
ness and genius coincide," which he so masterfully diagnosed in
Proust. For he was of course also speaking about himself when,
in complete agreement, he quoted what Jacques Rivière had
said about Proust: he "died of the same inexperience that permitted him to write his works. He died of ignorance . . . because he did not know how to make a fire or open a window"
("The Image of Proust"). Like Proust he was wholly incapable
of changing "his life's conditions even when they were about to
crush him." (With a precision suggesting a sleepwalker his
clumsiness invariably guided him to the very center of a misfortune, or wherever something of the sort might lurk. Thus, in
the winter of 1939–40 the danger of bombing made him decide to
leave Paris for a safer place. Well, no bomb was ever dropped
on Paris, but Meaux, where Benjamin went, was a troop center
and probably one of the very few places in France that was seriously endangered in those months of the phony war.) But like
Proust, he had every reason to bless the curse and to repeat the
strange prayer at the end of the folk poem with which he closes
his childhood memoir:

> Liebes Kindlein, ach, ich bitt,
> Bet fürs bucklicht Männlein mit.

> (O dear child, I beg of you,
> Pray for the little hunchback too.)

In retrospect, the inextricable net woven of merit, great gifts,
clumsiness, and misfortune into which his life was caught can be
detected even in the first pure piece of luck that opened Benjamin's career as a writer. Through the good offices of a friend, he

had been able to place "Goethe's *Elective Affinities*" in Hofmanns-thal's *Neue Deutsche Beiträge* (1924–25). This study, a master-piece of German prose and still of unique stature in the general field of German literary criticism and the specialized field of Goethe scholarship, had already been rejected several times, and Hofmannsthal's enthusiastic approval came at a moment when Benjamin almost despaired of "finding a taker for it" (*Briefe*, I, 300). But there was a decisive misfortune, apparently never fully understood, which under the given circumstances was neces-sarily connected with this chance. The only material security which this first public breakthrough could have led to was the *Habilitation*, the first step of the university career for which Benjamin was then preparing himself. This, to be sure, would not yet have enabled him to make a living—the so-called *Privat-dozent* received no salary—but it would probably have induced his father to support him until he received a full professorship, since this was a common practice in those days. It is now hard to understand how he and his friends could ever have doubted that a *Habilitation* under a not unusual university professor was bound to end with a catastrophe. If the gentlemen involved de-clared later that they did not understand a single word of the study, *The Origin of German Tragedy*, which Benjamin had sub-mitted, they can certainly be believed. How were they to under-stand a writer whose greatest pride it was that "the writing consists largely of quotations—the craziest mosaic technique imaginable"—and who placed the greatest emphasis on the six mottoes that preceded the study: "No one . . . could gather any rarer or more precious ones"? (*Briefe* I, 366). It was as if a real master had fashioned some unique object, only to offer it for sale at the nearest bargain center. Truly, neither anti-Semitism nor ill will toward an outsider—Benjamin had taken his degree in Switzerland during the war and was no one's disciple—nor the customary academic suspicion of anything that is not guaran-teed to be mediocre need have been involved.

However—and this is where bungling and bad luck come in—in the Germany of that time there was another way, and it was precisely his Goethe essay that spoiled Benjamin's only chance

for a university career. As often with Benjamin's writings, this
study was inspired by polemics, and the attack concerned Friedrich Gundolf's book on Goethe. Benjamin's critique was definitive, and yet Benjamin could have expected more understanding
from Gundolf and other members of the circle around Stefan
George, a group with whose intellectual world he had been quite
familiar in his youth, than from the "establishment"; and he
probably need not have been a member of the circle to earn his
academic accreditation under one of these men who at that time
were just beginning to get a fairly comfortable foothold in the
academic world. But the one thing he should not have done was
to mount an attack on the most prominent and most capable
academic member of the circle so vehement that everyone was
bound to know, as he explained retrospectively later, that he had
"just as little to do with academe . . . as with the monuments
which men like Gundolf or Ernst Bertram have erected" (*Briefe*
II, 523). Yes, that is how it was. And it was Benjamin's bungling
or his misfortune to have announced this to the world before he
was admitted to the university.

Yet one certainly cannot say that he consciously disregarded
due caution. On the contrary, he was aware that "Mr. Bungle
sends his regards" and took more precautions than anyone else
I have known. But his system of provisions against possible
dangers, including the "Chinese courtesy" mentioned by Scholem,[2] invariably, in a strange and mysterious way, disregarded
the real danger. For just as he fled from the safe Paris to the
dangerous Meaux at the beginning of the war—to the front, as
it were—his essay on Goethe inspired in him the wholly unnecessary worry that Hofmannsthal might take amiss a very
cautious critical remark about Rudolf Borchardt, one of the
chief contributors to his periodical. Yet he expected only good
things from having found for this "attack upon the ideology of
George's school . . . this one place where they will find it hard
to ignore the invective" (*Briefe* I, 341). They did not find it hard
at all. For no one was more isolated than Benjamin, so utterly

[2] Yearbook of the Leo Baeck Institute, 1965, p. 117.

alone. Even the authority of Hofmannsthal—"the new patron," as Benjamin called him in the first burst of happiness (*Briefe* I, 327)—could not alter this situation. His voice hardly mattered compared with the very real power of the George school, an influential group in which, as with all such entities, only ideological allegiance counted, since only ideology, not rank and quality, can hold a group together. Despite their pose of being above politics, George's disciples were fully as conversant with the basic principles of literary maneuvers as the professors were with the fundamentals of academic politics or the hacks and journalists with the ABC of "one good turn deserves another."

Benjamin, however, did not know the score. He never knew how to handle such things, was never able to move among such people, not even when "the adversities of outer life which sometimes come from all sides, like wolves" (*Briefe* I, 298), had already afforded him some insight into the ways of the world. Whenever he tried to adjust and be co-operative so as to get some firm ground under his feet somehow, things were sure to go wrong.

A major study on Goethe from the viewpoint of Marxism—in the middle twenties he came very close to joining the Communist Party—never appeared in print, either in the Great Russian Encyclopedia, for which it was intended, or in present-day Germany. Klaus Mann, who had commissioned a review of Brecht's *Threepenny Novel* for his periodical *Die Sammlung*, returned the manuscript because Benjamin had asked 250 French francs—then about 10 dollars—for it and he wanted to pay only 150. His commentary on Brecht's poetry did not appear in his lifetime. And the most serious difficulties finally developed with the Institute for Social Research, which, originally (and now again) part of the University of Frankfurt, had emigrated to America and on which Benjamin depended financially. Its guiding spirits, Theodor W. Adorno and Max Horkheimer, were "dialectical materialists" and in their opinion Benjamin's thinking was "undialectic," moved in "materialistic categories, which by no means coincide with Marxist ones," was "lacking in mediation" insofar as, in an essay on Baudelaire, he had related "certain conspicuous elements within the superstructure . . . directly, perhaps even causally, to corresponding elements in the substructure." The result was that Benjamin's original essay, "The Paris of the Second Empire in the Works of Baudelaire," was not printed, either then in the magazine of the Institute or in the posthumous two-volume edition of his writings. (Two parts of it have now been published, "Der Flâneur" in *Die Neue Rundschau*, December 1967, and "Die Moderne" in *Das Argument*, March 1968.)

Benjamin probably was the most peculiar Marxist ever produced by this movement, which God knows has had its full share of oddities. The theoretical aspect that was bound to fascinate him was the doctrine of the superstructure, which was only briefly sketched by Marx but then assumed a disproportionate role in the movement as it was joined by a disproportionately large number of intellectuals, hence by people who were interested only in the superstructure. Benjamin used this doctrine only as a heuristic-methodological stimulus and was hardly interested in its historical or philosophical background. What fascinated him about the matter was that the spirit and its material manifestation were so intimately connected that it seemed permissible to discover everywhere Baudelaire's *correspondances,* which clarified and illuminated one another if they were properly correlated, so that finally they would no longer require any interpretative or explanatory commentary. He was concerned with the correlation between a street scene, a speculation on the stock exchange, a poem, a thought, with the hidden line which holds them together and enables the historian or philologist to recognize that they must all be placed in the same period. When Adorno criticized Benjamin's "wide-eyed presentation of actualities" (*Briefe* II, 793), he hit the nail right on its head; this is precisely what Benjamin was doing and wanted to do. Strongly influenced by surrealism, it was the "attempt to capture the portrait of history in the most insignificant representations of reality, its scraps, as it were" (*Briefe* II, 685). Benjamin had a passion for small, even minute things; Scholem tells about his ambition to get one hundred lines onto the ordinary page of a notebook and about his admiration for two grains of wheat in the Jewish section of the Musée Cluny "on which a kindred soul had inscribed the complete *Shema Israel*." [3] For him the size of an object was in an inverse ratio to its significance. And this passion, far from being a whim, derived directly from the only world view that ever had a decisive influence on him, from Goethe's conviction of the factual existence of an *Urphänomen*, an archetypal phenomenon, a concrete thing to be discovered in the world of appearances in which "significance" (*Bedeutung*, the most Goethean of words, keeps recurring in Benjamin's writings) and appearance, word and thing, idea and experience, would coincide. The smaller the object, the more likely it seemed that it could contain in the most concentrated form everything else; hence his delight that two grains of wheat should contain the entire *Shema Israel*, the very essence of Judaism, tiniest essence appearing on tiniest entity, from which in both cases everything else originates that, however, in significance cannot be compared with its origin. In other words, what profoundly fascinated Benjamin from the beginning was never an idea, it was always a phenomenon. "What seems paradoxical about everything that is justly called beautiful is the fact that it appears" (*Schriften* I, 349), and this paradox—or, more simply, the wonder of appearance—was always at the center of all his concerns.

How remote these studies were from Marxism and dialectical materialism is confirmed by their central figure, the *flâneur*.[4] It is to him, aimlessly strolling through the crowds in the big cities in studied contrast to their hurried, purposeful activity, that things reveal themselves in their secret meaning: "The true picture of the past *flits* by" ("Philosophy of History"), and only the *flâneur* who idly strolls by receives the message. With great acumen Adorno has pointed to the static element in Benjamin: "To understand Benjamin properly one must feel behind his every sentence the conversion of extreme agitation into some-

[3] *Op. cit.*
[4] The classical description of the *flâneur* occurs in Baudelaire's famous essay on Constantin Guys "Le Peintre de la vie moderne"—see Edition Pléiade, pp. 877–83. Benjamin frequently refers to it indirectly and quotes from it in the Baudelaire essay.

thing static, indeed, the static notion of movement itself" (*Schrif-ten* I, xix). Naturally, nothing could be more "undialectic" than this attitude in which the "angel of history" (in the ninth of the "Theses on the Philosophy of History") does not dialectically move forward into the future, but has his face "turned toward the past." "Where a chain of events appears to *us, he* sees one single catastrophe which keeps piling wreckage upon wreckage and hurls it in front of his feet. The angel would like to stay, awaken the dead, and join together what has been smashed to pieces." (Which would presumably mean the end of history.) "But a storm is blowing from Paradise" and "irresistibly propels him into the future to which his back is turned, while the pile of ruins before him grows skyward. What we call progress is *this* storm." In this angel, which Benjamin saw in Klee's "Angelus Novus," the *flâneur* experiences his final transfiguration. For just as the *flâneur*, through the *gestus* of purposeless strolling, turns his back to the crowd even as he is propelled and swept by it, so the "angel of history," who looks at nothing but the ex-panse of ruins of the past, is blown backwards into the future by the storm of progress. That such thinking should ever have bothered with a consistent, dialectically sensible, rationally ex-plainable process seems absurd.

It should also be obvious that such thinking neither aimed nor could arrive at binding, generally valid statements, but that these were replaced, as Adorno critically remarks, "by metaphorical ones" (*Briefe* II, 785). In his concern with directly, actually demonstrable concrete facts, with single events and occurrences whose "significance" is manifest, Benjamin was not much inter-ested in theories or "ideas" which did not immediately assume the most precise outward shape imaginable. To this very com-plex but still highly realistic mode of thought the Marxian rela-tionship between superstructure and substructure became, in a precise sense, a metaphorical one. If, for example—and this would certainly be in the spirit of Benjamin's thought—the ab-stract concept *Vernunft* (reason) is traced back to its origin in the verb *vernehmen* (to perceive, to hear), it may be thought that a word from the sphere of the superstructure has been given back its sensual substructure, or, conversely, that a concept has been transformed into a metaphor—provided that "metaphor" is understood in its original, nonallegorical sense of *metapherein* (to transfer). For a metaphor establishes a connection which is sensually perceived in its immediacy and requires no interpretation, while an allegory always proceeds from an abstract notion and then invents something palpable to represent it almost at will. The allegory must be explained before it can become meaningful, a solution must be found to the riddle it presents, so that the often laborious interpretation of allegorical figures always unhappily reminds one of the solving of puzzles even when no more ingenuity is demanded than in the allegorical representation of death by a skeleton. Since Homer the metaphor has borne that element of the poetic which conveys cognition; its use establishes the *correspondances* between physically most remote things—as when in the *Iliad* the tearing onslaught of fear and grief on the hearts of the Achaians corresponds to the combined onslaught of the winds from north and west on the dark waters (Iliad IX, 1–8); or when the approaching of the army moving to battle in line after line corresponds to the sea's long billows which, driven by the wind, gather head far out on the sea, roll to shore line after line, and then burst on the land in thunder (Iliad IV, 422–28). Metaphors are the means by which the oneness of the world is poetically brought about. What is so hard to understand about Benjamin is that without being a poet he *thought poetically* and therefore was bound to regard the metaphor as the greatest gift of language. Linguistic "transference" enables us to give material form to the invisible—"A mighty fortress is our God"—and thus to render it capable of being experienced. He had no trouble understanding the theory of the superstructure as the final doctrine of metaphorical thinking—precisely because without much ado and eschewing all "mediations" he directly related the superstructure to the so-called "material" substructure, which to him meant the totality of sensually experienced data. He evidently was fascinated by the very thing that the others branded as "vulgar-Marxist" or "undialectical" thinking.

It seems plausible that Benjamin, whose spiritual existence had been formed and informed by Goethe, a poet and not a philosopher, and whose interest was almost exclusively aroused by poets and novelists, although he had studied philosophy, should have found it easier to communicate with poets than with theoreticians, whether of the dialectical or the metaphysical variety. And there is indeed no question but that his friendship with Brecht—unique in that here the greatest living German poet met the most important critic of the time, a fact both were fully aware of—was the second and incomparably more important stroke of good fortune in Benjamin's life. It promptly had the most adverse consequences; it antagonized the few friends he had, it endangered his relation to the Institute of Social Research, toward whose "suggestions" he had every reason "to be docile" (*Briefe* II, 683), and the only reason it did not cost him his friendship with Scholem was Scholem's abiding loyalty and admirable generosity in all matters concerning his friend. Both Adorno and Scholem blamed Brecht's "disastrous influence" [5] (Scholem) for Benjamin's clearly undialectic usage of Marxian categories and his determined break with all metaphysics; and the trouble was that Benjamin, usually quite inclined to compromises albeit mostly unnecessary ones, knew and maintained that his friendship with Brecht constituted an absolute limit not

[5] Both have recently reiterated this—Scholem in his Leo Baeck Memorial Lecture of 1965, in which he said, "I am inclined to consider Brecht's influence on Benjamin's output in the thirties baleful, and in some respects disastrous," and Adorno in a statement to his disciple Rolf Tiedemann according to which Benjamin admitted to Adorno that he had written "his essay on the Work of Art in order to outdo Brecht, whom he was afraid of, in radicalism" (quoted in Rolf Tiedemann, *Studien zur Philosophie Walter Benjamins*, Frankfurt, 1965, p. 89). It is improbable that Benjamin should have expressed fear of Brecht, and Adorno seems not to claim that he did. As for the rest of the statement, it is, unfortunately, all too likely that Benjamin made it because he was afraid of Adorno. It is true that Benjamin was very shy in his dealings with people he had not known since his youth, but he was afraid only of people he was dependent upon. Such a dependence on Brecht would have come about only if he had followed Brecht's suggestion that he move from Paris to Brecht's vicinity in considerably less expensive Denmark. As it turned out, Benjamin had serious doubts about such an exclusive "dependence on one person" in a strange country with a "quite unfamiliar language" (*Briefe* II, 596, 599).

only to docility but even to diplomacy, for "my agreeing with Brecht's production is one of the most important and most strategic points in my entire position" (*Briefe* II, 594). In Brecht he found a poet of rare intellectual powers and, almost as important for him at the time, someone on the Left who, despite all talk about dialectics, was no more of a dialectical thinker than he was, but whose intelligence was uncommonly close to reality. With Brecht he could practice what Brecht himself called "crude thinking" (*das plumpe Denken*): "The main thing is to learn how to think crudely. Crude thinking, that is the thinking of the great," said Brecht, and Benjamin added by way of elucidation: "There are many people whose idea of a dialectician is a lover of subtleties. . . . Crude thoughts, on the contrary, should be part and parcel of dialectical thinking, because they are nothing but the referral of theory to practice . . . a thought must be crude to come into its own in action." [6] Well, what attracted Benjamin to crude thinking was probably not so much a referral to practice as to reality, and to him this reality manifested itself most directly in the proverbs and idioms of everyday language. "Proverbs are a school of crude thinking," he writes in the same context; and the art of taking proverbial and idiomatic speech literally enabled Benjamin—as it did Kafka, in whom figures of speech are often clearly discernible as a source of inspiration and furnish the key to many a "riddle"—to write a prose of such singularly enchanting and enchanted closeness to reality.

Wherever one looks in Benjamin's life, one will find the little hunchback. Long before the outbreak of the Third Reich he was playing his evil tricks, causing publishers who had promised Benjamin an annual stipend for reading manuscripts or editing a periodical for them to go bankrupt before the first number appeared. Later the hunchback did allow a collection of magnifi-

---

[6] In the review of the *Dreigroschenroman*. Cf. *Versuche über Brecht*, Frankfurt, 1966, p. 90.

cent German letters, made with infinite care and provided with
the most marvelous commentaries, to be printed—under the title
Deutsche Menschen and with the motto *"Von Ehre ohne Ruhm/
Von Grösse ohne Glanz/Von Würde ohne Sold"* (Of Honor with-
out Fame/Of Greatness without Splendor/Of Dignity without
Pay); but then he saw to it that it ended in the cellar of the bankrupt Swiss publisher, instead of being distributed, as intended by
Benjamin, who signed the selection with a pseudonym, in Nazi
Germany. And in this cellar the edition was discovered in 1962,
at the very moment when a new edition had come off the press in
Germany. (One would also charge it to the little hunchback that
often the few things that were to take a good turn first presented
themselves in an unpleasant guise. A case in point is the translation of *Anabase* by Alexis Saint-Léger Léger [St.-John Perse]
which Benjamin, who thought the work "of little importance"
[*Briefe* I, 381], undertook because, like the Proust translation, the
assignment had been procured for him by Hofmannsthal. The
translation did not appear in Germany until after the war, yet
Benjamin owed to it his contact with Léger, who, being a dip-
lomat, was able to intervene and persuade the French government to spare Benjamin a second internment in France during
the war—a privilege that very few other refugees enjoyed.) And
then after mischief came "the piles of debris," the last of which
prior to the catastrophe at the Spanish border, was the threat he
had felt, since 1938, that the Institute for Social Research in New
York, the only "material and moral support" of his Paris existence
(*Briefe* II, 839), would desert him. "The very circumstances that
greatly endanger my European situation will probably make
emigration to the U.S.A. impossible for me," so he wrote in April
of 1939 (*Briefe* II, 810), still under the impact of the "blow"
which Adorno's letter rejecting the first version of the Baudelaire
study had dealt him in November of 1938 (*Briefe* II, 790).

Scholem is surely right when he says that next to Proust, Benjamin felt the closest personal affinity with Kafka among contemporary authors, and undoubtedly Benjamin had the "field of
ruins and the disaster area" of his own work in mind when he
wrote that "an understanding of [Kafka's] production involves,

among other things, the simple recognition that he was a failure" (*Briefe* II, 614). What Benjamin said of Kafka with such unique aptness applies to himself as well: "The circumstances of this failure are multifarious. One is tempted to say: once he was certain of eventual failure, everything worked out for him *en route* as in a dream" (*Briefe* II, 764). He did not need to read Kafka to think like Kafka. When "The Stoker" was all he had read of Kafka, he had already quoted Goethe's statement about hope in his essay on *Elective Affinities*: "Hope passed over their heads like a star that falls from the sky"; and the sentence with which he concludes this study reads as though Kafka had written it: "Only for the sake of the hopeless ones have we been given hope" (*Schriften* I, 140).

On September 26, 1940, Walter Benjamin, who was about to emigrate to America, took his life at the Franco-Spanish border. There were various reasons for this. The Gestapo had confiscated his Paris apartment, which contained his library (he had been able to get "the more important half" out of Germany) and many of his manuscripts, and he had reason to be concerned also about the others which, through the good offices of George Bataille, had been placed in the Bibliothèque Nationale prior to his flight from Paris to Lourdes in unoccupied France.[7] How was he to live without a library, how could he earn a living without the extensive collection of quotations and excerpts among his manuscripts? Besides, nothing drew him to America, where, as he used to say, people would probably find no other use for him than to cart him up and down the country to exhibit him as the "last European." But the immediate occasion for Benjamin's suicide was an uncommon stroke of bad luck. Through the armistice agreement between Vichy France and the Third Reich, ref-

[7] It now seems that nearly everything has been saved. The manuscripts hidden in Paris were, in accordance with Benjamin's instructions, sent to Theodor W. Adorno; according to Tiedemann (*op. cit.*, p. 212), they are now in Adorno's "private collection" in Frankfurt. Reprints and copies of most texts are also in Gershom Scholem's personal collection in Jerusalem. The material confiscated by the Gestapo has turned up in the German Democratic Republic. See "Der Benjamin-Nachlass in Potsdam" by Rosemarie Heise in *alternative*, October–December, 1967.

ugees from Hitler Germany—*les refugiés provenant d'Alle-magne*, as they were officially referred to in France—were in danger of being shipped back to Germany, presumably only if they were political opponents. To save this category of refugees —which, it should be noted, never included the unpolitical mass of Jews who later turned out to be the most endangered of all— the United States had distributed a number of emergency visas through its consulates in unoccupied France. Thanks to the ef-forts of the Institute in New York, Benjamin was among the first to receive such a visa in Marseilles. Also, he quickly obtained a Spanish transit visa to enable him to get to Lisbon and board a ship there. However, he did not have a French exit visa, which at that time was still required and which the French government, eager to please the Gestapo, invariably denied to German refu-gees. In general this presented no great difficulty, since a rela-tively short and none too arduous road to be covered by foot over the mountains to Port Bou was well known and was not guarded by the French border police. Still, for Benjamin, appar-ently suffering from a cardiac condition (*Briefe* II, 841), even the shortest walk was a great exertion, and he must have arrived in a state of serious exhaustion. The small group of refugees that he had joined reached the Spanish border town only to learn that Spain had closed the border that same day and that the border officials did not honor visas made out in Marseilles. The refugees were supposed to return to France by the same route the next day. During the night Benjamin took his life, whereupon the border officials, upon whom this suicide had made an impression, allowed his companions to proceed to Portugal. A few weeks later the embargo on visas was lifted again. One day earlier Benjamin would have got through without any trouble; one day later the people in Marseilles would have known that for the time being it was impossible to pass through Spain. Only on that particular day was the catastrophe possible.

II. THE DARK TIMES

"Anyone who cannot cope with life while he is alive needs one hand to ward off a little his despair over his fate . . . but with his

other hand he can jot down what he sees among the ruins, for he
sees different and more things than the others; after all, he is dead in
his own lifetime and the real survivor."

—FRANZ KAFKA, *Diaries,*
entry of October 19, 1921

"Like one who keeps afloat on a shipwreck by climbing to the top
of a mast that is already crumbling. But from there he has a chance
to give a signal leading to his rescue."

—WALTER BENJAMIN,
in a letter to Gerhard Scholem dated April 17, 1931

Often an era most clearly brands with its seal those who have
been least influenced by it, who have been most remote from it,
and who therefore have suffered most. So it was with Proust,
with Kafka, with Karl Kraus, and with Benjamin. His gestures
and the way he held his head when listening and talking; the
way he moved; his manners, but especially his style of speaking,
down to his choice of words and the shape of his syntax; finally,
his downright idiosyncratic tastes—all this seemed so old-fashioned, as though he had drifted out of the nineteenth century
into the twentieth the way one is driven onto the coast of a
strange land. Did he ever feel at home in twentieth-century Germany? One has reason to doubt it. In 1913, when he first visited
France as a very young man, the streets of Paris were "almost
more homelike" (*Briefe* I, 56) to him after a few days than the
familiar streets of Berlin. He may have felt even then, and he
certainly felt twenty years later, how much the trip from Berlin
to Paris was tantamount to a trip in time—not from one country
to another, but from the twentieth century back to the nineteenth. There was the *nation par excellence* whose culture had
determined the Europe of the nineteenth century and for which
Haussmann had rebuilt Paris, "the capital of the nineteenth century," as Benjamin was to call it. This Paris was not yet cosmopolitan, to be sure, but it was profoundly European, and thus
it has, with unparalleled naturalness, offered itself to all homeless
people as a second home ever since the middle of the last century.
Neither the pronounced xenophobia of its inhabitants nor the
sophisticated harassment by the local police has ever been able

to change this. Long before his emigration Benjamin knew how "very exceptional [it was] to make the kind of contact with a Frenchman that would enable one to prolong a conversation with him beyond the first quarter of an hour" (*Briefe* I, 445). Later, when he was domiciled in Paris as a refugee, his innate nobility prevented him from developing his slight acquaintances —chief among them was Gide—into connections and from making new contacts. (Werner Kraft—so we learned recently—took him to see Charles du Bos, who was, by virtue of his "enthusiasm for German literature," a kind of key figure for German emigrants. Werner Kraft had the better connections—what irony.[8]) In his strikingly judicious review of Benjamin's works and letters as well as of the secondary literature, Pierre Missac has pointed out how greatly Benjamin must have suffered because he did not get the "reception" in France that was due him.[9] This is correct, of course, but it surely did not come as a surprise.

No matter how irritating and offensive all this may have been, the city itself compensated for everything. Its boulevards, Benjamin discovered as early as 1913, are formed by houses which "do not seem made to be lived in, but are like stone sets for people to walk between" (*Briefe* I, 56). This city, around which one still can travel in a circle past the old gates, has remained what the cities of the Middle Ages, severely walled off and protected against the outside, once were: an interior, but without the narrowness of medieval streets, a generously built and planned open-air *intérieur* with the arch of the sky like a majestic ceiling above it. "The finest thing here about all art and all activity is the fact that they leave the few remainders of the original and the natural their splendor" (*Briefe* I, 421). Indeed, they help them to acquire new luster. It is the uniform façades, lining the streets like inside walls, that make one feel more physically sheltered in this city than in any other. The arcades which connect the great boulevards and offer protection from inclement weather exerted such an enormous fascination over Benjamin that he referred to

[8] Cf. "Walter Benjamin hinter seinen Briefen," *Merkur*, March 1967.
[9] Cf. Pierre Missac, "L'Eclat et le secret: Walter Benjamin," *Critique*, Nos. 231–32, 1966.

his projected major work on the nineteenth century and its capital simply as "The Arcades" (*Passagenarbeit*); and these passageways are indeed like a symbol of Paris, because they clearly are inside and outside at the same time and thus represent its true nature in quintessential form. In Paris a stranger feels at home because he can inhabit the city the way he lives in his own four walls. And just as one inhabits an apartment, and makes it comfortable, by living in it instead of just using it for sleeping, eating, and working, so one inhabits a city by strolling through it without aim or purpose, with one's stay secured by the countless cafés which line the streets and past which the life of the city, the flow of pedestrians, moves along. To this day Paris is the only one among the large cities which can be comfortably covered on foot, and more than any other city it is dependent for its liveliness on people who pass by in the streets, so that the modern automobile traffic endangers its very existence not only for technical reasons. The wasteland of an American suburb, or the residential districts of many towns, where all of street life takes place on the roadway and where one can walk on the sidewalks, by now reduced to footpaths, for miles on end without encountering a human being, is the very opposite of Paris. What all other cities seem to permit only reluctantly to the dregs of society—strolling, idling, *flânerie*—Paris streets actually invite everyone to do. Thus, ever since the Second Empire the city has been the paradise of all those who need to chase after no livelihood, pursue no career, reach no goal—the paradise, then, of bohemians, and not only of artists and writers but of all those who have gathered about them because they could not be integrated either politically—being homeless or stateless—or socially.

Without considering this background of the city which became a decisive experience for the young Benjamin one can hardly understand why the *flâneur* became the key figure in his writings. The extent to which this strolling determined the pace of his thinking was perhaps most clearly revealed in the peculiarities of his gait, which Max Rychner described as "at once advancing and

tarrying, a strange mixture of both." [10] It was the walk of a
flâneur, and it was so striking because, like the dandy and the
snob, the *flâneur* had his home in the nineteenth century, an
age of security in which children of upper-middle-class families
were assured of an income without having to work, so that they
had no reason to hurry. And just as the city taught Benjamin
flânerie, the nineteenth century's secret style of walking and
thinking, it naturally aroused in him a feeling for French literature as well, and this almost irrevocably estranged him from
normal German intellectual life. "In Germany I feel quite isolated
in my efforts and interests among those of my generation, while
in France there are certain forces—the writers Giraudoux and,
especially, Aragon; the surrealist movement—in which I see at
work what occupies me too"—so he wrote to Hofmannsthal in
1927 (*Briefe* I, 446), when, having returned from a trip to Moscow and convinced that literary projects sailing under the Communist flag were unfeasible, he was setting out to consolidate
his "Paris position" (*Briefe* I, 444–45). (Eight years earlier,
he had mentioned the "incredible feeling of kinship" which
Péguy had inspired in him: "No written work has ever touched
me so closely and given me such a sense of communion" [*Briefe*
I, 217].) Well, he did not succeed in consolidating anything, and
success would hardly have been possible. Only in postwar
Paris have foreigners—and presumably that is what everyone
not born in France is called in Paris to this day—been able to
occupy "positions." On the other hand, Benjamin was forced
into a position which actually did not exist anywhere, which,
in fact, could not be identified and diagnosed as such until afterwards. It was the position on the "top of the mast" from which the
tempestuous times could be surveyed better than from a safe harbor, even though the distress signals of the "shipwreck," of this

[10] Max Rychner, the recently deceased editor of the *Neue Schweizer
Rundschau*, was one of the most cultivated and most refined figures in the
intellectual life of the time. Like Adorno, Ernst Bloch, and Scholem, he
published his "Erinnerungen an Walter Benjamin" in *Der Monat*, Sept.
1960.

one man who had not learned to swim either with or against the tide, were hardly noticed—either by those who had never exposed themselves to these seas or by those who were capable of moving even in this element.

Viewed from the outside, it was the position of the free-lance writer who lives by his pen; however, as only Max Rychner seems to have observed, he did so in a "peculiar way," for "his publications were anything but frequent" and "it was never quite clear . . . to what extent he was able to draw upon other resources." [11] Rychner's suspicions were justified in every respect. Not only were "other resources" at his disposal prior to his emigration, but behind the façade of free-lance writing he led the considerably freer, albeit constantly endangered, life of an *homme de lettres* whose home was a library that had been gathered with extreme care but was by no means intended as a working tool; it consisted of treasures whose value, as Benjamin often repeated, was proved by the fact that he had not read them—a library, then, which was guaranteed not to be useful or at the service of any profession. Such an existence was something unknown in Germany, and almost equally unknown was the occupation which Benjamin, only because he had to make a living, derived from it: Not the occupation of a literary historian and scholar with the requisite number of fat tomes to his credit, but that of a critic and essayist who regarded even the essay form as too vulgarly extensive and would have preferred the aphorism if he had not been paid by the line. He was certainly not unaware of the fact that his professional ambitions were directed at something that simply did not exist in Germany, where, despite Lichtenberg, Lessing, Schlegel, Heine, and Nietzsche, aphorisms have never been appreciated and people have usually thought of criticism as something disreputably subversive which might be enjoyed—if at all—only in the cultural section of a newspaper. It was no accident that Benjamin chose the French language for expressing this ambition: "*Le but que je m'avais proposé . . . c'est d'être considéré comme le premier critique de la littérature allemande. La difficulté c'est que, depuis*

[11] *Ibid.*

plus de cinquante ans, la critique littéraire en Allemagne n'est plus considérée comme un genre sérieux. Se faire une situation dans la critique, cela . . . veut dire: la recréer comme genre." ("The goal I set for myself . . . is to be regarded as the foremost critic of German literature. The trouble is that for more than fifty years literary criticism in Germany has not been considered a serious genre. To create a place in criticism for oneself means to re-create it as a genre") (*Briefe* II, 505).

There is no doubt that Benjamin owed this choice of a profession to early French influences, to the proximity of the great neighbor on the other side of the Rhine which inspired in him so intimate a sense of affinity. But it is much more symptomatic that even this selection of a profession was actually motivated by hard times and financial woes. If one wants to express the "profession" he had prepared himself for spontaneously, although perhaps not deliberately, in social categories, one has to go back to Wilhelminian Germany in which he grew up and where his first plans for the future took shape. Then one could say that Benjamin did not prepare for anything but the "profession" of a private collector and totally independent scholar, what was then called *Privatgelehrter.* Under the circumstances of the time his studies, which he had begun before the First World War, could have ended only with a university career, but unbaptized Jews were still barred from such a career, as they were from any career in the civil service. Such Jews were permitted a *Habilitation* and at most could attain the rank of an unpaid *Extraordinarius;* it was a career which presupposed rather than provided an assured income. The doctorate which Benjamin decided to take only "out of consideration for my family" (*Briefe* I, 216) and his subsequent attempt at *Habilitation* were intended as the basis for his family's readiness to place such an income at his disposal.

This situation changed abruptly after the war: the inflation had impoverished, even dispossessed, large numbers of the bourgeoisie, and in the Weimar Republic a university career was open even to unbaptized Jews. The unhappy story of the *Habilitation* shows clearly how little Benjamin took these altered circum-

stances into account and how greatly he continued to be dominated by prewar ideas in all financial matters. For from the
outset the *Habilitation* had only been intended to call his father
"to order" by supplying "evidence of public recognition" (*Briefe*
I, 293) and to make him grant his son, who was in his thirties at
that time, an income that was adequate and, one should add,
commensurate with his social standing. At no time, not even
when he had already come close to the Communists, did he
doubt that despite his chronic conflicts with his parents he was
entitled to such a subvention and that their demand that he
"work for a living" was "unspeakable" (*Briefe* I, 292). When
his father said later that he could not or would not increase the
monthly stipend he was paying anyway, even if his son achieved
the *Habilitation*, this naturally removed the basis of Benjamin's
entire undertaking. Until his parents' death in 1930, Benjamin
was able to solve the problem of his livelihood by moving back
into the parental home, living there first with his family (he
had a wife and a son), and after his separation—which came
soon enough—by himself. (He was not divorced until 1930.) It
is evident that this arrangement caused him a great deal of
suffering, but it is just as evident that in all probability he never
seriously considered another solution. It is also striking that
despite his permanent financial trouble he managed throughout
these years constantly to enlarge his library. His one attempt to
deny himself this expensive passion—he visited the great auction
houses the way others frequent gambling casinos—and his res-
olution even to sell something "in an emergency" ended with his
feeling obliged to "deaden the pain of this readiness" (*Briefe* I,
340) by making fresh purchases; and his one demonstrable attempt to free himself from financial dependence on his family
ended with the proposal that his father immediately give him
"funds enabling me to buy an interest in a secondhand bookstore"
(*Briefe* I, 292). This is the only gainful employment that Benjamin ever considered. Nothing came of it, of course.

In view of the realities of the Germany of the twenties and
of Benjamin's awareness that he would never be able to make a
living with his pen—"there are places in which I can earn a

minimum and places in which I can live on a minimum, but there is no place where I can do both" (*Briefe* II, 563)—his whole attitude may strike one as unpardonably irresponsible. Yet it was anything but a case of irresponsibility. It is reasonable to assume that it is just as hard for rich people grown poor to believe in their poverty as it is for poor people turned rich to believe in their wealth; the former seem carried away by a recklessness of which they are totally unaware, the latter seem possessed by a stinginess which actually is nothing but the old ingrained fear of what the next day may bring.

Moreover, in his attitude to financial problems Benjamin was by no means an isolated case. If anything, his outlook was typical of an entire generation of German-Jewish intellectuals, although probably no one else fared so badly with it. Its basis was the mentality of the fathers, successful businessmen who did not think too highly of their own achievements and whose dream it was that their sons were destined for higher things. It was the secularized version of the ancient Jewish belief that those who "learn"—the Torah or the Talmud, that is, God's law—were the true elite of the people and should not be bothered with so vulgar an occupation as making money or working for it. This is not to say that in this generation there were no father-son conflicts; on the contrary, the literature of the time is full of them, and if Freud had lived and carried on his inquiries in a country and language other than the German-Jewish milieu which supplied his patients, we might never have heard of an Oedipus complex.[12] But as a rule these conflicts were resolved by the sons' laying claim to being geniuses, or, in the case of the numerous Communists from well-to-do homes, to being devoted to the welfare of mankind—in any case, to aspiring to things higher than making money—and the fathers were more than willing to

[12] Kafka, whose outlook on these matters was more realistic than that of any of his contemporaries, said that "the father complex which is the intellectual nourishment of many . . . concerns the Judaism of the fathers . . . the vague consent of the fathers (this vagueness was the outrage)" to their sons' leaving of the Jewish fold: "with their hind legs they were still stuck to the Judaism of their fathers, and with the forelegs they found no new ground" (Franz Kafka, *Briefe*, p. 337).

grant that this was a valid excuse for not making a living. Where such claims were not made or recognized, catastrophe was just around the corner. Benjamin was a case in point: his father never recognized his claims, and their relations were extraordinarily bad. Another such case was Kafka, who—possibly because he really was something like a genius—was quite free of the genius mania of his environment, never claimed to be a genius, and ensured his financial independence by taking an ordinary job at the Prague workmen's compensation office. (His relations with his father were of course equally bad, but for different reasons.) And still, no sooner had Kafka taken this position than he saw in it a "running start for suicides," as though he were obeying an order that says "You have to earn your grave." [13]

For Benjamin, at any rate, a monthly stipend remained the only possible form of income, and in order to receive one after his parents' death he was ready, or thought he was, to do many things: to study Hebrew for 300 marks a month if the Zionists thought it would do them some good, or to think dialectically, with all the mediating trimmings, for one thousand French francs if there was no other way of doing business with the Marxists. The fact that despite being down and out he later did neither is worthy of admiration, and so is the infinite patience with which Scholem, who had worked very hard to get Benjamin a stipend for the study of Hebrew from the university in Jerusalem, allowed himself to be put off for years. No one, of course, was prepared to subsidize him in the only "position" for which he was born, that of an *homme de lettres*, a position of whose unique prospects neither the Zionists nor the Marxists were, or could have been, aware.

Today the *homme de lettres* strikes us as a rather harmless, marginal figure, as though he were actually to be equated with the figure of the *Privatgelehrter* that has always had a touch of the comic. Benjamin, who felt so close to French that the language became for him a "sort of alibi" (*Briefe* II, 505) for his existence, probably knew about the *homme de lettres*'s origins in

[13] *Ibid.*, p. 55.

prerevolutionary France as well as about his extraordinary career in the French Revolution. In contrast to the later writers and literati, the *"écrivains et littérateurs"* as even Larousse defines the *hommes de lettres*, these men, though they did live in the world of the written and printed word and were, above all, surrounded by books, were neither obliged nor willing to write and read professionally, in order to earn a living. Unlike the class of the intellectuals, who offer their services either to the state as experts, specialists, and officials, or to society for diversion and instruction, the *hommes de lettres* always strove to keep aloof from both the state and society. Their material existence was based on income without work, and their intellectual attitude rested upon their resolute refusal to be integrated politically or socially. On the basis of this dual independence they could afford that attitude of superior disdain which gave rise to La Rochefoucauld's contemptuous insights into human behavior, the worldly wisdom of Montaigne, the aphoristic trenchancy of Pascal's thought, the boldness and open-mindedness of Montesquieu's political reflections. It cannot be my task here to discuss the circumstances which eventually turned the *hommes de lettres* into revolutionaries in the eighteenth century nor the way in which their successors in the nineteenth and twentieth centuries split into the class of the "cultured" on the one hand and of the professional revolutionaries on the other. I mention this historical background only because in Benjamin the element of culture combined in such a unique way with the element of the revolutionary and rebellious. It was as though shortly before its disappearance the figure of the *homme de lettres* was destined to show itself once more in the fullness of its possibilities, although—or, possibly, because—it had lost its material basis in such a catastrophic way, so that the purely intellectual passion which makes this figure so lovable might unfold in all its most telling and impressive possibilities.

There certainly was no dearth of reasons to rebel against his origins, the milieu of German-Jewish society in Imperial Germany, in which Benjamin grew up, nor was there any lack of justification for taking a stand against the Weimar Republic, in which he refused to take up a profession. In *A Berlin Childhood around 1900* Benjamin describes the house from which he came as a "mausoleum long intended for me" (*Schriften* I, 643). Characteristically enough, his father was an art dealer and antiquarian; the family was a wealthy and run-of-the-mill assimilated one; one of his grandparents was Orthodox, the other belonged to a Reform congregation. "In my childhood I was a prisoner of the old and the new West. In those days my clan inhabited these two districts with an attitude mingled of stubbornness and self-confidence, turning them into a ghetto which it regarded as its fief" (*Schriften* I, 643). The stubbornness was toward their Jewishness; it was only stubbornness that made them cling to it. The self-confidence was inspired by their position in the non-Jewish environment in which they had, after all, achieved quite a bit. Just how much was shown on days when guests were expected. On such occasions the inside of the sideboard, which seemed to be the center of the house and thus "with good reason resembled the temple mountains," was opened, and now it was possible "to show off treasures such as idols like to be surrounded with." Then "the house's hoard of silver" appeared, and what was displayed "was there not tenfold, but twentyfold or thirtyfold. And when I looked at these long, long rows of mocha spoons or knife rests, fruit knives or oyster forks, the enjoyment of this profusion struggled with the fear that those who were being expected might all look alike, just as our cutlery did" (*Schriften* I, 632). Even the child knew that something was radically wrong, and not only because there were poor people ("The poor—for the rich children of my age they existed only as beggars. And it was a great advance in my understanding when for the first time poverty dawned on me in the ignominy of poorly paid work" [*Schriften* I, 632]), but because "stubbornness" within and "self-confidence" without were producing an atmosphere of insecurity and self-consciousness which truly was anything but suitable for the raising of children. This was true not only of Benjamin or Berlin West[14] or Germany. With what passion did Kafka try to

---

[14] A fashionable residential area of Berlin.

persuade his sister to put her ten-year-old son in a boarding
school, so as to save him from "the special mentality which is
particularly virulent among wealthy Prague Jews and which cannot be kept away from children . . . this petty, dirty, sly mentality." [15]

What was involved, then, was what had since the 1870's or
1880's been called the Jewish question and existed in that form
only in the German-speaking Central Europe of those decades.
Today this question has been washed away, as it were, by the
catastrophe of European Jewry and is justly forgotten, although
one still encounters it occasionally in the language of the older
generation of German Zionists whose thinking habits derive from
the first decades of this century. Besides, it never was anything
but the concern of the Jewish intelligentsia and had no significance for the majority of Central European Jewry. For the intellectuals, however, it was of great importance, for their own Jewishness, which played hardly any role in their spiritual household,
determined their social life to an extraordinary degree and therefore presented itself to them as a moral question of the first
order. In this moral form the Jewish question marked, in Kafka's
words, "the terrible inner condition of these generations." [16] No
matter how insignificant this problem may appear to us in the
face of what actually happened later, we cannot disregard it
here, for neither Benjamin nor Kafka nor Karl Kraus can be understood without it. For simplicity's sake I shall state the problem
exactly as it was stated and endlessly discussed then—namely,
in an article entitled "German-Jewish Mt. Parnassus" ("Deutsch-
jüdischer Parnass") which created a great stir when Moritz Goldstein published it in 1912 in the distinguished journal *Der Kunst-
wart.*

According to Goldstein, the problem as it appeared to the Jewish intelligentsia had a dual aspect, the non-Jewish environment
and assimilated Jewish society, and in his view the problem was
insoluble. With respect to the non-Jewish environment, "We
Jews administer the intellectual property of a people which

[15] *Ibid.,* p. 339.
[16] *Ibid.,* p. 337.

denies us the right and the ability to do so." And further: "It is easy to show the absurdity of our adversaries' arguments and prove that their enmity is unfounded. What would be gained by this? That their hatred is *genuine*. When all calumnies have been refuted, all distortions rectified, all false judgments about us rejected, antipathy will remain as something irrefutable. Anyone who does not realize this is beyond help." It was the failure to realize this that was felt to be unbearable about Jewish society, whose representatives, on the one hand, wished to remain Jews and, on the other, did not want to acknowledge their Jewishness: "We shall openly drum the problem that they are shirking into them. We shall force them to own up to their Jewishness or to have themselves baptized." But even if this was successful, even if the mendacity of this milieu could be exposed and escaped—what would be gained by it? A "leap into modern Hebrew literature" was impossible for the current generation. Hence: "Our relationship to Germany is one of unrequited love. Let us be manly enough at last to tear the beloved out of our hearts, . . . I have stated what we *must* want to do; I have also stated why we *cannot* want it. My intention was to point up the problem. It is not my fault that I know of no solution." (For himself, Herr Goldstein solved the problem six years later when he became cultural editor of the *Vossische Zeitung*. And what else could he have done?)

One could dispose of Moritz Goldstein by saying that he simply reproduced what Benjamin in another context called "a major part of the *vulgar* anti-Semitic as well as the Zionist ideology" (*Briefe* I, 152–53), if one did not encounter in Kafka, on a far more serious level, a similar formulation of the problem and the same confession of its insolubility. In a letter to Max Brod about German-Jewish writers he said that the Jewish question or "the despair over it was their inspiration—an inspiration as respectable as any other but fraught, upon closer examination, with distressing peculiarities. For one thing, what their despair discharged itself in could not be German literature which on the surface it appeared to be," because the problem was not really a

German one. Thus they lived "among three impossibilities . . . : the impossibility of not writing" as they could get rid of their inspiration only by writing; "the impossibility of writing in German"—Kafka considered their use of the German language as the "overt or covert, or possibly self-tormenting usurpation of an alien property, which has not been acquired but stolen, (relatively) quickly picked up, and which remains someone else's possession even if not a single linguistic mistake can be pointed out"; and finally, "the impossibility of writing differently," since no other language was available. "One could almost add a fourth impossibility," says Kafka in conclusion, "the impossibility of writing, for this despair was not something that could be mitigated through writing"—as is normal for poets, to whom a god has given to say what men suffer and endure. Rather, despair has become here "an enemy of life *and* of writing; writing was here only a moratorium, as it is for someone who writes his last will and testament just before he hangs himself." [17]

Nothing could be easier than to demonstrate that Kafka was wrong and that his own work, which speaks the purest German prose of the century, is the best refutation of his views. But such a demonstration, apart from being in bad taste, is all the more superfluous as Kafka himself was so very much aware of it— "If I indiscriminately write down a sentence," he once noted in his Diaries, "it already is perfect" [18]—just as he was the only one to know that "*Mauscheln*" (speaking a Yiddishized German), though despised by all German-speaking people, Jews or non-Jews, did have a legitimate place in the German language, being nothing else but one of the numerous German dialects. And since he rightly thought that "within the German language, only the dialects and, besides them, the most personal High German are really alive," it naturally was no less legitimate to change from *Mauscheln*, or from Yiddish, to High German than it was to change from Low German or the Alemannic dialect. If one reads Kafka's remarks about the Jewish troupe of actors which so

[17] *Ibid.*, pp. 336–38.
[18] Franz Kafka, *Tagebücher*, p. 42.

fascinated him, it becomes clear that what attracted him were less the specifically Jewish elements than the liveliness of language and gesture.

To be sure, we have some difficulty today in understanding these problems or taking them seriously, especially since it is so tempting to misinterpret and dismiss them as mere reaction to an anti-Semitic milieu and thus as an expression of self-hatred. But nothing could be more misleading when dealing with men of the human stature and intellectual rank of Kafka, Kraus, and Benjamin. What gave their criticism its bitter sharpness was never anti-Semitism as such, but the reaction to it of the Jewish middle class, with which the intellectuals by no means identified. There, too, it was not a matter of the frequently undignified apologetic attitude of official Jewry, with which the intellectuals had hardly any contact, but of the lying denial of the very existence of widespread anti-Semitism, of the isolation from reality staged with all the devices of self-deception by the Jewish bourgeoisie, an isolation which for Kafka, and not only for him, included the often hostile and always haughty separation from the Jewish people, the so-called *Ostjuden* (Jews from Eastern Europe) who were, though one knew better, blamed by them for anti-Semitism. The decisive factor in all this was the loss of reality, aided and abetted by the wealth of these classes. "Among poor people," wrote Kafka, "the world, the bustle of work, so to speak, irresistibly enters the huts . . . and does not allow the musty, polluted, child-consuming air of a nicely furnished family room to be generated." [19] They fought against Jewish society because it would not permit them to live in the world as it happened to be, without illusions—thus, for example, to be prepared for the murder of Walther Rathenau (in 1922): to Kafka it was "incomprehensible that they should have let him live as long as that." [20] What finally determined the acuteness of the problem was the fact that it did not merely, or even primarily, manifest itself as a break between the generation from which one could have escaped by leaving home and family. To only very few

[19] Franz Kafka, *Briefe*, p. 347.
[20] *Ibid.*, p. 378.

German-Jewish writers did the problem present itself in this way, and these few were surrounded by all those others who are already forgotten but from whom they are clearly distinguishable only today when posterity has settled the question of who is who. ("Their political function," wrote Benjamin, "is to establish not parties but cliques, their literary function to produce not schools but fashions, and their economic function to set into the world not producers but agents. Agents or smarties who know how to spend their poverty as if it were riches and who make whoopee out of their yawning vacuity. One could not establish oneself more comfortably in an uncomfortable situation." [21]) Kafka, who exemplified this situation in the above-mentioned letter by "linguistic impossibilities," adding that they could "also be called something quite different," points to a "linguistic middle class" between, as it were, proletarian dialect and high-class prose; it is "nothing but ashes which can be given a semblance of life only by overeager Jewish hands rummaging through them." One need hardly add that the overwhelming majority of Jewish intellectuals belonged to this "middle class"; according to Kafka, they constituted "the hell of German-Jewish letters," in which Karl Kraus held sway as "the great overseer and taskmaster" without noticing how much "he himself belongs in this hell among those to be chastised." [22] That these things may be seen quite differently from a non-Jewish perspective becomes apparent when one reads in one of Benjamin's essays what Brecht said about Karl Kraus: "When the age died by its own hand, he was that hand" (*Schriften* II, 174).

For the Jews of that generation (Kafka and Moritz Goldstein were but ten years older than Benjamin) the available forms of rebellion were Zionism and Communism, and it is noteworthy that their fathers often condemned the Zionist rebellion more bitterly than the Communist. Both were escape routes from il-

[21] In "Der Autor als Produzent," a lecture given in Paris in 1934, in which Benjamin quotes an earlier essay on the intellectual Left. See *Versuche über Brecht*, p. 109.

[22] Quoted in Max Brod, *Franz Kafkas Glauben und Lehre*, Winterthur, 1948.

lusion into reality, from mendacity and self-deception to an honest existence. But this is only how it appears in retrospect. At the time when Benjamin tried, first, a half-hearted Zionism and then a basically no less half-hearted Communism, the two ideologies faced each other with the greatest hostility: the Communists were defaming Zionists as Jewish Fascists [23] and the Zionists were calling the young Jewish Communists "red assimilationists." In a remarkable and probably unique manner Benjamin kept both routes open for himself for years; he persisted in considering the road to Palestine long after he had become a Marxist, without allowing himself to be swayed in the least by the opinions of his Marxist-oriented friends, particularly the Jews among them. This shows clearly how little the "positive" aspect of either ideology interested him, and that what mattered to him in both instances was the "negative" factor of criticism of existing conditions, a way out of bourgeois illusions and untruthfulness, a position outside the literary as well as the academic establishment. He was quite young when he adopted this radically critical attitude, probably without suspecting to what isolation and loneliness it would eventually lead him. Thus we read, for example, in a letter written in 1918, that Walther Rathenau, claiming to represent Germany in foreign affairs, and Rudolf Borchardt, making a similar claim with respect to German spiritual affairs, had in common the *"will* to lie," "the objective mendacity" (*Briefe* I, 189 ff). Neither wanted to "serve" a cause through his works—in Borchardt's case, the "spiritual and linguistic resources" of the people; in Rathenau's, the nation— but both used their works and talents as "sovereign means in the service of an absolute will to power." In addition, there were the littérateurs who placed their gifts in the service of a career and social status: "To be a littérateur is to live under the sign of mere intellect, just as prostitution is to live under the sign of mere sex" (*Schriften* II, 179). Just as a prostitute betrays sexual love, a littérateur betrays the mind, and it was this betrayal of the mind which the best among the Jews could not forgive their

[23] Brecht, for instance, told Benjamin that his essay on Kafka gave aid and comfort to Jewish Fascism. See *Versuche*, p. 123.

colleagues in literary life. In the same vein Benjamin wrote five years later—one year after the assassination of Rathenau—to a close German friend: ". . . Jews today ruin even the best German cause which they publicly champion, because their public statement is necessarily venal (in a deeper sense) and cannot adduce proof of its authenticity" (*Briefe* I, 310). He went on to say that only the private, almost "secret relationships between Germans and Jews" were legitimate, while "everything about German-Jewish relations that works in public causes harm." There was much truth in these words. Written from the perspective of the Jewish question at that time, they supply evidence of the darkness of a period in which one could rightly say, "The light of the public darkens everything" (Heidegger).

As early as 1913 Benjamin weighed the position of Zionism "as a possibility and thus perhaps a necessary commitment" (*Briefe* I, 44) in the sense of this dual rebellion against the parental home and German-Jewish literary life. Two years later he met Gerhard Scholem, encountering in him for the first and only time "Judaism in living form"; soon afterwards came the beginning of that curious, endless consideration, extending over a period of almost twenty years, of emigration to Palestine. "Under certain, by no means impossible conditions I am ready if not determined [to go to Palestine]. Here in Austria the Jews (the decent ones, those who are not making money) talk of nothing else." So he wrote in 1919 (*Briefe* I, 222), but at the same time he regarded such a plan as an "act of violence" (*Briefe* I, 208), unfeasible unless it turned out to be necessary. Whenever such financial or political necessity arose, he reconsidered the project and did not go. It is hard to say whether he was still serious about it after the separation from his wife, who had come from a Zionist milieu. But it is certain that even during his Paris exile he announced that he might go "to Jerusalem in October or November, after a more or less definitive conclusion of my studies" (*Briefe* II, 655). What strikes one as indecision in the letters, as though he were vacillating between Zionism and Marxism, in truth was probably due to his bitter insight that all solutions were not only objectively false and inappropriate to reality, but would lead him personally to a false salvation, no matter whether that salvation was labeled Moscow or Jerusalem. He felt that he would deprive himself of the positive cognitive chances of his own position—"on the top of a mast that is already crumbling" or "dead in his own lifetime and the real survivor" among the ruins. He had settled down in the desperate conditions which corresponded to reality; there he wanted to remain in order to "denature" his own writings "like methylated spirits . . . at the risk of making them unfit for consumption" by anyone then alive but with the chance of being preserved all the more reliably for an unknown future.

For the insolubility of the Jewish question for that generation by no means consisted only in their speaking and writing German or in the fact that their "production plant" was located in Europe—in Benjamin's case, in Berlin West or in Paris, something about which he did "not have the slightest illusions" (*Briefe* II, 531). What was decisive was that these men did not wish to "return" either to the ranks of the Jewish people or to Judaism, and could not desire to do so—not because they believed in "progress" and an automatic disappearance of anti-Semitism or because they were too "assimilated" and too alienated from their Jewish heritage, but because all traditions and cultures as well as all "belonging" had become equally questionable to them. This is what they felt was wrong with the "return" to the Jewish fold as proposed by the Zionists; they could all have said what Kafka once said about being a member of the Jewish people: ". . . My people, provided that I have one." [24]

No doubt, the Jewish question was of great importance for this generation of Jewish writers and explains much of the personal despair so prominent in nearly everything they wrote. But the most clear-sighted among them were led by their personal conflicts to a much more general and more radical problem, namely, to questioning the relevance of the Western tradition as a whole. Not just Marxism as a doctrine but the Communist revolutionary movement exerted a powerful attraction on them because it

[24] Franz Kafka, *Briefe*, p. 183.

implied more than a criticism of existing social and political conditions and took into account the totality of political and spiritual
traditions. For Benjamin, at any rate, this question of the past
and of tradition as such was decisive, and precisely in the sense
in which Scholem, warning his friend against the dangers to his
thinking inherent in Marxism, posed it, albeit without being
aware of the problem. Benjamin, he wrote, was running the risk
of forfeiting the chance of becoming "the legitimate continuer
of the most fruitful and most genuine traditions of a Hamann
and a Humboldt" (*Briefe* II, 526). What he did not understand
was that such a return to and continuation of the past was the
very thing which "the morality of [his] insights," to which
Scholem appealed, was bound to rule out for Benjamin.[25]

It seems tempting to believe, and would indeed be a com-
forting thought, that those few who ventured out onto the most
exposed positions of the time and paid the full price of isolation
at least thought of themselves as the precursors of a new age.
That certainly was not the case. In his essay on Karl Kraus, Benjamin brought up this question: Does Kraus stand "at the
threshold of a new age?" "Alas, by no means. He stands at the
threshold of the Last Judgment" (*Schriften* II, 174). And at this
threshold there really stood all those who later became the masters of the "new age"; they looked upon the dawn of a new age
basically as a decline and viewed history along with the traditions which led up to this decline as a field of ruins.[26] No one

---

[25] In the above-mentioned article Pierre Missac deals with the same
passage and writes: "*Sans sous-estimer la valeur d'une telle réussite [d'être
le successeur de Hamann et de Humboldt], on peut penser que Benjamin
recherchait aussi dans le Marxisme un moyen d'y échapper.*" (Without
underestimating the value of such a success [being the successor of Hamann
and Humboldt], it is possible to think that Benjamin also sought in Marxism
a means of escaping it.)

[26] One is immediately reminded of Brecht's poem "On Poor B.B.—
*Von diesen Städten wird bleiben: der durch sie hindurchging, der Wind!
Fröhlich machet das Haus den Esser: er leert es.
Wir wissen, dass wir Vorläufige sind
Und nach uns wird kommen: nichts Nennenswertes.*
("Of these cities will remain that which blew through them, the wind. /
The house makes the feaster merry. He cleans it out. / We know we're only

has expressed this more clearly than Benjamin in his "Theses on the Philosophy of History," and nowhere has he said it more unequivocally than in a letter from Paris dated 1935: "Actually, I hardly feel constrained to try to make head or tail of this condition of the world. On this planet a great number of civilizations have perished in blood and horror. Naturally, one must wish for the planet that one day it will experience a civilization that has abandoned blood and horror; in fact, I am . . . inclined to assume that our planet is waiting for this. But it is terribly doubtful whether *we* can bring such a present to its hundred- or four-hundred-millionth birthday party. And if we don't, the planet will finally punish us, its unthoughtful well-wishers, by presenting us with the Last Judgment" [27] (*Briefe* II, 698).

Well, in this respect the last thirty years have hardly brought much that could be called new.

temporary and after us will follow / Nothing worth talking about." *The Manual of Piety*, New York, 1966.)

Worth noting, too, is a remarkable aphorism of Kafka in the "Notes from the Year 1920" under the title "HE": "Everything he does appears to him extraordinarily new but also, because of the impossible abundance of the new, extraordinarily amateurish, indeed hardly tolerable, incapable of becoming historical, tearing asunder the chain of generations, breaking off for the first time the music of the world which until now could at least be divined at in all its depth. Sometimes in his conceit he is more worried about the world than about himself."

The predecessor of this mood is, again, Baudelaire. "*Le monde va finir. La seule raison pour laquelle il pouvait durer, c'est qu'elle existe. Que cette raison est faible, comparée à toutes celles qui annoncent le contraire, particulièrement à celle-ci: qu'est-ce que le monde a désormais à faire sous le ciel? . . . Quant à moi qui sens quelquefois en moi le ridicule d'un prophète, je sais que je n'y trouverai jamais la charité d'un médecin. Perdu dans ce vilain monde, coudoyé par les foules, je suis comme un homme lassé dont l'oeil ne voit en arrière, dans les années profondes, que désabusement et amertume, et devant lui qu'un orage où rien de neuf n'est contenu, ni enseignement ni douleur.*" From *Journaux intimes*, Pléiade edition, pp. 1195–97.

[27] *Weltgericht* (Last Judgment) plays on the dual meaning of *Gericht* (judgment; dish). (Translator's note.)

III. THE PEARL DIVER

Full fathom five thy father lies,
Of his bones are coral made,
Those are pearls that were his eyes.
Nothing of him that doth fade
But doth suffer a sea-change
Into something rich and strange.
—*The Tempest*, I, 2

Insofar as the past has been transmitted as tradition, it possesses authority; insofar as authority presents itself historically, it becomes tradition. Walter Benjamin knew that the break in tradition and the loss of authority which occurred in his lifetime, were irreparable, and he concluded that he had to discover new ways of dealing with the past. In this he became a master when he discovered that the transmissibility of the past had been replaced by its citability and that in place of its authority there had arisen a strange power to settle down, piecemeal, in the present and to deprive it of "peace of mind," the mindless peace of complacency. "Quotations in my works are like robbers by the roadside who make an armed attack and relieve an idler of his convictions" (*Schriften* I, 571). This discovery of the modern function of quotations, according to Benjamin, who exemplified it by Karl Kraus, was born out of despair—not the despair of a past that refuses "to throw its light on the future" and lets the human mind "wander in darkness" as in Tocqueville, but out of the despair of the present and the desire to destroy it; hence their power is "not the strength to preserve but to cleanse, to tear out of context, to destroy" (*Schriften* II, 192). Still, the discoverers and lovers of this destructive power originally were inspired by an entirely different intention, the intention to preserve; and only because they did not let themselves be fooled by the professional "preservers" all around them did they finally discover that the destructive power of quotations was "the only one which still contains the hope that something from this period will survive—for no other reason than that it was torn out of it." In this form of "thought fragments," quotations have the double task of interrupting the flow of the presentation with "transcendent force" (*Schriften* I, 142–43) and at the same time of concentrating within themselves that which is presented. As to their weight in Benjamin's writings, quotations are comparable only to the very dissimilar Biblical citations which so often replace the immanent consistency of argumentation in medieval treatises.

I have already mentioned that collecting was Benjamin's central passion. It started early with what he himself called his "bibliomania" but soon extended into something far more characteristic, not so much of the person as of his work: the collecting of quotations. (Not that he ever stopped collecting books. Shortly before the fall of France he seriously considered exchanging his edition of the Collected Works of Kafka, which had recently appeared in five volumes, for a few first editions of Kafka's early writings—an undertaking which naturally was bound to remain incomprehensible to any nonbibliophile.) The "inner need to own a library" (*Briefe* I, 193) asserted itself around 1916, at the time when Benjamin turned in his studies to Romanticism as the "last movement that once more saved tradition" (*Briefe* I, 138). That a certain destructive force was active even in this passion for the past, so characteristic of heirs and latecomers, Benjamin did not discover until much later, when he had already lost his faith in tradition and in the indestructibility of the world. (This will be discussed presently.) In those days, encouraged by Scholem, he still believed that his own estrangement from tradition was probably due to his Jewishness and that there might be a way back for him as there was for his friend, who was preparing to emigrate to Jerusalem. (As early as 1920, when he was not yet seriously beset by financial worries, he thought of learning Hebrew.) He never went as far on this road as did Kafka, who after all his efforts stated bluntly that he had no use for anything Jewish except the Hasidic tales which Buber had just prepared for modern usage—"into everything else I just drift, and another current of air carries me away again." [28] Was he, then, despite all doubts, to go back to the

[28] Cf. Kafka, *Briefe*, p. 173.

German or European past and help with the tradition of its literature?

Presumably this is the form in which the problem presented itself to him in the early twenties, before he turned to Marxism. That is when he chose the German Baroque Age as a subject for his *Habilitation* thesis, a choice that is very characteristic of the ambiguity of this entire, still unresolved cluster of problems. For in the German literary and poetic tradition the Baroque has, with the exception of the great church chorales of the time, never really been alive. Goethe rightly said that when he was eighteen years old, German literature was no older. And Benjamin's choice, baroque in a double sense, has an exact counterpart in Scholem's strange decision to approach Judaism via the Cabala, that is, that part of Hebrew literature which is untransmitted and untransmissible in terms of Jewish tradition, in which it has always had the odor of something downright disreputable. Nothing showed more clearly—so one is inclined to say today—that there was no such thing as a "return" either to the German or the European or the Jewish tradition than the choice of these fields of study. It was an implicit admission that the past spoke directly only through things that had not been handed down, whose seeming closeness to the present was thus due precisely to their exotic character, which ruled out all claims to a binding authority. Obligative truths were replaced by what was in some sense significant or interesting, and this of course meant—as no one knew better than Benjamin—that the "consistence of truth . . . has been lost" (*Briefe* II, 763). Outstanding among the properties that formed this "consistence of truth" was, at least for Benjamin, whose early philosophical interest was theologically inspired, that truth concerned a secret and that the revelation of this secret had authority. Truth, so Benjamin said shortly before he became fully aware of the irreparable break in tradition and the loss of authority, is not "an unveiling which destroys the secret, but the revelation which does it justice" (*Schriften* I, 146). Once this truth had come into the human world at the appropriate moment in history—be it as the Greek *a-letheia*, visually perceptible to the eyes of the mind and comprehended by us as "un-concealment" ("*Unverborgenheit*"—Heidegger), or as the acoustically perceptible word of God as we know it from the European religions of revelation—it was this "consistence" peculiar to it which made it tangible, as it were, so that it could be handed down by tradition. Tradition transforms truth into wisdom, and wisdom is the consistence of transmissible truth. In other words, even if truth should appear in our world, it could not lead to wisdom, because it would no longer have the characteristics which it could acquire only through universal recognition of its validity. Benjamin discusses these matters in connection with Kafka and says that of course "Kafka was far from being the first to face this situation. Many had accommodated themselves to it, adhering to truth or whatever they regarded as truth at any given time and, with a more or less heavy heart, forgoing its transmissibility. Kafka's real genius was that he tried something entirely new: he sacrificed truth for the sake of clinging to the transmissibility" (*Briefe* II, 763). He did so by making decisive changes in traditional parables or inventing new ones in traditional style;[29] however, these "do not modestly lie at the feet of the doctrine," as do the haggadic tales in the Talmud, but "unexpectedly raise a heavy claw" against it. Even Kafka's reaching down to the sea bottom of the past had this peculiar duality of wanting to preserve and wanting to destroy. He wanted to preserve it even though it was not truth, if only for the sake of this "new beauty in what is vanishing" (see Benjamin's essay on Leskov); and he knew, on the other hand, that there is no more effective way to break the spell of tradition than to cut out the "rich and strange," coral and pearls, from what had been handed down in one solid piece.

Benjamin exemplified this ambiguity of gesture in regard to the past by analyzing the collector's passion which was his own. Collecting springs from a variety of motives which are not easily understood. As Benjamin was probably the first to emphasize, collecting is the passion of children, for whom things are not yet commodities and are not valued according to their usefulness,

---

[29] A selection appeared under the title *Parables and Paradoxes* in a bilingual edition (Schocken Books, New York, 1961).

and it is also the hobby of the rich, who own enough not to need anything useful and hence can afford to make "the transfiguration of objects" (*Schriften* I, 416) their business. In this they must of necessity discover the beautiful, which needs "disinterested delight" (Kant) to be recognized. At any rate, a collected object possesses only an amateur value and no use value whatsoever. (Benjamin was not yet aware of the fact that collecting can also be an eminently sound and often highly profitable form of investment.) And inasmuch as collecting can fasten on any category of objects (not just art objects, which are in any case removed from the everyday world of use objects because they are "good" for nothing) and thus, as it were, redeem the object as a thing since it now is no longer a means to an end but has its intrinsic worth, Benjamin could understand the collector's passion as an attitude akin to that of the revolutionary. Like the revolutionary, the collector "dreams his way not only into a remote or bygone world, but at the same time into a better one in which, to be sure, people are not provided with what they need any more than they are in the everyday world, but in which things are liberated from the drudgery of usefulness" (*Schriften* I, 416). Collecting is the redemption of things which is to complement the redemption of man. Even the reading of his books is something questionable to a true bibliophile: " 'And you have read all these?' Anatole France is said to have been asked by an admirer of his library. 'Not one-tenth of them. I don't suppose you use your Sèvres china every day?' " ("Unpacking My Library"). (In Benjamin's library there were collections of rare children's books and of books by mentally deranged authors; since he was interested neither in child psychology nor in psychiatry, these books, like many others among his treasures, literally were not good for anything, serving neither to divert nor to instruct.) Closely connected with this is the fetish character which Benjamin explicitly claimed for collected objects. The value of genuineness which is decisive for the collector as well as for the market determined by him has replaced the "cult value" and is its secularization.

These reflections, like so much else in Benjamin, have something of the ingeniously brilliant which is not characteristic of his essential insights, which are, for the most part, quite down-to-earth. Still, they are striking examples of the *flânerie* in his thinking, of the way his mind worked, when he, like the *flâneur* in the city, entrusted himself to chance as a guide on his intellectual journeys of exploration. Just as strolling through the treasures of the past is the inheritor's luxurious privilege, so is the "collector's attitude, in the highest sense, the attitude of the heir" ("Unpacking My Library") who, by taking possession of things—and "ownership is the most profound relationship that one can have to objects" (*ibid.*)—establishes himself in the past, so as to achieve, undisturbed by the present, "a renewal of the old world." And since this "deepest urge" in the collector has no public significance whatsoever but results in a strictly private hobby, everything "that is said from the angle of the true collector" is bound to appear as "whimsical" as the typically Jean Paulian vision of one of those writers "who write books not because they are poor, but because they are dissatisfied with the books which they could buy but don't like" (*ibid.*). Upon closer examination, however, this whimsicality has some noteworthy and not so harmless peculiarities. There is, for one thing, the gesture, so significant of an era of public darkness, with which the collector not only withdraws from the public into the privacy of his four walls but takes along with him all kinds of treasures that once were public property to decorate them. (This, of course, is not today's collector, who gets hold of whatever has or, in his estimate, will have a market value or can enhance his social status, but the collector who, like Benjamin, seeks strange things that are considered valueless.) Also, in his passion for the past for its own sake, born of his contempt for the present as such and therefore rather heedless of objective quality, there already appears a disturbing factor to announce that tradition may be the last thing to guide him and traditional values by no means be as safe in his hands as one might have assumed at first glance.

For tradition puts the past in order, not just chronologically but first of all systematically in that it separates the positive from the negative, the orthodox from the heretical, that which is obligatory and relevant from the mass of irrelevant or merely interesting opinions and data. The collector's passion, on the other hand, is not only unsystematic but borders on the chaotic, not so much because it is a passion as because it is not primarily kindled by the quality of the object—something that is classifiable—but is inflamed by its "genuineness," its uniqueness, something that defies any systematic classification. Therefore, while tradition discriminates, the collector levels all differences; and this leveling—so that "the positive and the negative . . . predilection and rejection are here closely contiguous" (*Schriften* II, 313)—takes place even if the collector has made tradition itself his special field and carefully eliminated everything not recognized by it. Against tradition the collector pits the criterion of genuineness; to the authoritative he opposes the sign of origin. To express this way of thinking in theoretical terms: he replaces content with pure originality or authenticity, something that only French Existentialism established as a quality *per se* detached from all specific characteristics. If one carries this way of thinking to its logical conclusion, the result is a strange inversion of the original collector's drive: "The genuine picture may be old, but the genuine thought is new. It is of the present. This present may be meager, granted. But no matter what it is like, one must firmly take it by the horns to be able to consult the past. It is the bull whose blood must fill the pit if the shades of the departed are to appear at its edge" (*Schriften* II, 314). Out of this present when it has been sacrificed for the invocation of the past arises then "the deadly impact of thought" which is directed against tradition and the authority of the past.

Thus the heir and preserver unexpectedly turns into a destroyer. "The true, greatly misunderstood passion of the collector is always anarchistic, destructive. For this is its dialectics: to combine with loyalty to an object, to individual items, to things sheltered in his care, a stubborn subversive protest against the typical, the classifiable." [30] The collector destroys the context in which

[30] Benjamin, "Lob der Puppe," *Literarische Welt*, Jan. 10, 1930.

his object once was only part of a greater, living entity, and since only the uniquely genuine will do for him he must cleanse the chosen object of everything that is typical about it. The figure of the collector, as old-fashioned as that of the *flâneur*, could assume such eminently modern features in Benjamin because history itself—that is, the break in tradition which took place at the beginning of this century—had already relieved him of this task of destruction and he only needed to bend down, as it were, to select his precious fragments from the pile of debris. In other words, the things themselves offered, particularly to a man who firmly faced the present, an aspect which had previously been discoverable only from the collector's whimsical perspective.

I do not know when Benjamin discovered the remarkable coincidence of his old-fashioned inclinations with the realities of the times; it must have been in the mid-twenties, when he began the serious study of Kafka, only to discover shortly thereafter in Brecht the poet who was most at home in this century. I do not mean to assert that Benjamin shifted his emphasis from the collecting of books to the collecting of quotations (exclusive with him) overnight or even within one year, although there is some evidence in the letters of a conscious shifting of emphasis. At any rate, nothing was more characteristic of him in the thirties than the little notebooks with black covers which he always carried with him and in which he tirelessly entered in the form of quotations what daily living and reading netted him in the way of "pearls" and "coral." On occasion he read from them aloud, showed them around like items from a choice and precious collection. And in this collection, which by then was anything but whimsical, it was easy to find next to an obscure love poem from the eighteenth century the latest newspaper item, next to Goecking's "Der erste Schnee" a report from Vienna dated Summer 1939, saying that the local gas company had "stopped supplying gas to Jews. The gas consumption of the Jewish population involved a loss for the gas company, since the biggest consumers were the ones who did not pay their bills. The Jews used the gas especially for committing suicide" (*Briefe* II, 820).

Here indeed the shades of the departed were invoked only from the sacrificial pit of the present.

The close affinity between the break in tradition and the seemingly whimsical figure of the collector who gathers his fragments and scraps from the debris of the past is perhaps best illustrated by the fact, astonishing only at first glance, that there probably was no period before ours in which old and ancient things, many of them long forgotten by tradition, have become general educational material which is handed to schoolboys everywhere in hundreds of thousands of copies. This amazing revival, particularly of classical culture, which since the forties has been especially noticeable in relatively traditionless America, began in Europe in the twenties. There it was initiated by those who were most aware of the irreparability of the break in tradition—thus in Germany, and not only there, first and foremost by Martin Heidegger, whose extraordinary, and extraordinarily early, success in the twenties was essentially due to a "listening to the tradition that does not give itself up to the past but thinks of the present." [31] Without realizing it, Benjamin actually had more in common with Heidegger's remarkable sense for living eyes and living bones that had sea-changed into pearls and coral, and as such could be saved and lifted into the present only by doing violence to their context in interpreting them with "the deadly impact" of new thoughts, than he did with the dialectical subtleties of his Marxist friends. For just as the above-cited closing sentence from the Goethe essay sounds as though Kafka had written it, the following words from a letter to Hofmannsthal dated 1924 make one think of some of Heidegger's essays written in the forties and fifties: "The conviction which guides me in my literary attempts . . . [is] that each truth has its home, its ancestral palace, in language, that this palace was built with the oldest *logoi*, and that to a truth thus founded the insights of the sciences will remain inferior for as long as they make do here and there in the area of language like nomads, as it were, in the conviction of the sign character of language which produces the

[31] See Martin Heidegger, *Kants These über das Sein*, Frankfurt, 1962, p. 8.

irresponsible arbitrariness of their terminology" (*Briefe* I, 329). In the spirit of Benjamin's early work on the philosophy of language, words are "the opposite of all communication directed toward the outside," just as truth is "the death of intention." Anyone who seeks truth fares like the man in the fable about the veiled picture at Saïs: "this is caused not by some mysterious monstrousness of the content to be unveiled but by the nature of truth before which even the purest fire of searching is extinguished as though under water" (*Schriften* I, 131, 152).

From the Goethe essay on, quotations are at the center of every work of Benjamin's. This very fact distinguishes his writings from scholarly works of all kinds in which it is the function of quotations to verify and document opinions, wherefore they can safely be relegated to the Notes. This is out of the question in Benjamin. When he was working on his study of German tragedy, he boasted of a collection of "over 600 quotations very systematically and clearly arranged" (*Briefe* I, 339); like the later notebooks, this collection was not an accumulation of excerpts intended to facilitate the writing of the study but constituted the main work, with the writing as something secondary. The main work consisted in tearing fragments out of their context and arranging them afresh in such a way that they illustrated one another and were able to prove their *raison d'être* in a free-floating state, as it were. It definitely was a sort of surrealistic montage. Benjamin's ideal of producing a work consisting entirely of quotations, one that was mounted so masterfully that it could dispense with any accompanying text, may strike one as whimsical in the extreme and self-destructive to boot, but it was not, any more than were the contemporaneous surrealistic experiments which arose from similar impulses. To the extent that an accompanying text by the author proved unavoidable, it was a matter of fashioning it in such a way as to preserve "the intention of such investigations," namely, "to plumb the depths of language and thought . . . by drilling rather than excavating" (*Briefe* I, 329), so as not to ruin everything with explanations that seek to provide a causal or systematic connection. In so doing Benjamin was quite aware that this new method of "drilling" resulted in a certain "forcing of insights . . . whose inelegant pedantry, however, is preferable to today's almost universal habit of falsifying them"; it was equally clear to him that this method was bound to be "the cause of certain obscurities" (*Briefe* I, 330). What mattered to him above all was to avoid anything that might be reminiscent of empathy, as though a given subject of investigation had a message in readiness which easily communicated itself, or could be communicated, to the reader or spectator: *"No poem is intended for the reader, no picture for the beholder, no symphony for the listener"* ("The Task of the Translator"; italics added).

This sentence, written quite early, could serve as motto for all of Benjamin's literary criticism. It should not be misunderstood as another dadaist affront of an audience that even then had already become quite used to all sorts of merely capricious shock effects and "put-ons." Benjamin deals here with thought things, particularly those of a linguistic nature, which, according to him, "retain their meaning, possibly their best significance, if they are not *a priori* applied exclusively to man. For example, one could speak of an unforgettable life or moment even if all men had forgotten them. If the nature of such a life or moment required that it not be forgotten, that predicate would not contain a falsehood but merely a claim that is not being fulfilled by men, and perhaps also a reference to a realm in which it *is* fulfilled: God's remembrance" (*ibid.*). Benjamin later gave up this theological background but not the theory and not his method of drilling to obtain the essential in the form of quotations—as one obtains water by drilling for it from a source concealed in the depths of the earth. This method is like the modern equivalent of ritual invocations, and the spirits that now arise invariably are those spiritual essences from a past that have suffered the Shakespearean "sea-change" from living eyes to pearls, from living bones to coral. For Benjamin to quote is to name, and naming rather than speaking, the word rather than the sentence, brings truth to light. As one may read in the preface to the *Origin of German Tragedy*, Benjamin regarded truth as an exclusively acoustical phenomenon: "Not Plato but Adam," who gave things their names, was to him the "father of philosophy." Hence tradition was the form in which these name-giving words were transmitted; it too was an essentially acoustical phenomenon. He felt himself so akin to Kafka precisely because the latter, current misinterpretations notwithstanding, had "no far-sightedness or 'prophetic vision,'" but listened to tradition, and "he who listens hard does not see" ("Max Brod's Book on Kafka").

There are good reasons why Benjamin's philosophical interest from the outset concentrated on the philosophy of language, and why finally naming through quoting became for him the only possible and appropriate way of dealing with the past without the aid of tradition. Any period to which its own past has become as questionable as it has to us must eventually come up against the phenomenon of language, for in it the past is contained ineradicably, thwarting all attempts to get rid of it once and for all. The Greek *polis* will continue to exist at the bottom of our political existence—that is, at the bottom of the sea—for as long as we use the word "politics." This is what the semanticists, who with good reason attack language as the one bulwark behind which the past hides—its confusion, as they say—fail to understand. They are absolutely right: in the final analysis all problems are linguistic problems; they simply do not know the implications of what they are saying.

But Benjamin, who could not yet have read Wittgenstein, let alone his successors, knew a great deal about these very things, because from the beginning the problem of truth had presented itself to him as a "revelation . . . which must be heard, that is, which lies in the metaphysically acoustical sphere." To him, therefore, language was by no means primarily the gift of speech which distinguishes man from other living beings, but, on the contrary, "the world essence . . . from which speech arises" (*Briefe* I, 197), which incidentally comes quite close to Heidegger's position that "man can speak only insofar as he is the sayer." Thus there is "a language of truth, the tensionless and even silent depository of the ultimate secrets which all thought is concerned with" ("The Task of the Translator"), and this is "the true language" whose existence we assume unthinkingly as soon as we translate from one language into another. That is why Benjamin places at the center of his essay "The Task of the Translator" the astonishing quotation from Mallarmé in which the spoken languages in their multiplicity and diversity suffocate, as it were, by virtue of their Babel-like tumult, the *"immortelle parole,"* which cannot even be thought, since "thinking is writing without implement or whispers, silently," and thus prevent the voice of truth from being heard on earth with the force of material, tangible evidence. Whatever theoretical revisions Benjamin may subsequently have made in these theological-metaphysical convictions, his basic approach, decisive for all his literary studies, remained unchanged: not to investigate the utilitarian or communicative functions of linguistic creations, but to understand them in their crystallized and thus ultimately fragmentary form as intentionless and noncommunicative utterances of a "world essence." What else does this mean than that he understood language as an essentially poetic phenomenon? And this is precisely what the last sentence of the Mallarmé aphorism, which he does not quote, says in unequivocal clarity: *"Seulement, sachons n'existerait pas le vers: lui, philosophiquement remunère le défaut des langues, complément supérieur"*—all this were true if poetry did not exist, the poem that philosophically makes good the defect of languages, is their superior complement.[32] All of which says no more, though in a slightly more complex way, than what I mentioned before—namely, that we are dealing here with something which may not be unique but is certainly extremely rare: the gift of *thinking poetically.*

And this thinking, fed by the present, works with the "thought fragments" it can wrest from the past and gather about itself. Like a pearl diver who descends to the bottom of the sea, not to excavate the bottom and bring it to light but to pry loose the rich and the strange, the pearls and the coral in the depths and to carry them to the surface, this thinking delves into the depths of the past—but not in order to resuscitate it the way it was and to contribute to the renewal of extinct ages. What guides this

[32] For the aphorism by Mallarmé, see "Variations sur un sujet" under the subtitle "Crise des vers," Pléiade edition, pp. 363–64.

thinking is the conviction that although the living is subject to the ruin of the time, the process of decay is at the same time a process of crystallization, that in the depth of the sea, into which sinks and is dissolved what once was alive, some things "suffer a sea-change" and survive in new crystallized forms and shapes that remain immune to the elements, as though they waited only for the pearl diver who one day will come down to them and bring them up into the world of the living—as "thought fragments," as something "rich and strange," and perhaps even as everlasting *Urphänomene.*

BERTOLT BRECHT

1898-1956

You hope, yes,
                    your books will excuse you,
save you from hell:
                    nevertheless,
without looking sad,
                    without in any way
seeming to blame
                    (He doesn't need to,
knowing well
                    what a lover of art
like yourself pays heed to),
                    God may reduce you
on Judgment Day
                    to tears of shame,
reciting by heart
                    the poems you would
have written, had
                    your life been good.

                                        W. H. Auden

I

WHEN Bertolt Brecht sought, and found, refuge in this country in 1941, he went to Hollywood "to join the sellers" on "the market where lies are bought," and wherever he went he heard the words "*Spell your name.*" [1] He had been famous in German-speaking countries since the early twenties, and he did not particularly like to be unknown and poor again. In 1947, he was called before the Committee on Un-American Activities; he appeared with a ticket to Zürich in his pocket, was greatly praised for being so

---

[1] Almost all of Brecht's poems exist in several versions. Unless otherwise noted I shall quote from the Collected Works published since the late nineteen-fifties by Suhrkamp in West Germany and the Aufbau-Verlag in East Berlin. The first two quotations are from "Hollywood" and "Sonett

"co-operative," and left the country. But when Brecht tried to settle in West Germany, the military-occupation authorities refused the necessary permission.[2] This turned out to be almost equally unfortunate for Germany and for Brecht himself. In 1949, he settled down in East Berlin, where he was given the direction of a theater and, for the first time in his life, ample opportunity to watch the Communist variety of total domination at close range. He died in August, 1956.

Since Brecht's death, his fame has spread all over Europe—even to Russia—and also to the English-speaking countries. With the exception of *The Seven Deadly Sins of the Petty Bourgeois*, a minor work translated by W. H. Auden and Chester Kallman (their superb translation of *The Rise and Fall of the City Mahagonny* was never published), and *Galileo*, translated by Charles Laughton and Brecht himself, none of his plays and, alas, few of his poems have appeared in an English translation worthy of this great poet and playwright; nor have any of his plays—except for the *Galileo*, with Charles Laughton, that lasted six performances in New York in the late forties, and, perhaps, *The Caucasian*

---

in der Emigration," *Gedichte 1941–1947*, vol. VI. The first two stanzas of the "Sonnet in the Emigration" are noteworthy because they contain a personal complaint—something very rare in Brecht's poetry.

Verjagt aus meinem Land muss ich nun sehn
Wie ich zu einem neuen Laden komme, einer Schenke
Wo ich verkaufen kann das, was ich denke.
Die alten Wege muss ich wieder gehn

Die glatt geschliffenen durch den Tritt der Hoffnungslosen!
Schon gehend, weiss ich jetzt noch nicht: zu wem?
Wohin ich komme hör' ich: Spell your name!
Ach, dieser "name" gehörte zu den grossen!

(Hunted out of my country, I now must see how to open a new shop, some place where I can sell what I think. I must take the old paths, worn smooth by the steps of the hopeless ones! Already on my way, I don't know yet: to whom am I going? Wherever I come, I hear: Spell your name! Oh, this "name" was one of the great ones.)

[2] Martin Esslin, author of *Brecht: The Man and His Work* (Anchor Books, 1961), stated recently that Brecht "could have gone back into Germany whenever he wanted . . . ; what was difficult at that time was for Germans to *leave* Germany, not to get in." ("Brecht at Seventy," in *tdr*, Fall 1967.) This is an error; but it is true that Brecht "wanted non-German travel documents precisely to keep his line of retreat open."

Chalk Circle at Lincoln Center in 1966—been given a worthy English-language production. An adequate, though not very distinguished, translation of Brecht's first book of poems—*Die Hauspostille*, which appeared in 1927—by Eric Bentley, with good annotations by Hugo Schmidt, has been published by Grove Press under the title *Manual of Piety*. (I shall use this translation in some of the following.) But fame has its own momentum, and although it has sometimes been a bit difficult to understand why people who don't know a word of German should get excited and enthusiastic about Brecht in English, the excitement and enthusiasm are welcome, because they are entirely deserved. Fame has also covered up the circumstances that made it necessary for Brecht to go to East Berlin, and this, too, is welcome to anyone who thinks back to the time when second-rate critics and third-rate writers could denounce him with impunity.[3]

Still, Brecht's political biography, a kind of case history of the uncertain relationship between poetry and politics, is no slight matter, and now, when his fame is secure, the time may have come when it is possible to raise certain questions without being misunderstood. To be sure, the fact of Brecht's doctrinaire and often ludicrous adherence to the Communist ideology as such need hardly cause serious concern. In a poem written in America during the war but published only recently, Brecht himself has defined the only point of importance. Addressing his German fellow poets under Hitler, he said, "Be on your guard, you who sing this man Hitler. I . . . know that he'll soon die and that, dying, he'll have outlived his fame. But even if he made the earth unfit for habitation by conquering it, no poem praising him could last. True, too quickly does the wail of pain of whole continents

---

[3] To avoid misunderstandings, Brecht fared no better with Communist literary critics, and what he said about them, in 1938, applies equally to "anti-Communists": "Lukács, Gabor, Kurella . . . are enemies of production. Productivity makes them suspicious. It is unreliable, it is unpredictable. You never know what is going to happen with productivity. And they themselves don't want to produce. They want to play at being *apparatchiks*, to have control over others. Each of their criticisms contains a threat." (See Walter Benjamin, "Gespräche mit Brecht," in *Versuche über Brecht*, Frankfurt, 1966.)

die down to drown out the hymn to the tormentor. True, those
who praise the outrage, they, too, have fine-sounding voices. And
yet it is the dying swan's song that is held to be the most beautiful: he sings without fear." [4] Brecht was right and wrong; no
poem praising Hitler or Hitler's war has survived Hitler's death,
because none of the hymnists had a "fine-sounding voice." (The
only German poem of the last war that will last is Brecht's own
"Children's Crusade 1939," a ballad written in the moving bitter-
sad tone of folk songs and telling the story of fifty-five war
orphans and a dog in Poland who set out for *"ein Land, wo Frie-
den war"*—"a country where peace was"—and didn't know the
way.) But Brecht's voice sounds fine enough in the lines to his
fellow poets, and one doesn't quite see why he did not publish
them—except that he might have known how a simple change of
name would cause the poem to boomerang upon him: How about
his ode to Stalin and his praise of Stalin's crimes, written and published while he was in East Berlin but mercifully omitted from
the collection of his works? Didn't he know what he was doing?
Oh, yes, he did: "Last night in a dream I saw fingers pointing
at me as though I were a leper. They were worn and they were
broken. 'You don't know!' I cried out, conscious of guilt." [5]

To talk about poets is an uncomfortable task; poets are there
to be quoted, not to be talked about. Those whose specialty is
literature, and among whom we now find the "Brecht scholars,"
have learned how to overcome their unease, but I am not one of
them. The voice of the poets, however, concerns all of us, not only
critics and scholars; it concerns us in our private lives and also
insofar as we are citizens. We don't need to deal with *engagé*
poets in order to feel justified in talking about them from a politi-

[4] "Briefe über Gelesenes," *Gedichte*, vol. VI.
[5] "Böser Morgen," *Gedichte 1948–1956*, vol. VII. Brecht's praise of Stalin
has been carefully eliminated from his *Collected Works*. The only traces are
to be found in *Prosa*, vol. V, the posthumously published *Me-ti* notes (see
note 33). There Stalin is praised as "the useful one" and his crimes are
justified (pp. 6off. and 100f.). Immediately after his death, Brecht wrote
that he had been "the incarnation of hope" for "the oppressed of five continents." (*Sinn und Form*, vol. 2, 1953, p. 10). Cf. also the poem in *op. cit.*,
II, 2, 1950, p. 128.

cal viewpoint, as citizens, but it seems easier for a non-literary person to engage in this activity if political attitudes and commitments have played an all-important role in the life and work of an author, as they did in Brecht's.

The first thing to be pointed out is that poets have not often made good, reliable citizens; Plato, himself a great poet in philosopher's disguise, was not the first to be sorely worried and annoyed by poets. There has always been trouble with them; they have often shown a deplorable tendency to misbehave, and in our century their misbehavior has on occasion been of even deeper concern to citizens then ever before. We need only remember the case of Ezra Pound. The United States government decided not to put him on trial for treason in wartime, because he could plead insanity, whereupon a committee of poets did, in a way, what the government chose not to—it judged him—and the result was an award to him for having written the best poetry of 1948. The poets honored him regardless of his misbehavior or insanity. They judged the poet; it was not their business to judge the citizen. And since they were poets themselves, they might have thought in Goethe's terms: *"Dichter sündgen nicht schwer;"* that is, poets do not shoulder such a heavy burden of guilt when they misbehave—one shouldn't take their sins altogether seriously. But Goethe's line had reference to different sins, light sins, such as Brecht speaks of when, in his irrepressible desire to tell the least welcome truths—which, indeed, was one of his great virtues—he says, addressing his womenfolk, "In me you have a man on whom you can't rely," [6] knowing so well that what women want most in their menfolk is reliability—the thing that poets can afford least. They can't afford it because those whose business it is to soar must shun gravity. They must not be tied down, and hence cannot bear as much responsibility as others must.

And Brecht, it now turns out, knew this very well though he never admitted it publicly. He often had thought, he said in a conversation in 1934, "of a tribunal before which I might be in-

---

[6] *"In mir habt ihr einen, auf den könnt ihr nicht bauen,"* in "Vom armen B.B.," the last poem of the *Hauspostille, Gedichte 1918–1929,* vol. I.

terrogated. 'How is it? Are you really serious?' I should then have to admit: Entirely serious I am not. There are too many artistic matters, matters concerning the theater, I think of to be entirely serious. But having said no to this important question I would add an even more important statement, namely, that my attitude is *legitimate*." In order to clarify what he meant he proposed the following: "Let's assume you read an excellent political novel and later learn that its author is Lenin; you would change your opinion on book and author to the detriment of both." [7] But there are sins and sins. Undeniably, Ezra Pound's sins were more serious; it was not merely a case of foolishly succumbing to Mussolini's exercises in oratory. In his vicious radio broadcasts, he went far beyond Mussolini's worst speeches, doing Hitler's business and proving to be one of the worst Jew-baiters among the intellectuals on either side of the Atlantic. To be sure, he had disliked Jews before the war and has disliked them since, and this dislike is his private affair, of hardly any political importance. It is quite another matter to trumpet this kind of aversion to the world at a moment when Jews are being killed by the millions. However, Pound could plead insanity and get away with things that Brecht, entirely sane and highly intelligent, was not able to get away with. Brecht's sins were smaller than Pound's, yet he sinned more heavily, because he was only a poet, not an insane one.

For, despite the poets' lack of gravity, reliability, and responsibility, they obviously can't get away with everything. But where to draw the line we, their fellow citizens, are hardly able to decide. Villon almost ended on the gallows—God knows, perhaps rightly so—but his songs still gladden our hearts, and we honor him for them. There is no surer way to make a fool of oneself than to draw up a code of behavior for poets, though quite a number of serious and respectable men have done it. Luckily for us and for the poets, we don't have to go to this absurd trouble, nor do we have to rely on our everyday standards of judgment. A poet is to be judged by his poetry, and while much is permitted

[7] Walter Benjamin, *op. cit.*, pp. 118–19.

him, it is not true that "those who praise the outrage have fine-sounding voices." At least, it was not true in Brecht's case; his odes to Stalin, that great father and murderer of peoples, sound as though they had been fabricated by the least gifted imitator Brecht ever had. The worst that can happen to a poet is that he should cease to be a poet, and that is what happened to Brecht in the last years of his life. He may have thought that the odes to Stalin did not matter. Weren't they written out of fear, and hadn't he always believed that almost everything is justified in the face of violence? This was the wisdom of his "Mr. Keuner," who, however, around 1930 was still a bit more fastidious in the choice of his means than his author twenty years later. In dark times, so one of the stories goes, there came an agent of the rulers to the home of a man who "had learnt how to say no." The agent claimed the man's home and food as his own and asked him, "Will you wait upon me?" The man put him to bed, covered him with a blanket, guarded his sleep, and obeyed him for seven years. But whatever he did, he never spoke a single word. After the seven years were over, the agent had grown fat with eating, sleeping, and giving orders, and he died. The man wrapped him in the rotten blanket, threw him out of the house, washed the bed, painted the walls, sighed with relief, and answered, "No." [8] Had Brecht forgotten Mr. Keuner's wisdom not to say "Yes"? In any event, what concerns us here is the sad fact that the few poems of his last years, published posthumously, are weak and thin. The exceptions are minor. There is the much-quoted witticism after the workers' rebellion of 1953: "After the rebellion of the seventeenth of June . . . one could read that the people had forfeited the government's confidence and could regain it only by redoubling their work efforts. Would it not be simpler for the government to dissolve the people and elect another one?" [9] There are a number of very touching lines in love poems and nursery rhymes. And, most important, there are praises of purposelessness, of which the best sounds like a half-conscious

[8] In the "Geschichten vom Herrn Keuner," *Versuche 1–3*, Berlin, 1930.
[9] *Gedichte*, vol. VII, entitled "Die Lösung."

variation on Angelus Silesius's famous "Ohne Warum." ("The rose is without why; it blooms because it blooms,/It cares not for itself, asks not if it is seen.")[10] Brecht writes:

> Ach, wie sollen wir die kleine Rose buchen?
> Plötzlich dunkelrot und jung und nah?
> Ach, wir kamen nicht, sie zu besuchen
> Aber als wir kamen, war sie da.
>
> Eh sie da war, ward sie nicht erwartet.
> Als sie da war, ward sie kaum geglaubt.
> Ach, zum Ziele kam, was nie gestartet.
> Aber war es so nicht überhaupt?[11]

That Brecht could write such verses at all indicates an unexpected and decisive shift in the poet's mood; only his early poetry, in the *Manual of Piety*, shows the same freedom from worldly purposes and cares, and in the place of the earlier tone of jubilation or defiance there is now the peculiar stillness of wonder and gratitude. The one perfect product of these last years, consisting of two four-line love stanzas, is a variation on a German nursery rhyme, and therefore untranslatable.[12]

> Sieben Rosen hat der Strauch
> Sechs gehör'n dem Wind
> Aber eine bleibt, dass auch
> Ich noch eine find.
>
> Sieben Male ruf ich dich
> Sechsmal bleibe fort
> Doch beim siebten Mal, versprich
> Komme auf ein Wort.

Everything indicated that the poet had found a new voice—perhaps "the dying swan's song that is held to be the most beau-

[10] Angelus Silesius, *Cherubinischer Wandersmann* (1657), Book I, 289, in *Werke*, München, 1949, vol. III.

[11] "How, oh how can we account for the little rose? Suddenly dark red and young and near? Oh, we didn't come to visit her, but when we came she was there.

"Before she was, she wasn't expected; when she appeared she was hard to believe in. Oh, something arrived that had never been started. But is that not the way it has always been?"
In *Gedichte*, vol. VII.

[12] *Ibid.*, p. 84.

tiful"—but when the moment came for the voice to be heard, it seemed to have lost its power. This is the only objective and therefore unquestionable sign we have that he had transgressed the rather wide limits set for poets, that he had crossed the line marking what was permitted to him. For these boundaries, alas, cannot be detected from the outside, and can hardly even be guessed at. They are like faint ridges, all but invisible to the naked eye, which, once a man has crossed them—or not even actually crossed them but just stumbled over them—suddenly grow into walls. There is no retracing of steps; whatever he does, he finds himself with his back against the wall. And even now, *après coup*, it is difficult to define the cause; our only evidence that the step was taken is supplied by the poetry, and all it tells us is the moment when it happened, when the punishment caught up with him. For the only meaningful punishment that a poet can suffer, short of death, is, of course, the sudden loss of what throughout human history has appeared a divine gift.

To Brecht the loss clearly came rather late, and hence it can teach us a lesson about the great permissiveness enjoyed by those who live under the laws of Apollo. It did not come when he became a Communist; to be a Communist in Europe in the twenties, and even the early thirties (at least for people who were not in the thick of things and could not know to what an extent Stalin had changed the Party into a totalitarian movement, ready to commit any crime and every betrayal, including the betrayal of the revolution), was no sin but merely an error. However, it did not come, either, when Brecht failed to break with the Party during the Moscow Trials, in which some of his friends were among the defendants, or during the Spanish Civil War, when he must have known that the Russians did everything they could to the detriment of the Spanish Republic, using the misfortunes of the Spanish to get even with anti-Stalinists inside and outside the Party. (He said in 1938, "Actually I have no friends there [in Moscow]; and the people in Moscow have no friends either—like the dead." [13]) And it did not come when, at the time of the Hitler-

[13] Benjamin, *op. cit.*, p. 133.

Stalin pact, Brecht failed to speak out, let alone to sever his relations to the Party; on the contrary, the years he spent in exile, first in the Danish city of Svendborg and then in Santa Monica, were creatively the best years of his life, comparable in sheer productivity only to his youth, when he was still uninfluenced by ideology and had not yet subjected himself to any political discipline. It came, finally, after he had settled down in East Berlin, where he could see, day after day, what it meant to the people to live under a Communist regime.

Not that he had wanted to settle down there; from December, 1947, until Fall, 1949, he had waited in Zürich for permission to settle in Munich,[14] and only when he had to give up all hope of getting it did he decide to go home as best he could—well provided against all hazards with a Czech passport soon to be exchanged for an Austrian one, a Swiss bank account, and a West German publisher. Up to that unfortunate moment, he had been quite careful not to come into close contact with his friends in the East. In 1933, when many of his friends foolishly believed they could find asylum in Soviet Russia, he went to Denmark, and when he fled Europe at the beginning of the war, though he came to America via Vladivostok, he hardly stopped in Moscow, never even considering Russia—this was the time of the Hitler-Stalin pact—as a possible place of refuge. Quite apart from the fact that he had never found favor with the Russian Communist Party—from beginning to end he was appreciated only by free audiences in Western countries—he must have had a foreboding that the poetic distance he had been able to keep from Communist politics even when he was most deeply committed to the "cause" (it seems he was never a member of the Party) would not withstand the onslaught of Soviet reality, as it did not withstand the infinitely less horrible onslaught of the reality of Ulbricht's Germany. The element of playfulness, so important in his work,

[14] Esslin, *op. cit.*, points out that "in the official East German version, Brecht's return to East Berlin is usually dated October 1948; at that time Brecht did indeed visit East Berlin, but he returned to Zürich again," and it was only "toward the end of 1949 [that] Brecht agreed to go to East Berlin." In October of that year, he still wrote: "I have no official function or obligation of any kind in East Berlin and receive no salary."

could not possibly survive in proximity with the very horrors he used to play with. It is, after all, one thing to tell your friends and acquaintances when they disagree with you, "We'll shoot you, too, when we seize power," and quite another thing to live where things worse than shooting happen to those who disagree with those who have indeed seized power. Brecht himself was not molested—not even in the years before Stalin's death. But since he was no fool, he must have known that his personal safety resulted from the fact that East Berlin was an exceptional place, the show window of the East during the fifties, and in desperate competition with the city's Western sector, just a couple of subway stops away. In this competition, the Berliner Ensemble—the repertory company that Brecht, under the aegis of the East German government, formed, headed, wrote for, and directed—was, and has remained to this day, the greatest asset of the East German regime, as it is also, perhaps, the only outstanding cultural achievement of postwar Germany. Thus, for seven years Brecht lived and worked in peace under the eyes—in fact, under the protection—of Western observers but now in infinitely closer contact with a totalitarian state than he had ever been in his life before, seeing the sufferings of his own people with his own eyes. And the consequence was that not a single play and not a single great poem was produced in those seven years, nor did he even finish the *Salzburger Totentanz*, which was begun in Zürich, and which—to judge by the fragments, which I know only in the English translation by Eric Bentley—might have become one of the great plays.[15] Brecht knew of his predicament, knew that he could not write in East Berlin. Shortly before his death, it is reported, he bought a house in Denmark and also considered moving to Switzerland.[16] No one had been more anxious to go home—"Put no nail into the wall, throw the jacket on the chair. . . . Why open the foreign grammar? The news that calls you home is written in familiar language"—and all he planned for when he lay dying was exile.

[15] In *The Jewish Wife and Other Short Plays*, Evergreen Paperbacks.
[16] See Marianne Kesting's monograph *Bertolt Brecht*, Hamburg, 1959, p. 155.

Hence, side by side with the great poet and playwright there is also the case of Bertolt Brecht. And this case is of concern to all citizens who wish to share their world with poets. It cannot be left to the literature departments but is the business of political scientists as well. The chronic misbehavior of poets and artists has been a political, and sometimes a moral, problem since antiquity. In the following discussion of this case, I shall stick to the two assumptions I have mentioned. First, although in general Goethe was right and more is permitted to poets than to ordinary mortals, poets, too, can sin so gravely that they must bear their full load of guilt and responsibility. And, second, the only way to determine unequivocally how great their sins are is to listen to their poetry—which means, I assume, that the faculty of writing a good line is not entirely at the poet's command but needs some help, that the faculty is granted him and that he can forfeit it.

II

To begin with, I must mention a few, a very few, biographical circumstances. We don't need to go into Brecht's personal life, about which he was more reticent—less willing to speak—than any other twentieth-century author (and this reticence, as we shall see, was one of his virtues, of which there were many), but we must, of course, follow the few exquisite hints in his poems. Brecht, born in 1898, belonged to what one might call the first of the three lost generations. Men of his generation whose initiation into the world had been the trenches and battlefields of the First World War invented or adopted the term because they felt that they had become unfit to live normal lives; normality was a betrayal of all the experience of horror, and comradeship in the midst of horror, that had made them into men, and, rather than betray what was most undoubtedly their own, they preferred to be lost—lost to themselves as well as to the world. This attitude, common to the war veterans of all countries, became a sort of climate of opinion when it turned out that they were succeeded by two more such "lost generations": the first, born about ten years

later, in the first decade of the century, was taught, through the
rather impressive lessons of inflation, mass unemployment, and
revolutionary unrest, the instability of whatever had been left intact in Europe after more than four years of slaughter; the next,
again born about ten years later, in the second decade of the century, had the choice of being initiated into the world by Nazi concentration camps, the Spanish Civil War, or the Moscow Trials.
These three groups, born, roughly, between 1890 and 1920, were
close enough together in age to form a single group during the
Second World War, whether as soldiers or as refugees and exiles,
as members of the resistance movements or as inmates of concentration and extermination camps, or as civilians under a rain of
bombs, survivors of cities of which Brecht, decades before, had
said in a poem:

We have been living, a light generation,
In houses that were thought beyond destruction.
(The lanky buildings of Manhattan Island and the fine antennae
That amuse the Atlantic Ocean are of our construction.)

Of these cities will remain that which blew through them, the wind.
The house makes the dinner guest merry. He cleans it out.
We know we're only temporary and after us will follow
Nothing worth talking about.

This, "On Poor B.B.," from the *Manual of Piety,* is the only
poem he ever wrote that is dedicated to the subject of lost generations. The title is, of course, ironic; he says in the concluding
lines that "in the earthquakes that will come I hope I won't let
my cigar go out in bitterness," and, in a way, that is characteristic
of his whole attitude, he turns the tables, as it were: What is lost
is not merely this weightless race of men but the world that was
supposed to house them. Because Brecht never thought in terms
of self-pity—not even on the highest level—he cut a rather solitary figure among all his contemporaries. When they called
themselves lost, they were looking upon the age and themselves
with the eyes of the nineteenth century; they were denied what
Friedrich Hebbel once called *"die ruhige reine Entwicklung"*—
the quiet, pure unfolding of all their faculties—and they reacted with bitterness. They resented the fact that the world did

not offer them shelter and the security to develop as individuals, and they began to produce their curious kind of literature, mostly novels in which nothing seems to be of interest but psychological deformation, social torture, personal frustration, and general disillusion. This is not nihilism; indeed, to call these authors nihilists would be to pay them an entirely undeserved compliment. They did not cut deep enough—they were too much concerned with themselves—to see the real issues; they remembered everything and forgot what mattered. There are two almost casual lines in another poem of the *Manual of Piety* in which Brecht said what he thought about this question of how to come to terms with one's own youth:

> *Hat er sein ganze Jugend, nur nicht ihre Träume vergessen*
> *Lange das Dach, nie den Himmel, der drüber war.*[17]

That Brecht never felt sorry for himself—hardly ever was even interested in himself—was one of his great virtues, but the virtue was rooted in something else, which was a gift and was, like all such gifts, part blessing and part curse. He speaks about it in the only strictly personal poem he ever wrote, and though it dates from the period of the *Manual of Piety*, he never published it; he did not want to be known. The poem, which belongs among his very best works, is entitled "Der Herr der Fische" [18]—that is to say, the lord and master of fishland, the land of silence. It tells how this lord comes up to the land of men, of the fishermen, rising and sinking with the regularity of the moon, a stranger and a friend to everybody (*allen unbekannt und allen nah*), and how he sits down with them, and can't remember their names but is interested in their business, in the price of the nets and the profit from the fish, in their women and their tricks of cheating the tax collector.

> *Sprach er so von ihren Angelegenheiten*
> *Fragten sie ihn auch: Wie stehn denn deine?*

[17] "Forgotten his whole youth but not its dreams, long forgotten the roof but never the sky above it." See "Ballade von den Abenteuern," *Gedichte*, I, 79.
[18] *Ibid.*, p. 42.

Und er blickte lächelnd um nach allen Seiten
Sagte zögernd: Habe keine.

For a while, everything goes well. "When they ask him 'And how about your own affairs?' he smiles hesitantly: 'I have none.'"
Until the day comes when they insist.

Eines Tages wird ihn einer fragen:
Sag, was ist es, was dich zu uns führt?
Eilig wird er aufstehn; denn er spürt:
Jetzt ist ihre Stimmung umgeschlagen.[19]

And he knows why their mood has changed; he has nothing to offer, and though he was welcome when he happened to come, he was never invited, for all he did was enrich their daily talk.

So, auf Hin- und Widerreden
Hat mit ihnen er verkehrt
Immer kam er ungebeten
Doch sein Essen war er wert.

When they want more of him, "he will take his leave, politely, like a dismissed servant. Nothing will remain of him, no shadow, no trace. But it is with his consent and permission that somebody else, richer than he is, takes his place. Truly, he prevents no one from talking where he remains silent."

Höflich wird, der nichts zu bieten hatte
Aus der Tür gehn: ein entlassner Knecht.
Und es bleibt von ihm kein kleinster Schatte
Keine Höhlung in des Stuhls Geflecht.

Sondern er gestattet, dass auf seinem
Platz ein anderer sich reicher zeigt.
Wirklich er verwehrt es keinem
Dort zu reden, wo er schweigt.

This self-portrait, Brecht's portrait of the poet as a young man —for this, of course, is what it really is—presenting the poet in all his remoteness, his mixture of pride and humility, "a stranger

[19] "One day one of them will ask him, 'And why, please, do you come to us?' He will get up in a hurry, knowing that their mood has changed."

and a friend to everybody," hence both rejected and welcome, good only for "*Hin- und Widerreden*" ("talk and countertalk"), useless for everyday life, silent about himself, as though there were nothing to talk about, curious and in desperate need of every bit of reality he can catch, gives us at least a hint of the enormous difficulties the young Brecht must have had in making himself at home in the world of his fellow men. (There exists another self-statement, a kind of prose poem of a later period: "I grew up as a son of well-to-do people. My parents placed a collar round my neck, educated me in the habits of being waited upon, and taught me the art of giving orders. But when I had grown up and looked around me, I didn't like the people of my class, neither the giving orders nor the being waited on. And I left my class and joined the company of low people." [20] This is probably true enough, though it sounds already a bit like a program. It is no self-portrait but a stylish way of speaking about himself.) It is altogether to his credit that we can only guess at who he was in this most personal way through some lines of the early poems. Still, there were certain aspects of his later, freely acknowledged behavior that these early lines may help us to understand.

There was first, and from the very beginning, Brecht's strange inclination toward anonymity, namelessness, and an extraordinary aversion to all fuss—to the pose of the ivory tower but also to the even more irritating bad faith of the "prophets of the people," or the "voices" of History, and to whatever else the "sale of values" ("*der Ausverkauf der Werte*" was a kind of slogan of the time) in the twenties offered its customers. But there was more to it than the natural distaste of a very intelligent and highly cultivated man for the bad intellectual manners of his surroundings. Brecht wished passionately to be (or, at any rate, to be taken for) an ordinary man—not to be marked as different by the possession of special gifts but to be like everybody else. And it is clear that these two closely connected personal dispositions—for anonymity and for ordinariness—were fully developed long

[20] "Verjagt mit gutem Grund," in *Hundert Gedichte,* Berlin, 1951.

before he adopted them as a pose. They predisposed him toward
two apparently opposed attitudes that later played a great role
in his work: his dangerous predilection for illegal work, which
demands that you wipe out your traces, hide your face, blot out
your identity, lose your name, "speak but conceal the speaker,
conquer but conceal the conqueror, die but hide death" [21]—quite
young, long before he thought of any "Praise of Illegal Work," [22]
he had written a poem on his late brother, who had "died secretly
and speedily disintegrated because he thought that no one saw
him" [23]—and his odd insistence on collecting around him so-called
"collaborators" who were often nondescript mediocrities, as
though he pleaded time and again, Everybody can do what I am
doing; it is a matter of learning, and no special gifts are needed,
or even wanted. In a very early "Epistle on Suicide," posthumously published, he discusses the reasons one could give for
the act, which should not be the true reasons, because they would
look too "grand": "At any rate, it shouldn't look as though one
had too high an opinion of oneself." [24] Precisely, and this is perhaps doubly true for people who, like Brecht, are tempted, not
by fame or flattery but by the objective manifestation of gifts
they can hardly ignore, to have a very high opinion of themselves. And if he carried this attitude to absurd extremes—absurd overestimation of the illegal apparatus of the Communist
Party, absurd demands upon his "collaborators" to learn what
was beyond learning—it must be admitted that the literary and
intellectual milieu of the twenties in Germany offered a temptation to puncture pomposity that, even without Brecht's special
disposition, was difficult to resist. The bantering lines on the behavior of his fellow poets in *The Threepenny Opera* hit the nail
right on the head:

Ich selber könnte mich durchaus begreifen
Wenn ich mich lieber gross und einsam sähe

[21] "Aus einem Lesebuch für Städtebewohner" (1930), in *Gedichte*, vol. I.
[22] In *Gedichte 1930–1933*, vol. III.
[23] The poem "Meines Bruders Tod," certainly written before 1920, in *Gedichte 1913–1929*, vol. II.
[24] The "Epistel über den Selbstmord," *ibid.*

Doch sah ich solche Leute aus der Nähe
Da sagt ich mir: Das musst du dir verkneifen.[25]

There is one more poem in which Brecht speaks explicitly of himself, and it is probably the most famous one. It belongs to the "Svendborger Gedichte," a sequence of poems written during the exile in Denmark in the thirties, and is entitled "To Those Born After Us." [26] As in the earlier "On Poor B.B.," the stress is on the catastrophes of the time in the world and on the need for stoicism with respect to everything that happens to oneself. But now that the "earthquakes to come" have arrived, all strictly biographical allusions have disappeared. ("On Poor B.B." begins and ends with the true story of his origins: "I, Bertolt Brecht, come from the black forests. My mother took me to the cities while I lay inside her. And the coldness of the forests will be with me till my dying day." His mother was from the Black Forest, and we know from posthumously published poems about her death that she was very close to him.[27]) It is the poem about those who "live in dark times," and its key lines read:

In the cities, I arrived at the time of disorder, when hunger ruled. Among men, I came at the time of upheaval, and I rebelled with them. Thus the time passed which was given me on earth.
I ate between battles, I slept among murderers, I was careless in loving, and I looked at nature without patience. Thus the time passed which was given me on earth.
When I lived, the street led to the morass. Speech betrayed me to the slaughterer. There was little I could do. But the rulers were safer without me, this I hoped. Thus the time passed which was given me on earth.
. . . You who will emerge from the flood in which we drowned remember when you speak of our weaknesses the dark time from which you escaped.

[25] "I too could understand myself quite well if I preferred to look great and solitary; but I saw such people rather close by and said to myself: This is not for you."
[26] The whole cycle, including "An die Nachgeborenen," in *Gedichte 1934–1941*, vol. IV.
[27] See the two poems "Von meiner Mutter" and "Meiner Mutter," in *Gedichte*, vol. II.

. . . Alas, we who wanted to prepare the ground for kindness
could not be kind.
. . . Remember us with forbearance.

Yes, indeed, let us do that, let us remember him with forbearance, if for no other reason than that he was so much more impressed by the catastrophes of the time in the world than by anything that concerned him. And let us not forget that success never
turned his head. He knew that "*wenn mein Glück aussetzt, bin
ich verloren*" ("when my luck leaves me, I'm lost"). And it was
his pride to rely on his luck rather than on his gifts, to believe
himself lucky rather than extraordinary. In a poem written a
few years later, during the war, when he counted his losses in
terms of friends who had died—to mention only the ones he
mentioned himself, Margarete Steffin, "little teacher from the
working class," whom he had loved and who had joined him
in Denmark; Walter Benjamin, Germany's most important literary
critic between the two wars, who, "tired of being persecuted,"
had taken his own life; and Karl Koch[28]—he spelled out for himself what had been implicit in an earlier poem: "I know, of
course: Only through luck did I survive so many friends. But to-
night in a dream I heard these friends say of me, 'Those who are
stronger survive.' And I hated myself."[29] This seems to have
been the only time his self-confidence was shaken; he compared
himself to others, and self-confidence always rests on a refusal
to indulge in such comparisons, whether they are for better or
worse. But it was only a dream.

So, in a sense, Brecht, too, felt lost—not because his individual
talents had failed to ripen as they should or could, or because
the world had hurt him, as indeed it had, but because the task
was too big. Hence, when he feels the flood rising, he does not
glance longingly backward, as no one did more beautifully than
Rilke in his later work, but appeals to those who will emerge from
it, and this appeal to the future—to posterity—has nothing to do
with "progress." What set him apart was that he realized how
deadly ridiculous it would be to measure the flood of events with

[28] "Die Verlustliste," in *Gedichte,* vol. VI.
[29] "Ich, der Überlebende," *ibid.*

the yardstick of individual aspirations—to meet, for instance, the international catastrophe of unemployment with a desire to make a career and with reflections on one's own success and failure, or to confront the catastrophe of the war with the ideal of a well-rounded personality, or to go into exile, as so many of his colleagues did, with complaints about lost fame or a broken-up life. There is not a shred of sentimentality left in Brecht's beautiful and beautifully precise definition of a refugee: *"Ein Bote des Unglücks"* ("a messenger of ill tidings").[30] A messenger's message, of course, does not concern himself. It was not merely their own misfortunes that the refugees carried with them from land to land, from continent to continent—"changing the countries more often than their shoes"—but the great misfortune of the whole world. If most of them were inclined to forget their message even before they learned that no one loves the bearer of ill tidings—well, hasn't this always been the trouble with messengers?

This ingenious, more than ingenious, phrase "messengers of ill tidings" for refugees and exiles may illustrate the great poetic intelligence of Brecht, that supreme gift of condensation which is the prerequisite of all poetry. Here are a few more instances of his utterly condensed and hence very tricky way of thinking. In a poem about the shame of being a German, written in 1933:

Hörend die Reden, die aus deinem Hause dringen, lacht man.
Aber wer dich sieht, der greift nach dem Messer.[31]

Or in a manifesto against war addressed to all German artists and writers, West and East, in the early fifties: "Great Carthage conducted three wars. It was still a great power after the first war, still habitable after the second. It was untraceable after the third." [32] In two simple statements, the whole atmosphere of the thirties and fifties, respectively, is caught with great accuracy. And the same illuminating trickiness shows up, perhaps even more

[30] In "Die Landschaft des Exils," in *Gedichte*, vol. VI.
[31] From "Deutschland," *Gedichte*, vol. III. "Hearing the speeches that ring from your house, the whole world laughs. But whoever sees you reaches for his knife."
[32] See M. Kesting, *op. cit.*, p. 139

strongly, in the following story, which appeared a number of years ago in a New York magazine. Brecht was in this country at the time of the Moscow Trials, and, so we are told, paid a visit to a man who was still of the Left but was violently anti-Stalinist and had become deeply involved in the counter-trials under the auspices of Trotsky. The conversation turned on the manifest innocence of the Moscow defendants, and Brecht, after maintaining a long silence, finally said, "The more innocent they are, the more they deserve to die." The sentence sounds outrage- ous. But what did he really say? The more innocent of what? Of what they were accused, of course. And what had they been accused of? Of conspiring against Stalin. Hence, precisely be- cause they had not conspired against Stalin, and were innocent of the "crime," there was some justice in the injustice. Hadn't it been the plain duty of the "old guard" to prevent one man, Stalin, from turning the revolution into one gigantic crime? Needless to say, Brecht's host did not catch on; he was outraged, and asked his guest to leave the house. Thus, one of the rare occasions when Brecht did speak out against Stalin, even though in his own teasingly cautious way, was lost. Brecht, I am afraid, might have sighed with relief when he found himself in the street: His luck had not yet left him.[33]

III

This, then, was the man: gifted with a penetrating, non-theoreti- cal, non-contemplative intelligence that went to the heart of the

[33] See Sidney Hook, "A Recollection of Bertholt Brecht," in *The New Leader*, October 10, 1960.—According to Benjamin (*op. cit.*, p. 131), Brecht was well informed of everything Trotsky wrote during the thirties; he said that these writings proved the existence of a justified suspicion that demanded a skeptical view of Russian developments. Should the suspicion prove true one would have to turn against the Russian regime *publicly*, but "fortunately or unfortunately, as you please," the suspicion was not yet a certainty. An interesting record of Brecht's desperate attempts to come to terms with Stalin's rule can now be found in an odd little volume of aphorisms, written chiefly during the thirties and found among his papers after his death. It was edited by Uwe Johnson and published in 1965 under the title *Me-ti, Buch der Wendungen*, which M. Esslin rightly translates "Book of Twists and Turns."

matter, silent and unwilling to show himself, remote and probably also shy, at any rate not much interested in himself but incredibly curious (indeed, "the knowledge-thirsty Brecht," as he called himself in the "Solomon Song" of *The Threepenny Opera*), and, first and foremost, a poet—that is, someone who must say the unsayable, who must not remain silent on occasions when all are silent, and who must therefore be careful not to talk too much about things that all talk about. He was sixteen years old at the outbreak of the First World War and was drafted as a medical orderly in the last war year, so the world first appeared to him as a scene of senseless slaughter, and speech appeared in the guise of ranting declamations. (His early "Legend of the Dead Soldier"—a soldier whom a military commission of doctors arouses from his grave and finds fit for active service—was inspired by a popular comment on draft policies at the end of the war, "*Man gräbt die Toten aus*" ["They're digging up the dead"], and has remained the only German First World War poem worthy of being remembered.)[34] But what became decisive for his early poetry was less the war itself than the world as it emerged from it after "the storms of steel," Ernst Jünger's *Stahlgewitter*, had done their work. This world possessed a property that is rarely taken into account but one that Sartre, after the Second World War, described with great precision: "When the instruments are broken and unusable, when plans are blasted and effort is meaningless, the world appears with a childlike and terrible freshness, suspended trackless in a void." (The twenties in Germany had much in common with the forties and fifties in France. What happened in Germany after the First World War was the breakdown of tradition—a breakdown that had to be recognized as an accomplished fact, a political reality, a point of no return—and that is what happened in France twenty-five years later. Politically speaking, it was the decline and downfall of the nation state; socially, it was the transformation of a class system into a mass society; and spiritually it was the rise of nihilism, which for a long time had been a concern

[34] "Die Legende vom toten Soldaten," in *Gedichte*, vol. I.

of the few but now, suddenly, had become a mass phenomenon.)
As it appeared to Brecht, four years of destruction had wiped
the world clean, the storms having swept along with them all
human traces, everything one could hold on to, including cultural
objects and moral values—the beaten paths of thought as well
as firm standards of evaluation and solid guideposts for moral
conduct. It was as though, fleetingly, the world had become as
innocent and fresh as it was on the day of creation. Nothing
seemed left but the purity of the elements, the simplicity of sky
and earth, of man and animals, of life itself. Hence it was life
that the young poet fell in love with—everything that the earth,
in its sheer thereness, had to offer. And this childlike, terrible
freshness of the postwar world is reflected in the horrible innocence of Brecht's early heroes—the pirates, adventurers, and infanticides, the "enamored pig Malchus," and Jakob Apfelböck,
who struck his father and his mother dead and then went on
living like "the lily of the field." [35]
   In this world swept clean and fresh, Brecht was at home to
begin with. If one wished to classify him, one might say that he
was an anarchist by disposition and inclination, but it would be
altogether wrong to see in him another member of that school
of decay and of morbid fascination with death which in his generation was perhaps best represented in Germany by Gottfried
Benn and in France by Louis-Ferdinand Céline. Brecht's characters—even his drowning girls who slowly swim down the rivers
until they are taken back into nature's great wilderness of all-
encompassing peace; even Mazeppa, bound to his own horse and
dragged to his death—are in love with life and with what earth
and sky have to offer, to the point where they willingly accept
death and destruction. The last two stanzas of the "Ballad
of Mazeppa" [36] are among the truly immortal lines of German
poetry:

> Drei Tage, dann musste alles sich zeigen:
> Erde gibt Schweigen und Himmel gibt Ruh.
> Einer ritt aus mit dem, was ihm zu eigen:

[35] All these in the *Hauspostille*, now vol. I of *Gedichte*.
[36] *Ibid.*

Mit Erde und Pferd, mit Langmut und Schweigen
Dann kamen noch Himmel und Geier dazu.

Drei Tage lang ritt er durch Abend und Morgen
Bis er alt genug war, dass er nicht mehr litt
Als er gerettet ins grosse Geborgen
Todmüd in die ewige Ruhe einritt.

Bentley's version of these lines seems inadequate to me, and I certainly cannot translate them properly. They speak of the end of the three days' ride into death: into silence, the gift of the earth; into rest, the gift of the sky. "One man rode out with the things that were most his own: with earth and horse, with endurance and silence, then he was joined by vultures and sky. For three days he rode, through evening and morning, until he was old enough not to suffer anymore, when, saved and tired to death, he rode into the great shelter, into eternal rest." There is a glorious, triumphant vitality in this death song, and it is the same vitality—the feeling that it is fun to be alive and that it is a sign of being alive to make fun of everything—that makes us delight in the lyrical cynicism and sarcasm of the songs in *The Threepenny Opera*. It was not for nothing that Brecht helped himself so generously to a Villon translation into German—something that German law, unhappily, called plagiarism. He is celebrating the same love of the world, the same gratitude for earth and sky, for the mere fact of being born and alive, and Villon, I am sure, would not have minded.

According to our tradition, the god of this careless, carefree, reckless love for earth and sky is the great Phoenician idol Baal, the god of the drunkards, the gluttons, the fornicators. "Yes, this planet pleases Baal if only because there's no other planet," says the young Brecht in the "Chorale of the Man Baal," of which the first and last stanzas are great poetry, especially when taken together:

Als im weissen Mutterschosse aufwuchs Baal
War der Himmel schon so gross und still und fahl
Jung und nackt und ungeheuer wundersam
Wie ihn Baal dann liebte, als Baal kam.

Als im dunklen Erdenschosse faulte Baal
War der Himmel noch so gross und still und fahl
Jung und nackt und ungeheuer wunderbar
Wie ihn Baal einst liebte, als Baal war.[37]

What matters, again, is the sky, the sky that was there before man was and will be there after he has gone, so that the best thing man can do is to love what for a short while is his. If I were a literary critic, I should go on from here to talk about the all-important part the sky plays in Brecht's poems, and especially in his few, very beautiful love poems. Love, in "Memory of Marie A.," [38] is the small, pure white of a cloud against the even purer azure blue of the summer sky, blooming there for some instants and vanishing with the wind. Or, in *The Rise and Fall of the City Mahagonny*, love is the flight of the cranes veering across the sky, side by side with the cloud, the sharing of the beautiful sky by crane and cloud for a few moments of flight.[39] To be sure, in this world there is no eternal love, or even ordinary faithfulness. There is nothing but the intensity of the moment; that is, passion, which is even a bit more perishable than man himself.

Baal cannot possibly be the god of any social order, and the kingdom he rules is peopled by the outcasts of society—the pariahs who, because they live outside civilization, have a more intense, and thus a more authentic, relation to the sun, which rises and sinks with majestic indifference and shines over all living creatures. There is, for instance, the "Ballad of the Pirates," with its shipful of wild, drinking, sinning, cursing men, hell-bent for destruction.[40] There they are on the doomed ship, mad with drink, with darkness, with unprecedented rains, sick from sun and from

---

[37] "Der Choral vom Grossen Baal," *ibid.* The translation of the first and last stanzas: "When Baal grew up inside the white maternal womb there was the sky, great and still and pale, young and naked and immensely wondersome, as Baal then loved it when Baal came.

"When Baal was left to rot inside the earth's dark womb, there still was the sky, great and still and pale, young and naked and immensely wonderful, as Baal had loved it when Baal was."

[38] "Erinnerung an die Marie A.," in *Gedichte*, vol. I.

[39] "Die Liebenden," in *Gedichte*, vol. II.

[40] The "Ballade von den Seeräubern" of the *Hauspostille*, in *Gedichte*, vol. I.

cold, at the mercy of all the elements, hurtling to their ruin. And then comes the refrain: "O Sky, radiant, unclouded blue! Tremendous wind in our sails! Let wind and sky fly away, if only the sea will stay around [the ship] Saint Mary."

> *Von Branntwein toll und Finsternissen!*
> *Von unerhörten Güssen nass!*
> *Vom Frost eisweisser Nacht zerrissen!*
> *Im Mastkorb, von Gesichten blass!*
> *Von Sonne nackt gebrannt und krank!*
> *(Die hatten sie im Winter lieb)*
> *Aus Hunger, Fieber und Gestank*
> *Sang alles, was noch übrig blieb:*
> *O Himmel, strahlender Azur!*
> *Enormer Wind, die Segel bläh!*
> *Lasst Wind und Himmel fahren! Nur*
> *Lasst uns um Sankt Marie die See!*

I chose the first stanza of this ballad—meant to be recited in a kind of singsong, for which Brecht wrote the music—because it illustrates another element very conspicuous in these hymns to life, namely, the element of hellish pride dear to all of Brecht's adventurers and outcasts, the pride of absolutely carefree men, who will yield only to the catastrophic forces of nature, and never to the daily worries of a respectable life, let alone to the higher worries of a respectable soul. Whatever philosophy Brecht may have been born with—as opposed to the doctrines he later borrowed from Marx and Lenin—is spelled out in the *Manual of Piety*, being clearly articulated in two perfect poems, the "Grand Hymn of Thanksgiving" and "Against Temptation," which was later incorporated into *The Rise and Fall of the City Mahagonny*. The "Grand Hymn" is an exact imitation of Joachim Neander's great baroque church hymn "Lobe den Herren," which every German child knows by heart. Brecht's fifth and last stanza reads:

> *Lobet die Kälte, die Finsternis und das Verderben!*
> *Schauet hinan:*
> *Es kommet nicht auf euch an*
> *Und ihr könnt unbesorgt sterben.*[41]

[41] "Grosser Dankchoral," *ibid*. "Praise ye the cold, the darkness, and

"Against Temptation" consists of four five-line stanzas praising life not in spite of but because of death:

> Lasst euch nicht verführen!
> Es gibt keine Wiederkehr.
> Der Tag steht in den Türen;
> Ihr könnt schon Nachtwind spüren:
> Es kommt kein Morgen mehr.
>
> .   .   .
>
> Was kann euch Angst noch rühren?
> Ihr sterbt mit allen Tieren
> Und es kommt nichts nachher.[42]

Nowhere else in modern literature, it seems to me, is there such a clear understanding that what Nietzsche called "the death of God" does not necessarily lead into despair but, on the contrary, since it eliminates the fear of Hell, can end in sheer jubilation, in a new "yes" to life. Two somewhat comparable passages come to mind. In one, by Dostoevski, the Devil speaks in almost identical terms to Ivan Karamazov: "Every man will know that he is altogether mortal, without resurrection, and he will receive death proudly and calmly, like a god." The other is Swinburne's thanks to

> Whatever gods may be
> That no life lives for ever;
> That dead men rise up never;
> That even the weariest river
> Winds somewhere safe to sea.

But in Dostoevski the thought is an inspiration of the Devil, and in Swinburne, a thought inspired by weariness, a rejection of life as something that no man would wish to have twice. In Brecht, the thought of no-God and no-hereafter spells not anxiety but a

the ruin. Look up to the skies: You do not matter and you may die without fear." According to Hugo Schmidt's notes to Eric Bentley's translations of the *Hauspostille* under the title *Manual of Piety*, its English version, "Praise ye the Lord the Almighty, the King of creation," is known from the Presbyterian Hymnal.

[42] "Gegen Verführung," *ibid.* "Do not let them tempt you! There is no recurrence of life. Day stands in the doors; the night wind blows through them: there will be no morrow. . . . How can fear still touch you? You die together with all animals, and there will be nothing thereafter."

233

liberation from fear. And Brecht must have grasped this aspect of the matter so readily because he grew up in Catholic surroundings; he obviously thought that anything would be preferable to sitting on earth hoping for Paradise and fearing Hell. What rebelled in him against religion was neither doubt nor desire; it was pride. In his enthusiastic denial of religion and his praise of Baal, the god of the earth, there is an almost explosive gratitude. Nothing, he says, is greater than life, and nothing more has been given us—and such gratitude one will hardly encounter either in the fashionable trend toward nihilism or in the reaction against it.

Yet there are nihilistic elements in Brecht's early poetry, and no one, probably, has ever been more aware of them than he was himself. Among the posthumous poems there are a few lines entitled "Der Nachgeborene," or "The Latecomer," which sum up nihilism better than whole volumes of arguments could do: "I admit I have no hope. Blind men talk of a way out. I see. When all the errors are used up, we shall be left with a last companion across the table—nothingness." [43] *The Rise and Fall of the City Mahagonny,* which is Brecht's only strictly nihilistic play, deals with the last error, his own, the error that what life has to give— the great pleasures of eating, drinking, fornicating, and boxing— could be enough. The city is a gold-digger sort of place, erected for the sole purpose of providing fun, of catering to man's happiness. Its slogan is *"Vor allem aber achtet scharf/Dass man hier alles dürfen darf"* ("First of all, understand that everything is permitted here"). There are two reasons for the city's downfall, the more obvious one being that even in the city where everything is permitted it is not permitted to lack the money to pay one's debts; underlying this banality is the second reason—the insight that the city of pleasure would end by creating the deadliest boredom imaginable, for it would be the place where "nothing ever happens" and where a man might sing, "Why should I not eat up my hat if there is nothing else to do?" [44]

[43] In *Gedichte,* vol. II.
[44] "Aufstieg und Fall der Stadt Mahagonny," now in *Stücke* (1927–1933), vol. III.

Boredom, then, was the end of the poet's first encounter with
the world, the end of the marvelous, life-praising, jubilant time
when he drifted weightlessly through the jungle of what had once
been one of the great cities of Europe, dreaming of the jungles
of all cities, dreaming of all continents and the seven seas, in love
with nothing but earth and sky and trees. As the twenties came to
a close, he must have begun to realize that, not poetically but
humanly speaking, this weightlessness condemned him to ir-
relevance—that the world was only metaphorically a jungle and
in reality a battlefield.

IV

What brought Brecht back to reality, and almost killed his
poetry, was compassion. When hunger ruled, he rebelled along
with those who were starving: "I am told: You eat and drink—
be glad you do! But how can I eat and drink when I steal my
food from the man who is hungry, and when my glass of water
is needed by someone who is dying of thirst?" [45] Compassion was
doubtless the fiercest and most fundamental of Brecht's passions,
hence the one he was most anxious to hide and also was least
successful in hiding; it shines through almost every play he
wrote. Even through the cynical fun of *The Threepenny Opera*
there sound the mighty, accusing lines:

> *Erst muss es möglich sein auch armen Leuten*
> *Vom grossen Brotlaib sich ihr Teil zu schneiden.*[46]

And what was sung mockingly there remained his leitmotiv up
to the end:

> *Ein guter Mensch sein! Ja, wer wär's nicht gern?*
> *Sein Gut den Armen geben, warum nicht?*
> *Wenn alle gut sind, ist Sein Reich nicht fern*
> *Wer sässe nicht sehr gern in Seinem Licht?* [47]

[45] In "An die Nachgeborenen," *op. cit.*
[46] "First it must be possible even for poor people to cut their slice
from the great bread of life." From the song "Denn wovon lebt der Mensch?"
in *Gedichte,* vol. II.
[47] "To be good! Yes, who wouldn't want that? To give your possessions

The leitmotiv was the fierce temptation to be good in a world and under circumstances that make goodness impossible and self-defeating. The dramatic conflict in Brecht's plays is almost always the same: Those who, compelled by compassion, set out to change the world cannot afford to be good. Brecht discovered by instinct what the historians of revolution have persistently failed to see: namely, that the modern revolutionists from Robespierre to Lenin were driven by the passion of compassion—*le zèle compatissant* of Robespierre, who was still innocent enough to admit openly this powerful attraction toward *"les hommes faibles"* and *"les malheureux."* "The classics," Marx, Engels, and Lenin, in Brecht's coded language, "were the most compassionate of all men," and what distinguished them from "ignorant people" was that they knew how to "transform" the emotion of compassion into the emotion of "anger." They understood that "pity is what one does not deny those whom one refuses to help." [48] Hence Brecht became convinced, probably without knowing it, of the wisdom of Machiavelli's precept for princes and statesmen, who must learn "how not to be good," and he shares with Machiavelli the sophisticated and seemingly ambiguous attitude toward goodness which has been open to so many simple-minded and learned misunderstandings—in his case as in the case of his predecessor.

"How not to be good" is the subject of *St. Joan of the Stockyards,* the marvelous early play about the Chicago girl in the Salvation Army who has to learn that on the day you must leave the world it will be of greater consequence to leave behind you a better world than to have been good. The purity, fearlessness, and innocence of Joan are matched in Brecht's plays by Simone in *The Visions of Simone Machard,* the child who dreams of Jeanne d'Arc under the German Occupation, and by the girl Grusche in *The Caucasian Chalk Circle,* where for once the whole predicament of goodness is spelled out: "Terrible is the tempta-

---

to the poor, why not? When all are good His kingdom is not far. Who wouldn't sit with pleasure in His light?" From "Über die Unsicherheit menschlicher Verhältnisse," *ibid.*

[48] The quotations are from *Me-ti, Buch der Wendungen.*

tion to be good" ("*Schrecklich ist die Verführung zur Güte*")—
well-nigh irresistible in its attraction, dangerous and suspect in
its consequences (Who knows the chain of events resulting from
what was done on the spur of the moment? Will not the simple
gesture distract him from more important tasks?), but also irrevocably terrible for him, too busy either with his own survival
or with saving the world, who resists temptation: "She who
doesn't listen to the cry for help but passes by with distracted
ear: never again will she hear the soft call of the beloved, or the
blackbird at dawn, or the happy sigh of the tired vintager when
the bells toll the Angelus." [49] Whether or not one should yield
to this temptation and how one is to resolve the conflicts that being good inevitably leads one into are the ever-recurring themes
of Brecht's plays. In *The Caucasian Chalk Circle,* the girl Grusche
yields to temptation, and everything ends well. In *The Good
Woman of Setzuan,* the problem is solved by the creation of a
double role: the woman, who is too poor to be good, who literally
cannot afford pity, becomes a tough businessman during the day,
makes a lot of money by cheating and exploiting the people, and
in the evening gives the earnings of the day away to the very
same people. This was a practical solution, and Brecht was a
very practical man. The theme is also present in *Mother Courage*
(Brecht's own interpretation notwithstanding), and even in *Galileo.* And any last doubts about the authenticity of this passionate
compassion should be dispelled when we read the last stanza of
the concluding song to the film version of *The Threepenny
Opera:*

> *Denn die einen sind im Dunkeln*
> *Und die andern sind im Licht.*
> *Und man siehet die im Lichte*
> *Die im Dunkeln sieht man nicht.*[50]

Ever since the French Revolution, when like a torrent the
immense stream of the poor burst for the first time into the

---

[49] *Der Kaukasische Kreisekreis,* written 1944–45, in *Stücke,* vol. X.

[50] "For some are in darkness, and others stand in the light. And you
see those in the light, those in darkness are not seen." *Gedichte,* vol. II.

streets of Europe, there have been many among the revolutionists who, like Brecht, acted out of compassion and concealed their
compassion, under the cover of scientific theories and hardboiled
rhetoric, out of shame. However, there have been very few
among them who understood the insult added to the poor's injured lives by the fact that their sufferings remained in the dark
and were not even recorded in the memory of mankind.

Mitkämpfend fügen die grossen umstürzenden Lehrer des Volkes
Zu der Geschichte der herrschenden Klassen die der beherrschten.[51]

This is how Brecht put it in his curiously baroque poetic version
of the "Communist Manifesto," which he planned as part of a
long didactic poem "On the Nature of Man," modeled after
Lucretius' "On the Nature of Things," and which is an almost
total failure. Anyway, he understood and was outraged by not
only the sufferings of the poor but their obscurity; like John
Adams, he thought of the poor man as the invisible man. And it
was out of this outrage, perhaps even more than out of pity and
shame, that he began to hope for the day when the tables would
be turned, when the words of Saint-Just—"*Les malheureux sont
la puissance de la terre*"—would come true.

Moreover, it was out of a feeling of solidarity with the downtrodden and oppressed that Brecht wrote so much of his poetry
in ballad form. (Like other masters of the century—W. H.
Auden, for instance—he had the latecomer's facility in the poetic
genres of the past, and hence was free to choose.) For the ballad,
grown out of folk and street songs, and, not unlike Negro spirit-
uals, out of endless stanzas in which servant girls in the kitchen
lamented unfaithful lovers and innocent infanticides—"*Die
Mörder, denen viel Leides geschah*" ("The murderers sorely af-
flicted with grief")—had always been the vein of unrecorded
poetry, the art form, if such it was, in which people condemned
to obscurity and oblivion attempted to record their own stories
and create their own poetic immortality. Needless to say, the

[51] "The great subversive teachers of the people, participating in its
struggle, add the history of the ruled class to that of the ruling classes."
In "Das Manifest," *Gedichte*, vol. VI.

folk song had inspired great poetry in the German language before Brecht. The servant girls' voices sound through some of the
most beautiful of German songs, from Mörike to the young
Hofmannsthal, and before Brecht the master of the Moritat was
Frank Wedekind. Also, the ballad in which the poet becomes a
storyteller had great predecessors, including Schiller and poets
before and after him, and, thanks to them, had lost, together with
its original crudeness, much of its popularity. But no poet before
Brecht had stuck with such consistency to these popular forms
and succeeded so thoroughly in gaining for them the rank of
great poetry.

If we add these things up—the weightlessness and the yearning
not so much for gravity as for gravitation, for a central point that
would be relevant within the setting of the modern world; plus
compassion, the almost natural, or, as Brecht would have said,
animal-like, inability to bear the sight of other people's suffering
—his decision to align himself with the Communist Party is easy
to understand, under the circumstances of the time. As far as
Brecht was concerned, the main factor in this decision was that
the Party not only had made the cause of the unfortunate ones
its own but also possessed a body of writings upon which one
could draw for all circumstances and from which one could
quote as endlessly as from Scripture. This was Brecht's greatest
delight. Long before he had read all the books—indeed, immediately upon joining his new comrades—he began to speak
of Marx, Engels, and Lenin as the "classics." [52] But the main
thing was that the Party brought him into daily contact with what
his compassion had already told him was reality: the darkness
and the great cold in this valley of tears.

Bedenkt das Dunkel und die grosse Kälte
In diesem Tale, das von Jammer schallt.[53]

---

[52] In Benjamin, *op. cit.*, one reads with pleasure that Brecht had his
doubts. He compares the Marxist theoreticians with the clerics (*Pfaffen*)
whom he hates with a deep-rooted hatred, inherited from his grandmother.
Like the priests, the Marxists will always form a camarilla; "Marxism offers
too many opportunities of interpretation."

[53] "Think of the darkness and the great cold in this valley that rings

From now on, he would not have to eat his hat; there was something else to do.

And this, of course, was where his troubles, and our troubles with him, began. He had scarcely joined the Communists before he found out that in order to change the bad world into a good world it was not enough "not to be good" but that you had to become bad yourself, that in order to exterminate meanness there should be no mean thing you were not ready to do. For— "Who are you? Sink into dirt, embrace the butcher, but change the world, the world needs change." Trotsky proclaimed even in exile, "We can only be right with and by the Party, for history has provided no other way of being in the right," and Brecht elaborated: "One man has two eyes, the Party has a thousand eyes, the Party sees seven countries, one man sees one city. . . . One man can be destroyed, but the Party can't be destroyed. For . . . it leads its struggle with the methods of the classics, which were drawn from the knowledge of reality." [54] Brecht's conversion was not quite as simple as it looks in retrospect. There were contradictions, heresies, that crept into even his most militant verses: "Let no one talk you into something, look for yourself; what you don't know yourself you don't know; examine the bill, you'll have to pay it." [55] (Hasn't the Party a thousand eyes to see what I can't see? Doesn't the Party know seven countries while I know only this city where I live?) However, these were only occasional slips, and when the Party—in 1929, after Stalin, at the Sixteenth Party Congress, had announced the liquidation of the right and left Opposition—began to liquidate its own members, Brecht felt that what the Party needed right then was a defense of killing one's own comrades and innocent people. In *Measure Taken* he shows how and for what reasons the innocent, the good, the humane, those who are outraged at injustice and come

with wails." From the "Schlusschoral" of the *Dreigroschenoper*. In *Gedichte*, vol. II.

[54] I quote from the songs of *Die Massnahme*, the only strictly Communist play Brecht ever wrote. See "Ändere die Welt: sie braucht es" and "Lob der Partei" in *Gedichte*, vol. III.

[55] "Lob des Lernens," *ibid*.

running to help are being killed. For the measure taken is the killing of a Party member by his comrades, and the play leaves no doubt that he was the best of them, humanly speaking. Precisely because of his goodness, it turns out, he had become an obstacle to the revolution.

When this play was first performed, in the early thirties, in Berlin, it aroused much indignation. Today we realize that what Brecht said in his play was only the smallest part of the terrible truth, but at the time—years before the Moscow Trials—this was not known. Those who even then were bitter opponents of Stalin, both inside and outside the Party, were outraged that Brecht had written a play defending Moscow, while the Stalinists denied vehemently that anything seen by this "intellectual" corresponded to the realities of Communism in Russia. God knows, Brecht never earned less thanks from his friends and comrades than with this play. The reason is obvious. He had done what poets will always do if they are left alone: He had announced the truth to the extent that this truth had then become visible. For the simple truth of the matter was that innocent people *were* killed and that the Communists, while they had not stopped fighting their foes (this came later), had begun to kill their friends. It was only a beginning, which most people still excused as an excess of revolutionary zeal, but Brecht was intelligent enough to see the method in the madness, although he certainly did not foresee that those who pretended to work for Paradise had just started establishing Hell on earth, and that there was no meanness, no treachery they were not prepared to perpetrate. Brecht had shown the rules according to which the infernal game was being played, and, of course, he expected applause. Alas, he had overlooked a small detail: It was by no means the intention of the Party, or in the Party's interests, to have the truth told, least of all by one of its loudly proclaimed sympathizers. On the contrary, the point, as far as the Party was concerned, was to deceive the world.

Rereading this play that once caused such an uproar, one becomes conscious of the terrible years that separate us from the time it was written and first produced. (Brecht did not produce it again later, in East Berlin, and, as far as I know, it has not appeared in other theaters; however, a few years ago it enjoyed a strange popularity on American campuses.) When Stalin made ready to liquidate the old guard of the Bolshevik Party, it may have taken the foresight of a poet to know that the best elements in the movement were going to be murdered during the next decade. But what then actually happened—and today is already half forgotten, overshadowed by even darker horrors—compared to Brecht's vision as a real storm compares to a storm in a teacup.

V

For my purpose, which is to present my thesis that a poet's real sins are avenged by the gods of poetry, *Measure Taken* is an important play. For from an artistic viewpoint this is by no means a bad play. It contains excellent lyrics, among them the "Rice Song," which was rightly famous and whose terse, hammering rhythms ring well enough even today:

> *Weiss ich, was ein Reis ist?*
> *Weiss ich, wer das weiss!*
> *Ich weiss nicht, was ein Reis ist*
> *Ich kenne nur seinen Preis.*
>
> *Weiss ich, was ein Mensch ist?*
> *Weiss ich, wer das weiss!*
> *Ich weiss nicht, was ein Mensch ist*
> *Ich kenne nur seinen Preis.*[56]

No doubt the play defends in all earnestness—not just for the fun of it, or in Swiftian sarcastic earnestness—things that are more than morally wrong, that are unspeakably hideous. And yet Brecht's poetic luck did not then forsake him, because he was still speaking the truth—a hideous truth, with which he wrongly tried to come to terms.

---

[56] "Do I know what rice is? Do I know who knows it! I don't know what rice is, I only know its price.

"Do I know what man is? Do I know who knows it! I don't know what man is, I only know his price."

From "Song von der Ware," *ibid.*

Brecht's sins were revealed for the first time after the Nazis had seized power and he had to confront the realities of the Third Reich from without. He went into exile on February 28, 1933, the day after the Reichstag fire. The "classics" by which he stubbornly tried to take his bearings did not permit him to recognize what Hitler actually did. He began to lie, and wrote the wooden prose dialogue in *Fear and Misery of the Third Reich* that anticipates later so-called poems, which are journalese divided into verse lines. By 1935 or 1936, Hitler had liquidated hunger and unemployment; hence, for Brecht, schooled in the "classics," there was no longer any pretext for not praising Hitler. In seeking one, he simply refused to recognize what was patent to everybody—that those really persecuted were not workers but Jews, that it was race, and not class, that counted. There was not a line in Marx, Engels, or Lenin that dealt with this, and the Communists denied it—it was nothing but a pretense of the ruling classes, they said—and Brecht, stolidly refusing to "look for himself," fell into line. He wrote a few poems about conditions in Nazi Germany, all of these poems quite bad, a representative one being entitled "Burial of the Agitator in the Zinc Coffin." [57] It deals with the Nazi custom of shipping home in sealed coffins the remains of people beaten to death in concentration camps. Brecht's agitator had suffered this fate because he had preached "eating your fill, a roof over your head, feeding your children"; in short, he was a madman, for no one went hungry in Germany at that time, and the Nazi slogan of the *Volksgemeinschaft* (folk community) was by no means mere propaganda. Who would have bothered to put him out of the way? The real horror, the only point to be made, was the way this man had died, that he had to be hidden in the zinc coffin. The zinc coffin was indeed important, but Brecht did not follow up the indication of the title; in his version, the agitator's fate was hardly any worse than the fate that an opponent of any kind of capitalist government was likely to suffer. And this was a lie. What Brecht wanted to say was that there was a difference only in degree between

[57] "Begräbnis des Hetzers im Zinksarg," in *Gedichte,* vol. III.

countries under capitalist rule. And this was a double lie, for in capitalist countries opponents were not beaten to death and shipped home in sealed coffins, and Germany was not a capitalist country any longer, as the Messrs. Schacht and Thyssen were to learn, to their sorrow. And how about Brecht? He had escaped from a country where everybody could eat his fill, had a roof over his head, and could feed his children. This is how it was, and this he did not dare to face. Even the anti-war poems of these years were undistinguished.[58]

However, bad as the work of this whole period was, it was not the end. The years of exile, as they went on and carried him farther and farther away from the turmoil that had been postwar Germany, had a very salutary effect upon his production. What could be more peaceful in the thirties than the Scandinavian countries? And whatever he might have said, rightly or wrongly, against Los Angeles, it was not a place famous for unemployed workers and hungry children. Although he would have denied it to his dying day, the poetic evidence is that he was slowly beginning to forget the "classics," and that his mind had started turning on themes that had nothing to do with capitalism or the class struggle. Out of Svendborg came poems like the "Legend on the Origin of the Book Tao-te Ching During Lao-tse's Journey Into Exile," which, narrative in form and making no attempt at experimenting with either language or thought, is among the stillest and—strange to say—most consoling poems written in our century.[59] Like so many of Brecht's poems, it wants to teach (in

[58] It appears that Brecht had second thoughts about the matter. In an article entitled "The Other Germany: 1943" and published by caw (an sds publication) in February 1968 without indication of source, he tried to explain why the German working class supported Hitler. The reason is that "unemployment was done away with [by the Third Reich] in short order. Indeed the speed and scope of the abolition were so extraordinary that it seemed like a revolution." The explanation, according to Brecht, was war industry, and "the truth is that war is in [the workers'] interest so long as they cannot or will not shake off the system under which they live." "The regime had to choose war because the whole people needed war only under this regime and therefore have to look for another way of life."

[59] "Legende von der Entstehung des Buches Taoteking auf dem Weg des Laotse in die Emigration," in *Gedichte,* vol. IV.

his world, poets and teachers lived close together), but this time
the lesson is of non-violence and wisdom:

> Dass das weiche Wasser in Bewegung
> Mit der Zeit den mächtigen Stein besiegt.
> Du verstehst, das Harte unterliegt.

"That soft water in movement defeats the mighty stone in
time. You understand, the tough are beaten." As indeed they
were. This poem had not yet been published when, at the beginning of the war, the French government decided to put its
refugees from Germany in concentration camps, but in the
spring of 1939, Walter Benjamin had brought it back to Paris
from a visit to Brecht in Denmark, and speedily, like a rumor
of good tidings, it traveled by word of mouth—a source of consolation and patience and endurance—where such wisdom was
most needed. It may be of some relevance that in the sequence
of the Svendborg poems the Lao-tse poem is followed by "Visit
with the Exiled Poets." Dante-like, the poet goes down to the
nether world and meets his dead colleagues, who were once in
trouble with the powers of the upper world. Ovid and Villon,
Dante and Voltaire, Heine, Shakespeare, and Euripides sit cheer-
fully together and give mocking advice, but then, "there came a
call from the darkest corner: 'You, there, do they know your
lines by heart? And those who know them, will they survive the
persecution?' And Dante explained softly, 'These are the forgotten poets; not only their bodies but even their works were
destroyed.' The laughter ceased abruptly. No one dared to look
at the guest. He had turned white." [60] Well, Brecht didn't need
to worry.

Even more noticeable than the poems were the plays he wrote
during these years of exile. After the war, no matter what the
Berliner Ensemble tried to do, whenever Galileo was staged in
East Berlin, every line sounded like an open declaration of hostility to the regime, and was understood as such. Up to this
period, Brecht had consciously avoided—by means of the so-
called epic theater—creating characters of any individuality,

[60] "Besuch bei den verbannten Dichtern," ibid.

but now, all of a sudden, his plays were peopled with real persons, who, if they were not characters in the old sense, were clearly unique and individual figures, such as Simone Machard, and the Good Woman of Setzuan, and Mother Courage, and the girl Grusche and Judge Azdak in *The Caucasian Chalk Circle*, and Galileo, and Puntila and his servant Matti. Today, all the plays in this group are part of the repertoire of good theater inside and outside Germany, though when Brecht wrote them they went unnoticed. No doubt this belated fame is a tribute to Brecht's own merits, and not only the merits of the poet and playwright but also those of the extraordinarily gifted theater director, who had at his disposition one of Germany's great actresses, Helene Weigel, who was his wife. But this does not alter the fact that everything he staged in East Berlin had been written outside Germany. Once he was back there, his poetic faculty dried up from one day to the next. He must finally have realized that he was confronted with circumstances that no quotation from the "classics" could explain or justify. He had stumbled into a situation in which his very silence—let alone his occasional praise of the butchers—was a crime.

Brecht's troubles had started when he became *engagé* (as we would say today, for the concept did not exist then), when he tried to do more than be a voice, which was how he began. A voice of what? Not of himself, to be sure, but of the world and of everything that was real. Yet that was not enough. To be a voice of what he thought was reality had carried him away from the real; wasn't he on the way to becoming what he liked least, one more solitary great poet in the German tradition, instead of what he wanted most to be, a bard of the people? And yet, when he went into the thick of things, his remoteness as a poet was what he carried, willy-nilly, into the newfound reality, his sharp and tricky intelligence notwithstanding. It was not so much lack of courage as this remoteness from the real that caused him not to break with a party that killed his friends and allied itself with his worst enemy, and to refuse to see, for the sake of the "classics," what was actually happening in his homeland—something that in his more prosaic moments he understood only too well.

In the concluding remarks to *The Resistible Rise of the Man Arturo Ui*—a satire on Hitler's "irresistible" rise to power, and not one of the great plays—he noted, "The great political criminals must be exposed by all means, and especially by ridicule. For they are above all no great political criminals but the perpetrators of great political crimes, which is not at all the same. . . . The failure of Hitler's enterprises does not mean that Hitler was an idiot, and the range of his enterprises does not mean that he was a great man." [61] This is considerably more than most intellectuals understood in 1941, and it is precisely this extraordinary intelligence, breaking like lightning through the rumble of Marxist platitudes, that has made it so difficult for good men to forgive Brecht his sins, or to reconcile themselves to the fact that he could sin *and* write good poetry. But, finally, when he went back to East Germany, essentially for artistic reasons, because its government would give him a theater—that is, for that "art for art's sake" he had vehemently denounced for nearly thirty years—his punishment caught up with him. Now reality overwhelmed him to the point where he could no longer be its voice; he had succeeded in being in the thick of it—and had proved that this is no good place for a poet to be.

This is what the case of Bertolt Brecht is likely to teach us, and what we ought to take into consideration when we judge him today, as we must, and pay him our respect for all that we owe him. The poets' relation to reality is indeed what Goethe said it was: They cannot bear the same burden of responsibility as ordinary mortals; they need a measure of remoteness, and yet would not be worth their salt if they were not forever tempted to exchange this remoteness for being just like everybody else. On this attempt Brecht staked his life and his art as few poets had ever done; it led him into triumph and disaster.

From the beginning of these reflections, I have proposed that we grant poets a certain latitude, such as we would hardly be

[61] The remarks "Zu *Der Aufhaltsame Aufstieg des Arturo Ui,*" in *Stücke,* vol. IX.

willing to grant each other in the ordinary course of events. I do not deny that this may offend many people's sense of justice; in fact, if Brecht were still among us he would certainly be the first to protest violently against any such exception. (In the posthumously published book *Me-ti,* which I mentioned before, he suggests a verdict for the "good man" gone wrong. "Listen," he says after the interrogation is completed, "we know you are our enemy. Therefore we shall now put you against a wall. But in consideration of your merits and virtues, it will be a good wall, and we shall shoot you with good bullets from good guns, and we shall bury you with a good shovel in good soil.") However, the equality before the law whose standard we commonly adopt for moral judgments as well is no absolute. Every judgment is open to forgiveness, every act of judging can change into an act of forgiving; to judge and to forgive are but the two sides of the same coin. But the two sides follow different rules. The majesty of the law demands that we be equal—that only our acts count, and not the person who committed them. The act of forgiving, on the contrary, takes the person into account; no pardon pardons murder or theft but only the murderer or the thief. We always forgive some*body,* never some*thing,* and this is the reason people think that only love can forgive. But, with or without love, we forgive for the sake of the person, and while justice demands that all be equal, mercy insists on inequality—an inequality implying that every man is, or should be, more than whatever he did or achieved. In his youth, before he adopted "usefulness" as the ultimate standard in judging people, Brecht knew this better than anybody else. There is a "Ballad About the Secrets of Each and Every Man" in the *Manual of Piety,* whose first stanza, in Bentley's translation, reads as follows:

> Everyone knows what a man is. He has a name.
> He walks in the street. He sits in the bar.
> You can all see his face. You can all hear his voice
> And a woman washed his shirt and a woman combs his hair.
> *But strike him dead! Why not indeed*
> *If he never amounted to anything more*
> *Than the doer of his bad deed or*
> *The doer of his good deed.*

The standard that rules in this domain of inequality is still contained in the old Roman saying *"Quod licet Iovi non licet bovi,"* what is permitted to Jove is not permitted to an ox. But, for our consolation, this inequality works both ways. One of the signs that a poet is entitled to such privileges as I here claim for him is that there are certain things he cannot do and still remain who he was. It is the poet's task to coin the words we live by, and surely no one is going to live by the words that Brecht wrote in praise of Stalin. The simple fact that he was capable of writing such unspeakably bad verse, worse by far than any fifth-rate scribbling versifier who was guilty of the same sins, shows that *quod licet bovi non licet Iovi,* what is permitted to an ox is not permitted to Jove. For whether or not you can praise tyranny in "fine-sounding voices," it is true that mere intellectuals or literati are not punished for their sins by loss of talent. No god leaned over their cradle; no god will take his revenge. There are a great many things that are permitted to an ox but not to Jove; that is, not to those who are a bit like Jove—or, rather, are blessed by Apollo. Hence the bitterness of the old saying cuts both ways, and the example of "poor B.B.," who never wasted a shred of pity on himself, may teach us how difficult it is to be a poet in this century or at any other time.

WALDEMAR GURIAN

1903-1954

He was a man of many friends and a friend to all of them, men and women, priests and laymen, people in many countries and from practically all walks of life. Friendship was what made him at home in this world and he felt at home wherever his friends were, regardless of country, language, or social background. Knowing how sick he was, he made his last trip to Europe because, as he said, "I want to say farewell to my friends before I die." He did the same when he came back and stayed a few days in New York, did it consciously and almost systematically, without a trace of fear or self-pity or sentimentality. He who throughout his life had never been able to express personal feeling without the greatest embarrassment could do this in a kind of impersonal manner, without feeling, and therefore without causing, embarrassment. Death must have been very familiar to him.

He was an extraordinary and extraordinarily strange man. The temptation is great to illustrate this judgment by insisting on the range and depth of his intellectual capacities, and to explain the strange feeling one always had that he came from nowhere, by reciting the few data we have of his early life. Yet, all such attempts

251

would fall hopelessly short of the man. Not his mind, but his person was extraordinary, and his early history would not sound strange if he had not treated it with the same reticent indifference he showed toward all personal facts and circumstances of his private and professional life, as though these like all mere facts could only be boring.

Not that he ever tried to hide anything. He always answered readily enough all direct questions put to him. He came from a Jewish family in St. Petersburg (the name Gurian is the Russification of the more commonly known Lurie) and since he was born at the beginning of the century in Tsarist Russia, the birthplace itself indicates that he came from an assimilated and well-to-do family, because only such Jews—usually merchants and physicians—were permitted to settle outside the pale in one of the great cities. He must have been about nine years old when, a few years before the outbreak of the First World War, his mother took him and his sister to Germany and into the Catholic Church. I do not think that, when I first met him in Germany in the early thirties, I was aware of either the Russian background or the Jewish origin. He was already well known as a German Catholic publicist and writer, a pupil of Max Scheler, the philosopher, and of Carl Schmitt, the famous professor of constitutional and international law who later became a Nazi.

One cannot say that the events of 1933 changed him in the sense that they threw him back to his origins. The point is not that he was made conscious of his Jewish extraction, but that he now thought it necessary to talk about it publicly because it was no longer a fact of personal life; it had become a political issue and it was a matter of course for him to solidarize himself with those who were persecuted. He kept this solidarity and a constant interest in the Jewish fate up until the first postwar years; an outstanding brief account of the history of German anti-Semitism, published in *Essays on Antisemitism* (New York, 1946), is witness to this preoccupation and at the same time to the rare facility with which he could become an "expert" in any matter which aroused his interest. Yet, when the years of persecution were over and anti-Semitism ceased to be a central political issue, his interest faded.

The same is not true for the Russian background, which has played an altogether different, truly predominant role all his life. Not only did he look vaguely "Russian" (whatever that may be), but he never lost the language of his early childhood although the complete and radical change in his surroundings made him spend his whole adult life in a German-speaking milieu. His wife being a German, the language spoken at his home in Notre Dame remained German. So strong was the hold of everything Russian on his taste, imagination, and mentality that he spoke English and French with a marked Russian, not German accent, although I am told that he spoke Russian fluently but not like someone whose mother tongue it is. No poetry and literature—perhaps with the exception of Rilke in his later years—could equal his love of and familiarity with Russian writers. (In the small but significant Russian section of his library there was still a battered copy of *War and Peace* in a children's edition, illustrated in the manner of the beginning of the century, with loose pages to which he returned throughout his life and which at his death was found on the night table.) And in the company of Russians, even if they were strangers, he was more at his ease than in other milieus, as if he belonged and was at home. His vast intellectual and political interests seemingly sent him in all directions. Actually they were centered around Russia, her intellectual and political history, her impact on the Western world, her unusual spiritual heritage, her religious passions as they are expressed first in the strange sectarianism of her people and later in her great literature. He became an outstanding expert in Bolshevism because nothing attracted him more and concerned him more deeply than the Russian spirit in all its ramifications.

I do not know whether the threefold break which occurred in his early life, the break-up of the family, the break from homeland and mother tongue, and the complete change of social milieu which conversion to the Catholic faith implied (for religious conflicts he was not only too young, he probably had hardly any religious education prior to his conversion), caused any deep wound in his personality, and I am certain they are hopelessly inadequate to explain its strangeness. But I think that from the few things I have mentioned it should be apparent that if such wounds existed, he had healed them through faithfulness, simply by his being loyal to the essentials of his early memories. At any event, faithfulness to his friends, to everybody he had ever known, to everything he had ever liked, became so much the dominant note on which his life was tuned that one is tempted to say that the crime most alien to him was the crime of oblivion, perhaps one of the cardinal crimes in human relationships. His memory had a haunting and haunted quality, as though it had never been permitted to let go of anything or anybody. It was much more than the capacity needed for scholarship and erudition, where it became one of his chief instruments for objective achievement. His erudition, on the contrary, was only another form of his enormous capacity for loyalty. This loyalty made him follow the writings of every author who ever had aroused his interest and given him some satisfaction, even though he might never have met him, just as it compelled him to give his help unconditionally not only to friends when they were in need, but to their children after their death, even though he had never seen or ever wished to see them. As he grew older, it was only natural that the number of dead friends should increase; and although I never saw him violently stricken with grief, I was aware of the almost calculated carefulness with which he kept mentioning their names as though he were afraid that through some fault of his they would slip away altogether from the company of the living.

All this was real and noticeable enough when one came to know him, but it gives no notion of the odd strangeness of the huge man with the even larger head, the broad cheeks divided by a surprisingly small, slightly turned-up nose—the only humorous trait in his face, for his eyes were rather somber despite their clearness and the smile which suddenly could melt away the flesh of cheeks and chin was too much the smile of a boy whom delight has caught unaware to contain humor, perhaps one of the most adult qualities. That he was a strange man, everyone must have noticed immediately, even those who knew him only in later years when strangeness and shyness—not timidity and never, to be sure, any sense of inferiority, but an instinctive movement of both soul and body of shying-away from the world—had already given way, yielded, as it were, to the burdens of official position and public recognition. What surprised as strange at first glance was, I think, the fact that he was a complete stranger in the world of things, which we use and handle constantly, among which we move without noticing them, so that we are hardly aware that all life in each of its movements is implanted in, surrounded, guided, and conditioned by non-moving, non-living things. If we stop to think of it, we may become aware of a discrepancy between living animate bodies and unmoving objects, a discrepancy which is constantly bridged through using, handling, dominating the world of inanimate matter. But here this discrepancy had widened into something like an open conflict between the humanity of man and the re-ity of things, and his awkwardness had such a touching, convincing human quality because it showed all things up as mere matter, as objects in the most literal sense of the word, namely, as *ob-jecta,* thrown against man and hence objectionable and objecting to his humanity. It was as though a battle was constantly going on between this man whose very humanity would not allow for the existence of things, who refused to recognize in himself their potential fabricator and habitual ruler, and the objects themselves, a battle in which, curiously and actually inexplicably, he never won a victory or was crushed by defeat. The things used to survive rather better than one dared to expect; and he never got caught to the point of plain catastrophe. And this conflict, strange and moving in itself, became all the more typical since his huge body was like the first, the quasi-primordial "thing" in which the objectionable *res*-quality of the world had first been incarnated.

We moderns, for whom the ability to manipulate things and to move in an object-ridden world has become so important a part of our way of life, are easily tempted to misunderstand awkwardness and shyness as semi-psychopathological phenomena, especially if they cannot be traced to feelings of inferiority which we assume to be "normal." Yet, pre-modern times must have known certain combinations of human traits which strike us as strange to belong to a perhaps not common, but still well-known type. The many serious and humorous medieval tales about very fat men, and the fact that gluttony had to be counted among the cardinal sins (which we find a little hard to understand), bear witness to this. For the obvious alternative to making, using, handling, and dominating things is the attempt to get rid of the obstacles by devouring them—and he was a perfect example of this quasi-medieval solution in the midst of the modern world. (Chesterton it seems was another one, and I suspect that much of his great insight into, not so much the philosophy, but the person of St. Thomas sprang from the sheer sympathy of one very awkward and very fat man with another.) In this case too, it started, as it should if it was at all genuine, with eating and drinking for which, as long as he was in good health, he had a gargantuan capacity and in which he took a kind of triumphant delight. However, his capacity for the food of the mind was even greater, and his curiosity, abetted by a memory of likewise gargantuan dimensions, had the same devouring, insatiable quality. He was like a walking reference library, and this had some intimate connection with the bulk of his body. The slowness and awkwardness of his bodily movements corresponded with a swiftness to absorb, digest, communicate, and retain information—the like of which I have never seen in anybody else. His curiosity was like his appetite, not at all the often lifeless curiosity of the scholar and expert, but aroused by nearly everything that mattered in the strictly human world, politics and literature, philosophy and theology, as well as plain gossip, the trifles of anecdote, and the innumerable newspapers he felt compelled to read every day. To devour and assimilate mentally everything related to human affairs and, at the same time, to leave out with sublime indifference everything in the realm of the physical—whether the subjects of natural sciences or the "knowledge" of how to drive a nail into the wall—this appeared to be his kind of revenge upon the common human fact that demands of a soul to live in a body and of a living body to move in an environment of "dead" things.

It is this attitude toward the world which made him so very human and sometimes so very vulnerable. If we say that somebody is human, we ordinarily think of some special kindness and gentleness, of easy approachability or something of this sort. For the same reason I have mentioned, because we are so used to and move with such ease in a world of man-made things, we are inclined to identify ourselves with what we make and do, and frequently forget that it remains the greatest prerogative of every man to be essentially and forever more than anything he can produce or achieve, not only to remain, after each work and achievement, the not yet exhausted, sheer inexhaustible source of further achievements, but to be in his very essence beyond all of them, untouchable and unlimited by them. We know how people daily and gladly forfeit this prerogative and identify themselves wholly with what they do, proud of their intelligence or work or genius, and it is true that remarkable results can be the outcome of such identification. Yet, impressive as such results may be, this attitude invariably loses the specifically human quality of greatness, of being greater than anything done. True greatness, even in works of art, where the struggle between the greatness of genius and the even greater greatness of man is most acute, appears only where we sense behind the tangible and comprehensible product a being that remains greater and more mysterious because the work itself points to a person behind it whose essence can be neither exhausted nor fully revealed by whatever he may have the power to do.

This specifically human quality of greatness, the very level, intensity, depth, passionateness of existence itself, was known to him to an extraordinary degree. Because he had it himself as the most natural thing in the world, he was an expert at detecting it in others, and this quite regardless of any position or achievement. He never failed in this, and it remained his ultimate standard of judgment in whose favor he discarded not only the more superficial yardsticks of worldly success, but also the legitimate objective standards, which he knew, on the other hand, to perfection. To say of a man that he had an unerring sense for quality and relevance sounds like nothing, like a complimentary conventional phrase. And yet, in the not frequent cases where men have possessed it and have chosen not to exchange it for more easily recognizable and acceptable values, it infallibly has led them far —far beyond conventions and established standards of society— and carried them directly into the dangers of a life that is no longer protected by the walls of objects and the supports of objective evaluations. It means to be friends with people who at first, and even second, sight have nothing in common, to discover constantly persons whom only bad luck or some queer trick of talent has prevented from coming fully into their own, it means to discard systematically, though not necessarily consciously, all, even the most respectable standards of respectability. It leads invariably into a kind of life that will offend many, be vulnerable to many objections, open to frequent misunderstandings; there always will be conflicts with those in power, and this without willed intention from the offender and without any ill will from the offended, but simply because power must be exerted in accordance with objective standards.

What used to save him from getting into trouble was not only, and perhaps not even primarily, his enormous intellectual capacity and the eminence of his achievements. It was even more that curiously boyish, at times slightly mischievous innocence which was so unexpected in this complicated and difficult person and which shone in convincing purity whenever his smile lit up an otherwise rather melancholy facial landscape. What finally convinced even those he had antagonized by some flare of temper was that he never meant any real harm. To him, provocation, being provoked no less than provoking, was essentially a means to bring out into the open the real and relevant conflicts we are so careful to stifle in polite society, to cover up with meaningless civilities, with that sham-considerateness we call "not hurting anybody's feelings." He was delighted when he could break down these barriers of so-called civilized society, because he saw in them barriers between human souls. At the source of this delight were innocence and courage, innocence all the more captivating as it occurred in a man who was so extremely well versed in the ways of the world, and who therefore needed all the courage he could muster to keep his original innocence alive and intact. He was a very courageous man.

Courage was viewed by the ancients as the political virtue *par excellence*. Courage, understood in the fullest sense of its many meanings, probably drove him into politics, which may appear bewildering in a man whose original passion was doubtless for ideas and whose deepest concern was clearly the conflicts of the human heart. To him, politics was a battlefield not of bodies, but of souls and ideas, the only realm where ideas could take form and shape until they would fight each other, and in this fight emerge as the true reality of the human condition and the innermost rulers of the human heart. In this sense, politics was to him a kind of realization of philosophy, or to put it more correctly the realm where the mere flesh of material conditions for men's living-together is consumed by the passion of ideas. His political sense therefore became essentially a sense for the dramatic in history, in politics, in all contacts between man and man, soul and soul, idea and idea. And just as in his scholarly work he sought out the high-spots of drama where all coverings are burnt away and ideas and men clash in a kind of immaterial nakedness (i.e., under conditions of absence of those material circumstances without which we commonly can no more bear the light of the spirit than we can bear the light of the sun in a cloudless sky), so he sometimes appeared in his intercourse with friends to be almost possessed by an urge to seek out the potentialities for drama, the opportunities for a big, blazing battle of ideas, for one gigantic fight of souls in which everything would come to light.

He did not do this often. What kept him from it was never lack of courage, of which he had rather too much than too little, but a highly developed sense of considerateness which was much more than politeness, and which combined itself with the early shyness which he never lost altogether. What he dreaded most was embarrassment, a situation in which he would embarrass somebody or be embarrassed by others. The embarrassing situation, whose whole depth was explored probably only by Dostoevski, is in a sense the reverse side of that blazing triumphant battle

259

of souls and ideas in which the human spirit can sometimes free itself of all conditions and conditionings. Whereas in the battle of ideas, in the nakedness of confrontation, men soar freely above their conditions and protections in an ecstasy of sovereignty, not defending but confirming with absolutely no defenses *who* they are, the embarrassing situation exposes them and points to them at a moment when they are least ready to show themselves, when things and circumstances have unexpectedly conspired to deprive the soul of its natural defenses. The trouble is that the embarrassing situation drags into the limelight the same defenseless self which man can bear to show freely only in the supreme effort of courage. Embarrassment played a great role in his life (he was not only afraid of it, but also attracted by it), because it repeats on the level of human relations, the one level he always and in all respects was ready to recognize, the alienation of man from the world of things. Just as things were to him dead objects, hostile to man's living existence to the point of making him their helpless victim, so in the embarrassing situation men are victims of circumstance. This in itself is humiliating, and it scarcely matters whether what is dragged into the light is something shameful or honorable. It was the greatness of Dostoevski's genius to sum up in a single situation these different aspects of embarrassment: When the prince in the famous party scene in *The Idiot* breaks the precious vase, he is exposed in his clumsiness, his inability to fit into the world of man-made things; at the same time this exposure shows most conclusively his "goodness," that he is "too good" for this world. The humiliation lies in the fact that he is exposed as somebody who *is* good, and cannot help being good, just as he cannot help being clumsy.

Humiliation is the extreme of embarrassment. Combined in him, closely connected in fact with his impulse of defiance against conventions and powers-that-be, was a veritable passion for the dispossessed, the disinherited and downtrodden, those whom life or men had treated badly, who had been dealt with unjustly. He who ordinarily would feel himself attracted only where he saw intelligence and spiritual creativity, forgot in such cases all his other standards; even his great fear of boredom would not pre-

vent his going out of his way to meet such people. He always became their friend, following the later events in their lives with
an intensity which was as removed from indiscretion as it was
from sheer compassion. It was not so much the people, it was
the story that fascinated him, the drama itself, as though, listening
to some new bit of information, he said breathlessly to himself
over and over again—such is life, such is life. He had a deep and
genuine respect for those whom life had singled out to write its
own story that then has not only its normal sad end but is like a
sequence of bad endings, and he never showed such people any
pity as though he would not have dared to pity them. The only
thing he did (apart from helping, of course, wherever he could)
was to bring them purposely into society, into contact with his
other friends in order to undo, as far as it was in his power, the
insult of humiliation which society invariably adds to the injury
of misfortune. The dramatic reality of life and world as he saw
it could never be complete, could not even begin to unfold itself,
outside the company of the dispossessed and disinherited.

This insight into the true quality of humiliation and this passion for the downtrodden are so well known to us through the
great Russian writers that we can hardly fail to notice how
"Russian" he was in his being a Christian. Yet, in him this Russian feeling for what the essence of human life is was intimately
blended with his altogether Western sense of reality. And it was
precisely in this sense that he was a Christian and a Catholic.
His uncompromising realism, which formed perhaps the outstanding trait of his contributions to history and political science, was
to him the natural result of Christian teachings and Catholic train-
ing. (He had a deep contempt for all sorts of perfectionists and
never tired of denouncing their lack of courage to face reality.)
He knew very well what he owed to them for having been able
to remain what he was, a stranger in the world, never quite at
home in it, and at the same time a realist. It would have been
easy for him to conform, for he knew the world very well; it
would have been easier for him, a greater temptation in all probability, to escape into some utopianism. His whole spiritual existence was built on the decision never to conform and never to

escape, which is only another way of saying that it was built on courage. He remained a stranger and whenever he came it was as though he arrived from nowhere. But when he died, his friends mourned him as though a member of the family had gone and left them behind. He had achieved what we all must: he had established his home in this world and he had made himself at home on the earth through friendship.

RANDALL JARRELL

1914-1965

I MET HIM shortly after the end of the war when he had come to New York to edit *The Nation*'s book section while Margaret Marshall was away, and when I was working for Schocken Books. What brought us together was "business"—I had been very impressed by some of his war poems and asked him to translate some German poems for the publishing house, and he edited (translated into English, I should say) some book reviews of mine for *The Nation*. Thus, like people in business, we made it a habit of lunching together, and these lunches, I suspect but do not remember, were paid for in turn by our employers; for this was still the time when we were all poor. The first book he gave to me was *Losses*, and he inscribed it "To Hannah (Arendt) from her translator Randall (Jarrell)," reminding me jokingly of his first name which I was slow to use, but not, as he suspected, because of any European aversion to first names; to my un-English ear Randall sounded not a bit more intimate than Jarrell, in fact, the two sounded very much alike.

I don't know how long it took me to invite him to our home; his letters are of no help since they are all undated. But for some years he came at regular intervals, and when he announced his next visit he would for instance write, "You could enter in your engagement book Sat. Oct. 6, Sun. Oct. 7—American Poetry Weekend." And this is precisely what it always turned out to be. He read English poetry to me for hours, old and new, only rarely his own, which, however, for a time, he used to mail as soon as the poems came out of the typewriter. He opened up for me a whole new world of sound and meter, and he taught me the specific gravity of English words, whose relative weight, as in all languages, is ultimately determined by poetic usage and standards. Whatever I know of English poetry, and perhaps of the genius of the language, I owe to him.

What originally attracted him not just to me or to us but to the house was the simple fact that this was a place where German was spoken. For

> I believe—
> I do believe, I do believe—
> The country I like best of all is German.

The "country," obviously, was not Germany but German, a language he barely knew and stubbornly refused to learn—"Alas, my German isn't a *bit* better: if I translate, how can I find time to learn German? if I don't translate, I forget about German," he wrote after my last not very convinced attempt at making him use a grammar and a dictionary.

> It is by Trust and Love and reading Rilke
> Without *ein Wörterbuch*, that man learns German.

For him, all things considered, this was true enough, for he had read in this way Grimm's tales and *Des Knaben Wunderhorn,* as though he was completely at home in the strange and intense poetry of German folk tales and folk songs, which are as untranslatably German as, well, *Alice in Wonderland* is untranslatably English. Anyhow, it was this folk element in German poetry that he loved and recognized in Goethe and even in Hölderlin and Rilke. I often thought that the country the German language represented to him was actually where he came from, for he was, down to the details of physical appearance, like a figure from fairyland; it was as though he had been blown down by some charmed wind into the cities of men or had emerged from the enchanted forests in which we spent our childhood, bringing with him the magic flute, and now not just hoping but *expecting* that everybody and everything would come to join in the midnight dance. What I mean to say is that Randall Jarrell would have been a poet if he had never written a single poem— just as that proverbial Raphael born without hands would still have been a great painter.

I knew him best during some winter months in the early fifties when he stayed at Princeton, which he found "*much* more Princetonian than—than Princeton, even." He came to New York on weekends, leaving behind, as he described it, a whole house of undone rooms and dishes and God knows how many street cats whom he had befriended. The moment he entered the apartment I had the feeling that the household had become bewitched. I never found out how he actually did it, but there was no solid object, no implement or piece of furniture, which did not undergo a subtle change, in the process of which it lost its everyday prosaic function. This poetic transformation could be annoyingly real when he decided, as he often did, to follow me into the kitchen to entertain me while I was preparing our dinner. Or, he might decide to visit my husband and engage him in some long, fierce debate about the merits and the rank of writers and poets, and the voices of the two rang lustily as they tried to outdo and especially outshout each other—who knew better how to appreciate *Kim*, who was a greater poet, Yeats or Rilke? (Randall, of course, voting for Rilke and my husband for Yeats), and so on, for hours. As Randall wrote after one such shouting match "it's always awing (for an enthusiast) to see someone more enthusiastic than yourself—like the second fattest man in the world meeting the fattest."

In his poem about Grimm's tales, "The Märchen," he has described the land he came from:

Listening, listening; it is never still.
This is the forest . . .

where

> The sunlight fell to them, according to our wish,
> And we believed, till nightfall, in that wish;
> And we believed, till nightfall, in our lives.

His was not at all the case of the man who flees the world and builds himself a dream castle; on the contrary, he met the world head-on. And the world, to his everlasting surprise, was as it was—not peopled by poets and readers of poetry, who according to him belonged to the same race, but by television watchers and readers of *Reader's Digest* and, worst of all, by this new species, the "Modern Critic," who no longer exists "for the sake of the plays and stories and poems [he] criticizes" but for his own sake, who knows "how poems and novels are put together," whereas the poor writer "had just put them together. In the same way, if a pig wandered up to you during a bacon-judging contest, you would say impatiently, 'Go away, pig! What do you know about bacon?'" The world, in other words, did not welcome the poet, was not grateful to him for the splendor he brought, seemed unneedful of his "immemorial power to make the things of this world seen and felt and living in words," and therefore condemned him to obscurity, complaining then that he was too "obscure" and could not be understood, until finally "the poet said, 'Since you won't read me, I'll make sure you can't.'" All these complaints were ordinary enough, so ordinary indeed that I at first could not understand why he bothered with them at all. Only slowly did it dawn upon me that he did not want to belong among "the happy few, who grow fewer and unhappier day by day," for the simple reason that he was a democrat at heart with "a scientific education and a radical youth," who was "old-fashioned enough to believe, like Goethe, in Progress." And it took me even longer, I must confess, to realize that his marvelous wit, by which I mean the precision of his laughter, was not the simple outgrowth of his unbelief in cheapness and vulgarity of every kind or of his belief that everybody he came in contact with had his own absolute feeling (like absolute pitch) for quality, this infallible judgment in all artistic as well as human matters, but that there was also, as he himself pointed out in "The Obscurity of the Poet," the mocking and self-mocking "tone of someone accustomed to helplessness." I trusted the very exuberance of his cheerfulness, thought or hoped that it would be sufficient to ward off all dangers to which he was so obviously exposed, because I found his laughter so exactly right. How, after all, could any of the learned or sophisticated rubbish about "adjustment" hope to survive this one sentence of his (in *Pictures from an Institution*), "President Robbins was so well adjusted to his environment that sometimes you could not tell which was the environment and which was President Robbins"? And if you can't laugh away the rubbish, what help is there? To disprove point by point all the nonsense our century has produced would demand ten life-spans, and in the end the disprovers would be as little distinguishable from their victims as was the College President from his environment. Randall, at any rate, had nothing to protect him against the world but his splendid laughter, and the immense naked courage behind it.

When I last saw him, not long before his death, the laughter was almost gone, and he was almost ready to admit defeat. It was the same defeat he had foreseen more than ten years earlier in the poem entitled "A Conversation with the Devil."

> Indulgent, or candid, or uncommon reader
> —I've some: a wife, a nun, a ghost or two—
> If I write for anyone, I wrote for you;
> So whisper, when I die, *We was too few;*
> Write over me (if you can write; I hardly knew)
> That I—that I—but anything will do,
> I'm satisfied . . . And yet—
>   and yet, you *were* too few:
> Should I perhaps have written for your brothers,
> Those artful, common, unindulgent others?

INDEX

Adams, John, 238
Adorno, Theodor W., 154, 162, 163, 165, 167, 170n., 175n.
Aquinas, Thomas, 256
Aragon, Louis, 175
Aristotle, 7, 15, 24
Auden, W. H., 207, 208, 238
Augustine, 88, 132

Bataille, George, 170
Baudelaire, Charles, 156, 162, 163, 164n., 169, 192n.
Bebel, August, 34, 37, 51
Benjamin, Walter, 153–206, 225, 227n., 239n., 245
Benn, Gottfried, 229
Bentley, Eric, 209, 217, 230, 233n., 248
Bernstein, Eduard, 46n., 48, 49, 50, 52
Bertram, Ernst, 161
Bespaloff, Rachel, 114n.
Blixen, Hans Bror, 106

Bloch, Ernst, 175
Borchardt, Rudolf, 161, 188
Bos, Charles du, 173
Brecht, Bertolt, viii, 154, 162, 167, 168, 187, 188n., 191n., 200, 207–49
Broch, Hermann, 111–51
Brod, Max, 184, 204
Buber, Martin, 194
Bullock, Alan, 34n.

Capovilla, Mgr. Loris, 64
Carroll, Lewis, 264
Céline, Louis-Ferdinand, 229
Chesterton, G. K., 256
Cicero, 15, 71, 154
Clausewitz, Karl von, 53n.
Cole, Berkeley, 101

Dante, 120, 245
Deutscher, Isaac, 34n.

Diefenbach, Hans, 45
Dinesen, Isak, 95–109
Dostoevski, Fyodor, 67, 233, 259, 260
Duncker, Hermann, 55
Dzerzhynski, Feliks, 41

Engels, Friedrich, 236, 239, 243
Erzberger, Matthias, 36
Esslin, Martin, 208n., 216n., 227n.
Euripides, 245

Faulkner, William, 20, 104
Finch-Hatton, Denys, 96, 100, 101, 103, 104, 109
Fischer, Ruth, 55
France, Anatole, 197
Freud, Sigmund, 179

George, Stefan, 161
Gide, André, 118, 173
Giovanni XXIII, Pope, 57–69
Giraudoux, Jean, 175
Goethe, Johann Wolfgang von, 5, 21, 40, 107, 109, 116n., 130, 154, 155, 156, 161, 164, 167, 170, 195, 201, 211, 218, 247, 264, 266
Goldstein, Moritz, 183, 187
Grimm, Jakob and Wilhelm, 264, 265
Gundolf, Friedrich, 161
Guys, Constantin, 164n.

Haase, Hugo, 36
Halberg, Werner, 53n.
Hatch, Alden, 66, 68
Haussmann, Georges, 172
Hebbel, Friedrich, 219
Hebel, Johann, 98
Hegel, Georg Friedrich, 39, 86, 91, 92, 93

Heidegger, Martin, ix, 189, 196, 201, 204
Heiden, Konrad, 34n.
Heine, Heinrich, 107, 176, 245
Heise, Rosemarie, 170n.
Hemingway, Ernest, 99
Hessel, Franz, 156
Hitler, Adolf, 18, 33–34n., 122, 154, 209, 210, 212, 243, 244n., 247
Hobbes, Thomas, 126
Hochhuth, Rolf, 63
Hofmannsthal, Hugo von, 114, 115, 116n., 120, 121, 130, 154, 155, 160, 161, 162, 169, 175, 201, 239
Hölderlin, Johann Christian Friedrich, 264
Homer, 107, 166
Hook, Sidney, 227n.
Horkheimer, Max, 162
Husserl, Edmund, 137

Jarrell, Randall, 263–67
Jaspers, Karl, 71–94
Jaurès, Jean, 34, 44
Jesus of Nazareth, 58, 59, 60, 62, 125
Jogiches, Leo, 36, 44, 45, 46, 47, 54
Johnson, Uwe, 227n.
Joyce, James, 118, 120, 134
Jünger, Ernst, 228

Kafka, Franz, 28, 117, 118, 154, 155, 168, 169, 170, 172, 179, 180, 182, 183, 185, 186, 187, 188n., 190, 192n., 194, 196, 200, 201, 204
Kallman, Chester, 208
Kant, Immanuel, 26, 27, 73, 74, 77, 82, 84, 91, 92, 93, 129, 132, 139, 156, 197
Kautsky, Karl, 34, 50, 52
Kempis, Thomas à, 68

Kierkegaard, Sören, 67
Kipling, Rudyard, 265
Klee, Paul, 165
Kleist, Heinrich von, 98
Klinger, Kurt, 60
Knopf, Alfred A., 114
Kraft, Werner, 173
Kraus, Karl, 172, 183, 186, 187,
    191, 193

Landauer, Gustav, 36
Langbaum, Robert, 100, 108
La Rochefoucauld, 181
Laughton, Charles, 208
Léger, Alexis Saint-Léger, see
    Perse, St.-John
Leibniz, Gottfried, 136, 137
Lenin, 34, 38, 40, 41, 45, 46, 47,
    53, 54, 55, 212, 232, 236,
    239, 243
Leo XIII, Pope, 65
Leskov, Nikolai, 196
Lessing, Gotthold Ephraim, vii,
    3–31, 92, 176
Leviné, Eugene, 36, 47
Levi, Paul, 54
Lichtenberg, Georg, 176
Lichtheim, George, 36
Liebknecht, Karl, 34, 35, 36, 46,
    47, 55
Lucretius, 238
Lukács, Georg, 209n.
Luxemburg, Rosa, 33–56

Machiavelli, Niccolò, 236
Madison, James, 91
Mallarmé, Stéphane, 205
Mann, Klaus, 162
Marchlewski, Julian, 41
Marshall, Margaret, 263
Marx, Karl, 38–39, 48, 50, 53n., 92,
    163, 232, 236, 239, 243
Mehring, Franz, 39, 45, 55
Migel, Parmenia, 98, 99, 103, 106

Millerand, Alexandre, 34
Missac, Pierre, 173, 191n.
Montaigne, Michel de, 181
Montesquieu, Charles L. de, 181
Mörike, Eduard, 40, 239
Mussolini, 212

Neander, Joachim, 232
Nero, 122
Nettl, J. P., 34, 36, 37, 38, 40,
    41, 42, 43, 44, 45, 49, 52, 56
Nietzsche, Friedrich, 42, 43, 67,
    121, 176, 233
Noske, Gustav, 35

Oelssner, Fred, 55
Ovid, 245

Pabst, Captain, 35
Papen, Franz von, 62
Parmenides, ix, 27
Parvus, 50
Pascal, Blaise, 181
Péguy, Charles, 175
Perse, St.-John (Alexis Saint-Léger
    Léger), 156, 169
Pilsudski, Józef, 42
Pius XII, Pope, 63
Plato, ix, 27, 91, 123, 124, 211
Plekhanov, Georgi V., 34, 46, 50
Pound, Ezra, 211, 212
Proust, Marcel, 156, 159, 169, 172

Raphael, 265
Rathenau, Walther, 36, 186, 188,
    189
Rilke, Rainer Maria, 120–21, 225,
    253, 264, 265
Rivière, Jacques, 159
Robespierre, Maximilien, 14, 236
Rosenfeld, Kurt, 37
Rousseau, Jean Jacques, 12, 14, 24
Runge, 35
Rychner, Max, 174, 175n., 176

St. John of the Cross, 58
Saint-Just, Louis de, 238
Sarraute, Nathalie, 77
Sartre, Jean Paul, viii
Schacht, Hjalmar, 244
Scheler, Max, 252
Schiller, Friedrich, 239
Schlegel, Friedrich, 30, 176
Schmidt, Hugo, 233n.
Schmitt, Carl, 252
Scholem, Gerhard (Gershom),
    154, 156, 161, 163, 167, 169,
    170n., 172, 175n., 180, 189,
    191, 194, 195
Seneca, 155
Shakespeare, William, 103, 193,
    245
Silesius, Angelus, 214
Souvarine, Boris, 34n.
Stalin, Joseph, 33–34n., 38, 210,
    213, 215, 241, 242, 249
Steffin, Margarete, 225
Stifter, Adalbert, 80

Swinburne, Algernon, 233

Thyssen, Fritz, 244
Tiedemann, Rolf, 167n., 170n.
Tocqueville, Alexis de, 193
Tolstoy, Leo, 118, 253
Trotsky, Leon, 34, 47, 227n., 240

Villon, François, 212, 230, 245
Vogel, Lieutenant, 35
Voltaire, François Marie Arouet, 245
Voss, Johann Heinrich, 107

Wedekind, Frank, 239
Weigel, Helene, 246
Welty, Eudora, 98
Westarp, Graf, 45
Wittgenstein, Ludwig, 204
Wolf, Julius, 48

Yeats, W. B., 265

Zetkin, Clara, 37